Crisis and Husserlian Phenomenology

Also Available from Bloomsbury

Husserl's Ethics and Practical Intentionality, Susi Ferrarello
Phenomenology and the Social Context of Psychiatry, Magnus Englander
Hermeneutics and Phenomenology, edited by Saulius Geniusas and Paul Fairfield
Heidegger and the Problem of Phenomena, Fredrik Westerlund

Crisis and Husserlian Phenomenology

A Reflection on Awakened Subjectivity

Kenneth Knies

BLOOMSBURY ACADEMIC
LONDON • NEW YORK • OXFORD • NEW DELHI • SYDNEY

BLOOMSBURY ACADEMIC
Bloomsbury Publishing Plc
50 Bedford Square, London, WC1B 3DP, UK
1385 Broadway, New York, NY 10018, USA
29 Earlsfort Terrace, Dublin 2, Ireland

BLOOMSBURY, BLOOMSBURY ACADEMIC and the Diana logo are trademarks of
Bloomsbury Publishing Plc

First published in Great Britain 2021
This paperback edition published in 2022

Copyright © Kenneth Knies, 2021

Kenneth Knies has asserted his right under the Copyright, Designs and Patents Act,
1988, to be identified as Author of this work.

For legal purposes the Acknowledgments on p. viii constitute
an extension of this copyright page.

Cover design by Jade Barnett
Cover image by Rene Böhmer/Unsplash

All rights reserved. No part of this publication may be reproduced
or transmitted in any form or by any means, electronic or mechanical,
including photocopying, recording, or any information storage or retrieval
system, without prior permission in writing from the publishers.

Bloomsbury Publishing Plc does not have any control over, or responsibility for, any
third-party websites referred to or in this book. All internet addresses given in this
book were correct at the time of going to press. The author and publisher regret any
inconvenience caused if addresses have changed or sites have ceased to exist, but can
accept no responsibility for any such changes.

A catalogue record for this book is available from the British Library.

Library of Congress Cataloging-in-Publication Data

Names: Knies, Kenneth, author.
Title: Crisis and Husserlian phenomenology: a reflection on awakened
subjectivity / Kenneth Knies.
Description: London; New York: Bloomsbury Academic, 2020. |
Includes bibliographical references and index. | Summary: "Shedding new light on the theme of "crisis" in
Husserl's phenomenology, this book reflects on the experience of awakening to one's own naïveté. Beginning from
everyday examples, Knies examines how this awakening makes us culpable for not having noticed what was
noticeable. He goes on to apply this examination to fundamental issues in phenomenology, arguing that the
appropriation of naïve life has a different structure from the reflection on pre-reflective life. Husserl's work on the "crisis" is
presented as an attempt to integrate this appropriation into a systematic transcendental philosophy. Crisis and Husserlian
Phenomenology brings Husserl into dialogue with other key thinkers in Continental philosophy such
as Descartes, Kant, Heidegger, Merleau-Ponty and Derrida. It is suitable for students and scholars alike, especially
those interested in subjectivity, responsibility and the philosophy of history"– Provided by publisher.
Identifiers: LCCN 2020019586 (print) | LCCN 2020019587 (ebook) | ISBN 9781350145214 (hb) |
ISBN 9781350145221 (ePDF) | ISBN 9781350145238 (ebook)
Subjects: LCSH: Husserl, Edmund, 1859-1938. | Crises (Philosophy) | Phenomenology. | Subjectivity.
Classification: LCC B3279.H94 K57 2020 (print) | LCC B3279.H94 (ebook) | DDC 142/.7–dc23
LC record available at https://lccn.loc.gov/2020019586
LC ebook record available at https://lccn.loc.gov/2020019587

ISBN: HB: 978-1-3501-4521-4
PB: 978-1-3502-0137-8
ePDF: 978-1-3501-4522-1
eBook: 978-1-3501-4523-8

Typeset by Newgen KnowledgeWorks Pvt. Ltd., Chennai, India

To find out more about our authors and books visit www.bloomsbury.com
and sign up for our newsletters.

Contents

Acknowledgments	viii
Introduction	1
Part 1 Awakened Subjectivity	11
Division A The Phenomenology of Having Presupposed	13
1. Bringing Presuppositions Back to Life	13
2. Realization and Reflection	17
3. Realization and Having Presupposed	20
4. Awakening and Naïveté	23
5. The "I" Who Presupposed	27
6. The Devaluation of Naïve Life	33
7. Basic Integrity	35
8. Jeopardy	43
9. The Finality of Wakeful Life	45
10. Appropriative Reflection	49
11. Illusions	55
Division B Levels of Awakening and Appropriation	59
1. Awakening and Reality: The Mundane Attitude	59
2. Reality and World	62
3. Provinciality and Worldliness	64
4. The Ideal of Reclaiming the World	72
5. Transition to the Phenomenological Level	80
6. The Consuming Interest of the Natural Attitude	82
7. Naïve World-Belief as a Transcendental Accomplishment	90
8. Self-Reflection, Self-Creation, Self-Realization	96
9. The Finality of Phenomenological Wakefulness	98
10. Complete Maturation	106
11. The Devaluation of Natural-Attitude Life	108
12. Phenomenological Awakening and Jeopardy	111

13. The Idea of an Enlightenment Project — 118
14. The Presupposition of an Enlightenment Project — 120
15. Critical-Historical Appropriation — 124
16. The History of Philosophy and Philosophical History — 128
17. Crisis and Hope — 129
18. Phenomenological and Critical-Historical Appropriation — 131

Part 2 The Crisis Problematic — 135

Division A Husserl and the Ultimate Presuppositions — 137
1. The Idea of an Independent Introduction — 137
2. From Philosophical Epoché to Historical Intervention — 139
3. Philosophical Epoché versus Historical Intervention — 142
4. The Inevitability of Crisis — 146
5. Crisis as a Medical Concept — 150
6. Husserl's Appropriative Concepts — 154
7. The Practical Extension of Phenomenological Reason — 155
8. Historical Teleology: Contemplative and Interventionist — 159
9. Mythmaking and the Will to Believe — 164
10. Relation between the Two Dimensions of Appropriation — 167
11. Relation between the Practical Extension and Phenomenology Proper — 170

Division B Husserl and the Subject of Crisis — 173
1. Two Ideas of Science — 174
2. Descartes — 176
3. Hume — 178
4. Kant — 180
5. Decision between the Two Scientific Ideas — 182
6. The Definition of Europe — 187
7. The Nation and Political Historicity — 189
8. Denationalization — 196
9. Renaissance — 199
10. Europeanization — 202

11.	The Problem of European Hypocrisy	204
12.	The Problem of European Exceptionalism	210
13.	Philosophical Seriousness	214

Conclusion: Owning Philosophy 217

Notes 221
References 235
Index of Names 243
Index of Subjects 245

Acknowledgments

I am grateful to have known so many insightful and patient conversationalists who never tire of talking philosophy. Without their companionship, it would have been difficult to continue believing in the importance of ideas that don't make anything run. I am especially indebted to two former colleagues, Ed Papa and Marcello Kilani, for keeping me focused on this book. I am also mindful of the many people who made it possible for me to continue professionally in philosophy by giving generously of their time, advice, and resources. Special thanks in this regard to Donn Welton and George Heffernan. Finally, I want to acknowledge an anonymous reviewer from whose thoroughness I benefited greatly.

Introduction

Consider the experience of realizing something that had previously escaped notice. Such realizations bring to light a strange kind of failure. It is not just that I did not notice something that I now notice. Instead, I am aware that what I now realize was previously noticeable for me but somehow inaccessible. I was blind to something that I now see to have been available all along. Of what I now realize, it seems true both that I was able and that I was unable to notice it before. It is as if I were kept from grasping something within my reach. In the experience under consideration, nothing external kept me from noticing what I now realize. I who realize hold myself responsible. We call "naïveté" this peculiar way of failing to notice and "awakening" the process of discovering this failure.

Reflecting on the awakening to naïveté raises difficulties about subjectivity and responsibility of special concern to phenomenology. We can anticipate these difficulties by noting that phenomenology is at once a philosophy of consciousness and a philosophy of crisis. Phenomenology is a philosophy of consciousness not in the sense that it is the philosophical study of a particular topic, consciousness. Phenomenology is rather a philosophy according to which the philosophical study of any topic proceeds via the study of consciousness. It is through actual and possible consciousness that whatever is not consciousness is what it truly is. This insight that consciousness functions transcendentally for all objectivity is the epicenter from which phenomenological researches radiate. Having established this insight, phenomenology has access to its subject matter in a unique way. Everything that exists in the material, animal, and spiritual realms can be elucidated in its being with reference to conscious activities that are open to reflection for the one who takes these things to be. Some consciousness is clear and some obscure. But they are both equally available as what they are to reflection. If consciousness is, nothing needs to happen for it to be available. The methods that make manifest its contents move within the availability of consciousness to itself.

Phenomenology is a philosophy of crisis because consciousness emerges from a life of transcendental naïveté. This is a philosophy according to which philosophical thinking begins by disengaging the default attitude of all human existence. In this natural attitude, the transcendental function of consciousness is concealed such that it has to be realized in the sense described above. Taking responsibility for transcendental naïveté ultimately involves reflections quite different from those that elucidate philosophical subject matter from the perspective of consciousness. The availability of that subject matter is itself the result of an awakening. And this awakening requires the phenomenologist to reorient herself to the history in which she stands. This history is not external to phenomenology. It is the history that phenomenology makes as philosophy. Phenomenology is of historical significance insofar as it necessitates the transformation of human projects that cannot achieve their aims in transcendental naïveté. To be in crisis is to face the practical necessity of this transformation, the impossibility of going forward without it. In clarifying the crisis, the phenomenologist regards herself as an agent of the projects she critiques. As such, she attempts to discern what these projects are and who she has become by sharing responsibility for their fate.

This study tries to understand how phenomenology is at once a philosophy of consciousness and of crisis. We will develop both dimensions of philosophical concern beginning from an examination of presuppositions. We define a presupposition as a necessary condition that is realized in an awakening to naïveté. The one who realizes a presupposition takes responsibility for her naïveté by regarding herself as the subject of a past act of presupposing. This thought that it was I, the awakened I, who presupposed opens an appropriative relation to my own history. To resume wakefully what I was doing naively, I have to comprehend the course of my naïve activity from the perspective of its previously inaccessible condition. We will explore these dynamics beginning from presuppositions realizable within the natural attitude. This exploration will prepare us to see how the phenomenological attitude is founded on the realization of consciousness as the universal presupposition of natural-attitude life. This account of the phenomenological attitude will, in turn, prepare an argument for the perennial importance of the crisis problematic to the philosophy of consciousness. Thinking through the crisis is the only way to appropriate certain "ultimate presuppositions" that condition that philosophy.

The tradition of Husserlian phenomenology guides this study from beginning to end. Indeed, we proceed in the conviction that our account generally harmonizes with what Husserl thought about the philosophy of consciousness.

However, our primary aim is not to show that this conviction is true. It will be enough if Husserl's thought proves suggestive for the thesis that reflections on crisis and consciousness belong together in any systematic phenomenological philosophy. Whether and how they belong together will not be treated here as a hermeneutical question about the unity of Husserl's corpus. Instead, we will make what progress we can by defining the relevant topics of inquiry and describing things as we see them.

Summary of Contents

This study is organized into two parts, each in two divisions.[1] The *first part* gains access to the dynamics of awakening by developing a phenomenology of having presupposed. Its first division works out a general analysis that the second division specifies according to three different attitudes. The *first division* begins by delimiting the concept of presupposition. I define presupposition formally as the potentially independent part of a whole it forms with a part that depends upon it (its ground). I define presupposition epistemically in terms of a cognitive interest. One is interested in the truth of the presupposition because one is interested in the truth of the ground. Finally, I define the developmental structure in which the ground-presupposition relation unfolds. The initial assertion of the ground precedes the discovery of its presupposition and thereby the discovery that the ground is a ground. The presupposition is the correlate of an "act" of presupposing only for a retroactive realization. It is impossible to presuppose in the present. I introduce the concepts of naïveté and awakening to capture how one holds oneself responsible in the present for having presupposed in the past.

The remainder of the first division pursues a detailed analysis of holding oneself responsible for having presupposed. I first focus on the realization of having presupposed, then the demand to appropriate the naïve life-phase, and finally the appropriation that satisfies this demand. Presuppositions originally become evident in realizations, which apprehend states of affairs as having not been ready to be apprehended. I examine the distinct experience of inability that distinguishes realization from reflection, discovery, and correction. The distinction between reflection and realization is of particular importance. Each makes the implicit explicit, but in very different ways. In light of this distinction, I clarify awakening as a reflection within realization that shifts focus from what is realized to one's having been unable to apprehend it. The object of awakening is one's own past naïveté.

The demand to appropriate the naïve life-phase arises from the disvalue of naïveté. I address the question of why it is bad to have been naïve by examining the affective experience of jeopardy that attends realization. This experience reveals an intrinsic disvalue of naïveté apart from considerations of correctness and success. I argue that the realization of naïveté jeopardizes the subject, not only as the accomplisher of a cognitive or practical task, but in its very being as an ego. As soon as it emerges on the scene of experience, the ego lays claim to an in-principle ability to appropriate its life. This in-principle ability is analogous to, and underlies, the in-principle accessibility of remote objects in space and time. Such an ability makes intelligible the factual constraints on its own exercise. It is this "basic integrity" of the ego that is compromised in the realization of naïveté and that must be reclaimed in wakeful appropriation. Basic integrity supports an unconditional will to wakefulness: *I do not want to be naïve, but if I am, I want to realize that I have been, no matter the consequences.*

I treat the expression "I presupposed" as a clue to how the awakened ego reclaims its naïve life. The "I" in "I presupposed" refers to the emergent ego of the present awakening. This ego has the presupposition in its purview and projects its capacity for apprehension back into the naïve life-phase such that it holds itself responsible for failing to apprehend. My consideration of how appropriative reflection can discover this negligence is guided by models of narrative explanation drawn from the analytic philosophy of history. These models help define the problem by analyzing true statements that describe past events such that they could not have been witnessed at the time. However, they cannot illuminate how the appropriation of naïveté differs from historical retrospect. Appropriation makes evident the actual missing of an implication that lay in the purview of the naïve ego according to the very meanings it relied upon in its naïve accomplishment. In doing so, it discovers a "consuming interest" failing which the presupposition would have been apparent. The formula for wakeful responsibility for naïveté runs: *though I was factually unable, I was in principle able just because I am now able.* I conclude by showing why the wakeful resumption of naïve projects requires teleological interpretations that identify the aims of the naïve ego with those of the wakeful ego. The difficulty of this identification can be masked by illusions that I outline.

The *second division* specifies the general account of the first division in terms of three basic attitudes: the natural attitude, the phenomenological attitude, and the critical-historical attitude. Each attitude frames endless tasks for the appropriation of naïveté that higher attitudes cannot usurp, even as they expose the fundamental presuppositions of their predecessors. Special problems thus emerge for appropriative reflections that move between basic attitudes. The awakened ego understands naïveté as a deficient mode of its own life but cannot advance the tasks to which the naïve ego stood committed. These tasks, and the basic attitude to which they are appropriate, thus retain a final legitimacy. This ambiguous situation will complicate the ideal of wakeful self-responsibility and its systematic pursuit in philosophy.

For the natural attitude, human wakefulness is the state of a diurnal animal and is essentially attentiveness to the world. The awakening to naïveté is accordingly construed as a development within this general world-oriented wakefulness that is the opposite of sleep. The horizon structure of the world determines the nature of awakenings to naïveté in the natural attitude. I distinguish between world and world context. The former is the correlate of an infinity of concordant experiences, the latter of a finite set of experiences organized into routines. Inattentiveness to the world because of a consuming interest in a world context is the canonical form of naïveté for which life in the natural attitude holds itself responsible. With reference to Welton, Steinbock, and Waldenfels, I define worldliness and provinciality as the natural-attitude specifications of wakefulness and naïveté. Because all world-directed wakefulness is potentially provincial, but cannot anticipate how, the natural attitude tends toward a relativistic interpretation of wakefulness itself. I explore attempts to overcome this relativity through an appropriation of world-directed life as a whole. I consider two opposed strategies, each of which pushes mundane wakefulness to its limits. This exploration reveals (via Descartes) the epistemic problem of certainty and (via Heidegger) the existential problem of life-significance as issues that no higher attitude can ignore.

I characterize the phenomenological attitude in terms of the awakening to transcendental naïveté on which it is founded and the transformation it brings about in the very idea of wakefulness. I argue that reflection can achieve the phenomenological attitude only when complex modifications of interest are at the disposal of the ego. Phenomenological reflection is first made possible by the jeopardizing realization of transcendental naïveté, the inability to notice transcendental constitution. Husserl's claim that transcendental life is intrinsically ready to become an object of immanent perception is not false. However, I emphasize that this intrinsic readiness is first revealed through the annexation of naïve life in wakeful appropriation. The view that transcendental life lies within the purview of natural life, perhaps at its margins or in its background, is vulnerable to Merleau-Ponty's critique of "philosophies of reflection." Transcendental subjectivity is a new domain in which to appropriate naïve accomplishments, not a lost origin to which one returns. Here as elsewhere, *appropriative reflection exhausts what naïve life was like in terms of the new evidence won through awakening.*

Phenomenological wakefulness is unique in its finality. I distinguish this finality from the complete appropriation of natural-attitude life. The phenomenological attitude is "presuppositionless," not because one has overcome all presuppositions but because one has realized an apodictic presupposition in terms of which to conduct an endless appropriation of naïveté. Revisiting Cartesian doubt, I argue that dream skepticism is conceivable once wakefulness is no longer tethered to world-directedness. It is in this context that I defend Husserl's experiments in world-annihilation. Such experiments reveal the formal relationship between the world and consciousness. The presupposition, here as elsewhere, is potentially independent from the whole it forms with the ground. Finally, I show how the phenomenological devaluation of the natural attitude differs from the devaluation of naïve attitudes within the natural attitude. The natural attitude continues to guide involvement in the domain to which it pertains after phenomenological awakening. The phenomenological attitude cannot appropriate the natural-attitude ideals of worldliness and existential responsibility.

Part I concludes by describing how the issue of phenomenology's own life-significance can occasion a new basic attitude and a new form of appropriative reflection. Phenomenological awakening is genuine insofar as it uproots projects to which one stood committed in the natural attitude. Because the interests of the natural and phenomenological attitudes fundamentally diverge, neither attitude can understand such projects. I develop an account of a "critical-historical" attitude directed toward how phenomenology itself transforms ramified projects in the human world. These projects include special sciences (especially psychology), universal science (philosophy), as well as the civilizational pursuit of scientific culture (Enlightenment). In order for these projects to be uprooted because of their transcendental naïveté, they must have been oriented toward wakefulness as a value that transcends the interests of natural-attitude life. Revisiting the discussion of teleology, I outline the problems appropriative reflection confronts in discovering such an orientation.

The *second part* of the study takes stock of Husserl's innovative attempt to provide systematic finish to a transcendental philosophy through the critical-historical appropriation of a "crisis." The first division defines the crisis problematic, a group of interconnected problems, perennial for phenomenology, that Husserl's crisis writings engage from a particular perspective. The second division considers the sort of concepts that emerge in solving these problems, with particular attention to those employed by Husserl.

The *first division* begins by considering various ways that Husserl relates the program of phenomenological reflection to the goal of "science" or "philosophy." Husserl's most comprehensive view recognizes that the interpretation of phenomenology as philosophy depends upon certain "ultimate presuppositions." Their appropriation, he argues, requires a teleological reconstruction of our shared history that exhibits in it an orientation toward absolute self-responsibility. With reference to the work of Carr and Dodd, I explore the importance of historical reflection in the crisis problematic. I argue that history is here at issue primarily as a domain in which to cultivate clarity of purpose in the pursuit of inalienable but unstable goals. The first task for a phenomenological philosophy is not to respond to the crisis, as if it were an external exigency, but to show that there is a crisis, one internal to a history oriented toward wakefulness as an absolute value. The ultimate presuppositions may be summed up as the conviction that such a crisis is possible.

I interpret the crisis that concerns Husserl in his late philosophy in terms of the dynamics of awakened subjectivity. To be in crisis is to be jeopardized in one's dedication to a project one cannot let go, but which has become untenable because of the naïveté with which it has been pursued. According to Husserl's formula, crisis is the *painful existential contradiction* of needing to believe in a goal, but facing the question of whether one can believe. I show why the "crisis of science" ultimately encompasses the entire movement of Enlightenment in its transcendental naïveté. Engaging competing accounts of Husserl's crisis reflections, I argue for taking seriously Husserl's own medical conception of the crisis. In spiritual medicine, diagnosing the sickness is already part of the cure. The critical-historical appropriation accomplishes this diagnosis by making us responsible for the wakeful transformation of the Enlightenment project that has its engine in science. It disabuses us of false consolations that might conceal the necessity of this transformation while winning a teleological comprehension of a history in which the life-significance of science is at stake.

I further clarify the function of critical-historical appropriation in the crisis problematic through a series of comparisons. Husserl turns to philosophical history in order to enable belief in a project that cannot be abandoned. This suggests a comparison with Kant's extension of theoretical reason for practical purposes. Husserl, like Kant, holds that certain problematic assertions are justified if they are not false and if they orient the pursuit of an apparently futile, but practically necessary project. However, because Husserl has no recourse to Kant's phenomenal/noumenal distinction, both the apparent futility of the project and its actual attainability are products of historical understanding. The "end derived from reason" is also derived from history. This result suggests a comparison with Hegel's philosophy of history. Husserl, like Hegel, has a teleological conception of human history as a "spiritual" development, rather than a merely anthropological evolution. However, whereas Hegel contemplates the sovereignty of reason in history, the crisis reflections illuminate everything at stake for one who wills that sovereignty. With reference to James, I consider the relationship between purposive and theoretical clarity, suggesting "mission statements" as a model for understanding the evidential standards for Husserl's history.

The *second division* argues that the existence of a crisis ultimately depends upon there being a subject of crisis, a historical community for whom science *has* the life-significance that might be lost. I examine the problems that beset the discovery of any such subject and how Husserl negotiates them in his crisis writings. I begin by showing that Husserl's history of philosophy takes its bearings from a philosophical history. This latter pertains to a historical community that charges philosophy with responsibilities it cannot satisfy without overcoming its transcendental naïveté. I contend that Husserl's most concrete conception of philosophical subjectivity is to be a bearer of this history who struggles for its true sense against false consolations. We who philosophize are neither generic human beings nor transcendental spectators, but rather participants in a community committed to an endangered vision of scientific culture.

The latter sections of the final division consider the kind of teleological reconstruction by which one can take responsibility for belonging to this community. Any engagement with the crisis problematic has to specify the historical provenance, limits, and prospects of its "we." It interprets specific events, persons, and social formations available in the historical background so that they express an unconditional commitment to wakefulness. At the same time, because this historical community is at issue precisely as the bearer of this unconditional commitment, its historical specificity must be reconciled with an anthropological indeterminacy that allows for participation irrespective of lineage or inheritance. Identifying with this history is a difficult exercise of willing autonomy by cultivating a tradition. I argue that Husserl's conception of "European humanity" should be understood as responding to these demands of the crisis problematic. I contest the standard view that Husserl's Europe is an "idea in the Kantian sense," arguing that it is rather a historical community oriented toward such ideas. Husserl's European history traces the transformations in human culture that result when the realization of naïveté expands the purview of human responsibility into an infinite dimension. I distinguish between the conventional conception of being European and the conception that emerges from Husserl's appropriation. The latter is tied to the shaking of national allegiance, the critique of both traditionalism and the sophistic corruption of tradition, and the struggle against the finitization of infinite ideas.

In concluding, I argue that any appropriation of the ultimate presuppositions is contentious and evaluate the controversies peculiar to Husserl's appropriation. Of particular importance are the problems of hypocrisy and exceptionalism as they pertain to the subject of crisis. The first problem arises because philosophical humanity, to use Husserl's formula, *lives in finitude but toward poles of infinity*. Orientation toward these poles entails a routinized subjection of finite ideas to an infinite framework of critique. Hypocrisy would mean that the appeal to infinite ideas actually functions within the purview of finite interests. The question of whether a purportedly philosophical history is hypocritical is a matter for historical judgment (I consider representatives on both sides of the "Europe" question), as is whether one revitalizes or departs from that history in critiquing its hypocrisy (again, I consider representatives on both sides). The second problem arises because pluralism threatens to undermine the entire crisis problematic by finitizing philosophy as an expression of culture. This threat, however, does not require the claim (which Husserl makes) that there is only one historical formation that sustains an orientation toward infinity. That claim, too, is based on historical judgement. The virtue of the crisis problematic is that it does not allow for a pretended resolution to these problems from a theoretical perspective. Instead, it demands an interpretation of the life-significance of the program of transcendental reflection in light of the ideals of worldliness and existential responsibility. It demands maximal wakefulness of the philosopher.

Philosophical Style

Husserl once summed up his pedagogical approach by saying that he seeks not to instruct but to lead by drawing attention to what he sees (1970, 8/17). This study tries to follow Husserl without taking instruction from him. I turn to Husserl's texts for guidance in the discipline of phenomenological seeing, treating them as pointers, not subject matter. The reader familiar with Husserl will notice that I often struggle to articulate in my own terms dimensions of experience for which Husserl himself has provided detailed accounts. By developing original descriptive themes and concepts, I try to open up a trajectory in Husserlian thinking that might remain concealed in explications of what Husserl thought. Even the second part of this study, which closely examines Husserl's work on the crisis, is a proposal for how to understand the significance of that work, not an attempt to reconstruct it and its intellectual context. My construal of "the crisis problematic" seeks to pursue the trajectory opened up by the investigations of Part I.

In the interest of writing a study of manageable length, I have tried to develop phenomenological descriptions that strike a balance between exploring and surveying their territory. I often work out formulations that are simultaneously summary and suggestive and employ them moving forward. I intend such formulations as invitations to, not substitutes for, further thinking. For the same reason, this study cannot settle the questions it raises about how to situate Husserlian phenomenology with respect to its Cartesian and Kantian heritage and its existentialist, hermeneutical, and realist critics. Rather than say nothing about these matters, I occasionally indicate how a broader discussion might take them up.

Phenomenological description poses special difficulties for the use of personal pronouns. In the body of this work, I use the authorial "we" and reserve "I" for the description of egoic phenomena. In connection with the crisis problematic, the meaning of the authorial "we" in phenomenology becomes an issue in its own right and acquires a new sense that I indicate with scare quotes. In good eidetic fashion, "he" and "she" are arbitrarily employed to refer to an individual person, but I stick with "he" when tracking Husserl's usage.

This study does not aim to discover much in the way of philology. Where possible, I cite translations of Husserl's work, making modifications in rare instances when a point of importance turns on the language. I have provided my own translations of material unavailable in English. When citing a translation of Husserl's work, I provide pagination in the corresponding *Husserliana* volume following a forward slash. In line with Carr (1970), Dodd (2004), and Moran (2012), I refer to Husserl's unfinished final treatise simply as "*Crisis*." I use "*Crisis I*," "*Crisis II*," and "*Crisis III*" to refer to the parts of that treatise as translated and organized by Carr in *The Crisis of European Sciences and Transcendental Phenomenology* (1970). The phrase "crisis writings" refers to the appendixes to that volume as well as additional materials in *Husserliana* 6 and 29.

Part One

Awakened Subjectivity

Division A

The Phenomenology of Having Presupposed

1. Bringing Presuppositions Back to Life

Some preliminary distinctions will help fix the terms that describe our topic. We will be using the term "presupposition" to pick out one of the many phenomena to which it refers in ordinary and philosophical usage. We do not mean to imply that the phenomena covered by these other uses are reducible to presuppositions in our sense. We rather wish to isolate and examine a particular phenomenon with special importance for phenomenology. We will delimit this phenomenon, first in terms of its formal and epistemological features, then its developmental structure, and finally its significance for someone's life. From here, we can move from delimitation to description and begin the investigation.

Treated as a strictly formal topic, presuppositions have one basic feature. A presupposition is a potentially independent part of a whole it forms with a part (its ground) that depends upon it. For instance, the grass's being green is a ground upon the presupposition of its being colored. We may apply the same terms to the moments of a judgment that articulates such a whole. We can then treat the ground-presupposition judgment as if it were composed of two separate judgments, A ("the grass is green") and B ("the grass is colored"), and attend to their truth values. If we do this, the compound judgment will share certain features with the truth-functional conditional. For instance, there can be no true statement that "A presupposes B" when "A" is true and "B" is false. However, to judge "A presupposes B" is to see *that* the ground depends upon its presupposition, not to notice the patterns of truth values correlated with this dependency. The ground-presupposition judgment discerns a whole comprised of parts in just this way. Then, when we state of the analyzed judgment itself that "'A' presupposes 'B'" the word "presupposes" expresses our understanding that the truth of the judgment's ground moment requires that of its presupposition moment.

To stand in these relationships, the contents formed as ground and presupposition must be expressible as assertions. Not only the whole but also each part contains a thought about what is, is not, or might be the case. With respect to the presupposition in particular, it can be true without the ground's being true, and refers to a state of affairs that is a potentially independent part of the ground-presupposition whole. We will therefore avoid using the term "presupposition" for the hypothetical conditions expressed in counterfactual clauses. "If I were young again …" is not a presupposition in our sense, nor is "… I would do things differently" a ground, whereas "If I were young again I would do things differently" is a possible presupposition and a possible ground. We reserve the term "supposition" for hypothetical conditions and their expression. Grounds and presuppositions are beliefs in the broad sense that they bear a rational commitment.

Conditional relationships guide various kinds of inquiry, only one of which deals with presuppositions in our sense. Antecedent and consequent are ground and presupposition only when one is interested in the truth of the latter in order to determine the truth of the former. The truth of the ground is at stake in the consideration of the presupposition. This excludes from our topic not only the converse interest that looks into the antecedent in order to determine the truth of the consequent but also several other directions of inquiry. Given some reliable truth, one may, for instance, search for whatever it entails. What one finds are its necessary conditions but not its presuppositions in our sense. Because the truth of the ground is at stake in the consideration of the presupposition, the ground must be able to turn out false. The presupposition, however, may be a judgment that is perfectly certain. This is an exceptional case that we will examine. For now, we may distinguish our use of "presupposition" from that which designates assertions that lack sufficient evidence. Such "suspicions" are presuppositions only if they have the formal and epistemological features outlined above.

Presuppositions enter into concrete episodes of reasoning in a remarkable way. The assertion of the ground precedes any consideration of the ground-presupposition whole in which the ground is ground. During the initial assertion of the ground (or the content that will become ground), the presupposition is neither affirmed nor denied, nor entertained at all. It is during this phase that the presupposition will count as the correlate of an "act" of presupposing. Among necessary conditions, we thus distinguish presuppositions in our sense from every freely posited "assumption" and every habitually functioning "conviction" to which one can voluntarily direct attention. For the reasoning subject, the presupposition is not available while it is presupposed, but only in a retroactive realization. Only then does the one who has presupposed confront the whole truth of which the ground is a part, if the ground is true. We use the term "ground" for the dependent part of the ground-presupposition whole because it comes to attention as what was naively relied upon. The realization of the presupposition uproots the ground. We will explore the possibility of attributing unrealized presuppositions to someone in order to explain what she thinks or does. However, the presupposition actually enters into an episode of reasoning through a realization that retroactively assigns it to a naïve life-phase that the realization itself puts to an end. The presupposition is a moment of the larger phenomenon of having presupposed.

As is already clear, the term "presupposition" refers to a multidimensional subject matter. Ontologically, it refers to the potentially independent part of a whole it forms with a part that depends upon it (its ground). Logically, it refers to the moment of a judgment that discerns the presupposition in the former sense and that, when analyzed, mirrors the consequent in the truth-functional conditional. Epistemically, it refers to an object of inquiry in which the truth of the ground is at stake. Mentally, it refers to the "act," constituted retroactively in a realization of naïveté, of not noticing the presupposition in the prior senses. It is this final sense that encompasses the others and is decisive for a study of realizing presuppositions *as one's own*.

Having presupposed is the object of retroactive realization, and thus belongs to an experiential development in the life of a subject. What has been presupposed has a definite logical form. However, this form need not concern the one who realizes a presupposition. The fact of having presupposed, on the other hand, necessarily concerns her. Having presupposed is of concern because it puts something at risk to which one was committed. The ground is embodied in an ongoing project that has become questionable in its viability, the presupposition in an unnoticed circumstance the realization of which has transformed the viable project into a dependent moment of a new practical whole. As judgment moments, ground and presupposition refer, respectively, to dependent and potentially independent parts of this situation, which we will term a "predicament." Thinking about the predicament can, but need not, involve the explicit consideration of propositions that bear upon it. So long as this situation is thematic as the subject's own, even the formal analysis of ground and presupposition is bound up with a trial of subjectivity we will call "jeopardy." For a subject committed to a project she cannot let go, this trial takes on special existential importance—it becomes a "crisis."

Having presupposed ultimately concerns the subjectivity of the realizing subject. The realization "I have presupposed ..." always includes a definite presuppositional content. It is this content and its relation to its ground that ordinarily captures attention. However, attention to presuppositional content is undergirded by a narrative and evaluative self-understanding. Whoever has presupposed takes responsibility for failing to have noticed the presupposition. This negligence is apparent in the realization itself. When a presupposition is realized, it exposes a fault in the one who has presupposed. Having presupposed involves a devaluation of the life-phase during which one was presupposing, a positive valuation of the realization itself, and a need to revisit one's uprooted commitments from a perspective no longer dominated by the presupposition. It will prove difficult to fix criteria that distinguish genuine presuppositions from "pseudo-presuppositions" that fail to prompt this self-assessment. In any case, the devaluation and valuation at work here, as well as the tasks they orient, concern the one who has presupposed not only as the author of something uprooted in the predicament but as an I. Presuppositions in our sense are necessary conditions, the retroactive realization of which places in question the very "I" of the one who has presupposed.[1]

We can now offer a preliminary description of our topic: a presupposition is a necessary condition that becomes evident in a realization that I am jeopardized by my past naïveté. The analyses of this division will develop this description by examining the experience from which it is drawn. We can begin only by targeting its most general features. Further, because the experience is composed of intertwined moments, our initial findings will complement and reinforce one another rather than build in a linear progression. They will be like snapshots whose overlapping edges indicate their place in an arrangement. Only in subsequent divisions can we think in terms of the comprehensive view they afford. We also have to forestall critical questions about our method of trying to understand what something really is by reflecting on the experience in which it becomes evident. One teaching of phenomenology is that the meaning of such questions depends upon the extent to which we have interrogated presuppositions so elementary that they shape every subject matter available to attention. In these initial explorations, however, we will ignore those responsibilities phenomenology entrusts to the "reflection on experience." This way of proceeding is necessary because these initial explorations, while naïve from a phenomenological standpoint, will indicate a broader development that illuminates the significance of that very standpoint.

2. Realization and Reflection

The similarities, differences, and relations between realization and reflection are of great importance to this study. Realizations apprehend a state of affairs as only now coming to attention for the first time. The "for the first time" distinguishes realizations from forms of consideration that grasp what was previously attended to as such. The "only now" distinguishes them from forms of taking notice that move within a purview, a field of what is potentially noticeable in familiar ways. This "only now ... for the first time" character inheres in what is realized and is not derived from an additional judgment directed toward it. It is thus different from receiving a piece of news that I subsequently decide has arrived too late. This character can inhere in the realization because of the way it builds upon a prior history of understanding. The realization that x entails that x was not ready to be noticed, was not held in a purview that indicated it as potential object of attention. Yet, the realization that x builds upon a previous acquaintance with the rational motives that could have prompted its being noticed. Because what is now realized was implied but not discerned as implied in the previous acquaintance, realization supplies what the realizing subject was *missing* in a special sense.[2] Realization is an apprehension that lags behind what it apprehends.

The sudden character of realization is due to this lag. Whereas the discovering explication of what is now implied fulfills or disappoints expectations, the realization only now of what was implied sneaks up without expectation. This sneaking up is the passive undercurrent of realization: something dawning. What dawns eludes the monitoring of potentialities that guides ordinary finding out about things. It breaks into an object of realization without following any train of thought. But what dawns is not incomprehensible or even unforeseeable. What is realized was before it was realized. It dawns out of the past. The paradigm for the sudden is not the intrusion of something novel that catches one off guard. If we go far enough in this direction, we find events that would lack any meaningful contrast with expectations and produce no effect. The paradigm for the sudden is rather the appearance of something that was implied but missed as implied. When we go further in this direction, by multiplying the implications and extending the period during which they obtain, as do certain plot forms, we enhance the effect. Realization emerges on the basis of this passive undercurrent of something suddenly dawning. But it itself is a realization *that*, a directedness toward how things stand, not a mere sensation of surprise. In this respect, realization is similar to a remembering that breaks into an otherwise occupied course of experience. The essential difference is that any remembering is based upon a previous apprehension of what is now remembered.

Like realization, reflection makes explicit what was implicit in a previous acquaintance. However, the pre-reflective acquaintance already held what is seen in reflection in the purview of potential attention. The shift in focus that brings the reflected upon object into view does not supply what was missing, but rather brings into the foreground something already available. Yet it is a *shift* in focus because it breaks with the course of explication projected in the pre-reflective acquaintance. In doing so, it engages other points of view already at the disposal of the one reflecting. For everything experienced, certain of its features and connections are salient and others are in the background, depending upon the concerns that govern unreflective involvement with it. Most reflection steps back from the courses of explication suggested by what is salient and showcases its object in view of something pertinent to, but not prominent in, this initial involvement. As a special case, simple reflection showcases merely that and how the object of pre-reflective acquaintance is. In either case, reflection is the suspension of a governing interest that freely returns to its object in order to consider it in a new light. In the case of simple reflection, the light "shines" directly from the object of pre-reflective acquaintance itself.

This account of reflection conforms in many ways to Husserl's in *Ideas I* (§§ 38, 45, 77). However, it differs in one important respect. Whereas Husserl defines reflection as the way in which consciousness knows itself, we define it, by way of contrast with realization, in terms of how it notices the unnoticed, leaving the nature of its object open. On our definition, many reflections do not concern consciousness at all. In using an appliance, one can reflect that such appliances did not exist just fifty years ago, so long as this fact was not salient during the initial use and one is familiar with it. This approach will allow us to consider problems concerning the role of both reflection and realization in the discovery of subjectivity at various levels.[3] "Know thyself!" may be an insufficient slogan for the task of self-responsibility if it means "Reflect! Turn within!" It may require supplementation with: "Want to realize what you cannot now reflect upon!" This latter is an appeal to desire, rather than an effective imperative, because it points beyond what is within one's own power.[4]

Let us now spell out the most crucial differences between reflection and realization. First, their temporal character differs. Reflection is a free return to what was there before, which it now "takes up again in a new light." Realization, on the other hand, is overtaken by what was previously unnoticed, which it confronts "only now for the first time." Second, their relation to the implicit differs. What was implicit in the unreflective acquaintance was already familiar to the one who now reflects in its light. Reflection only finds what the one reflecting held in the background of the unreflective acquaintance and does so by actualizing an available direction of possible attention. Realization, by contrast, brings something into view that was outside the purview of the previous acquaintance, and thus missing. Third, their starting points differ. Reflection begins from a free stepping back that suspends a governing interest. Realization begins from an uncanny dawning that delivers what is realized in advance of all method.

Realization and reflection are different ways of taking notice of any object. While it is clear that any object of realization can become an object of reflection, it might seem that certain objects cannot be realized because they are by their nature already available to reflection. The case of consciousness is especially difficult and will occupy us at length. It is also tempting to suppose that lawful connections between objects or object moments guarantee that in thinking of the one, one is already implicitly thinking of the other, so that the lawfully connected whole cannot be realized only now for the first time. But unless we conceive the thinking subject as the executive of every ideal law, such connections only determine what one ought to think, not what one does. It is the purview of the subject alone that decides how what was implied comes to notice, either discovered from out of the background or dawning as having been missed. It is in principle possible to realize only now for the first time that *A* follows from *A and B*. When one does, it is not primarily because of lawful necessity that one thinks one could have noticed, but because of what one finds in reflecting upon how one came to notice.

Realization and reflection not only overlap, they also encompass one another in various ways. Reflection can take as its object a realization or an object of realization. It can also take as its object the reflection on realization. But a reflective attitude also courts realizations. By suspending governing interests and reconfiguring objects of attention, it provides space for the familiar to unfold its unnoticed implications. There are no methods of realization, but methods of reflection at least inhibit the ossification of attention that prohibits realization. Finally, realizations demand reflection. To be understood, what has been realized and the realization itself require the attention of the subject now ready to apprehend them.

3. Realization and Having Presupposed

A presupposition is originally given for a realization. This is important to emphasize because one way of explaining presuppositions is to treat them as prior convictions that have become obvious and mostly unavailable. We will consider the place of such explanations, which do have their place. For now, we only want to point out that the presuppositional content itself, what becomes evident as presupposed, is essentially the correlate of a process of realization. It becomes evident as something to which I have never attended. The realization of a presupposition can break into a course of experience on its own. Typically, however, it occurs in the modification of an initial realization. I realize something, and in so realizing, it dawns on me that I have presupposed. We will focus on this complex case because it includes the simpler one.

Anything can be an object of realization so long as the rational motive for its discovery was given in a previous acquaintance blind to its implications. What is realized may be some present or future state of affairs (*tomorrow is a holiday*) and it may involve people other than the realizing subject (*he has been planning to leave*). The presupposition that builds on an initial realization also has its content. This need not be, but often is, opposed to that of the initial realization (*tomorrow is a workday; he is intending to stay*). The presupposition is the object of its own realization, however, not only because its content can differ from that of the initial realization but also because it essentially concerns the past life of the realizing subject. By this relation of concern, we refer to the way that certain prominent objects of value or disvalue draw attention toward the subject for whom they matter. This draw on attention is there as a draw, even if it is not followed. The presupposition inculpates me in the past from which the initial realization dawns. At issue is my history of understanding, which was blind in precisely such a way as to allow for the "only now for the first time" of the initial realization. Generally, the one who realizes a presupposition is first of all interested in its truth as it bears upon the uprooted ground. However, underlying this interest is a self-concern that brings one's history of blindness within one's purview.

Though we cannot yet see how, having presupposed is discoverable in this history. That it can *only* be discovered in this history follows from our stipulated definition. As an act, my having presupposed is essentially past. The first-person present tense of the verb "to presuppose" is absurd. One commonly uses this form of the verb to refer to assumptions, suppositions, or suspicions. But we have employed fixed terminology precisely to emphasize that assumptions, suppositions, and suspicions, unlike presuppositions, are wakefully accomplished and are not bound to retroactive realization. If first-person evidence for my having presupposed is possible, then the present realization of the presupposition indicates a past occurrence in my mental life, somehow related to the presuppositional content, of which I had no awareness at the time. Presupposing thus seems to belong to a class of phantom acts including forgetting and mistaking that are only converted into first-person accomplishments after the fact, and that, by becoming accessible now as complete, become inaccessible to direct representation. It is true that realizing a presupposition entails that I am no longer presupposing and that I cannot remember having presupposed. However, this hardly settles the question of whether I "really" presupposed. We will soon consider whether Danto's conception of narrative sentences elucidates how "I have presupposed" can be true. The narrative sentence describes an event in light of a later event such that the prior event could not have been witnessed under this description. It thus furnishes actions "with descriptions which the actor himself could not have given of them at the time" (1985, 183). Whatever it yields, this analysis at the level of the statement must be tempered by Carr's reminder that verbal narration does not impose narrative structure on experience, but rather articulates story-like features internal to experience itself (1986, 29). This applies also to the retrospective revision of one's life expressed in "I have presupposed."

The realization of a presupposition opens an encounter with oneself that has peculiar narrative and evaluative characteristics. Subsequent sections will consider how this self-understanding is pursued through reflections that treat my having presupposed as a past accomplishment. For now, we can guard against the tendency to confuse this self-understanding with analogous interpretive attitudes. Confusion arises because the realized presupposition indicates a mental occurrence (having presupposed) of which I had no awareness at the time. It thus seems plausible to detach the act of presupposing from the self-concerned, pastward realization in which it is disclosed. Detached in this manner, presupposing is attributable to subjects who have not realized their having presupposed. I judge, for instance, that someone else is currently missing something implied in what she is attending to. Or I judge that I myself am probably missing something right now, although I have not yet realized what. Such judgments are indeed possible and have their justification. However, they also have their own ways of addressing the subject who apparently presupposes. These ways are quite different from how one becomes a problem for oneself in the realization of having presupposed. The analysis goes astray if we substitute the former for the latter. We can anticipate some important differences by looking at a few cases of the attribution of unrealized presuppositions.

An historical account of a military conflict may state that the generals had presupposed that the enemy would not approach the city by land. Evidence can be marshaled for this claim. The heavy artillery was pointed toward the sea, fortifications were constructed on the coast, but not along the city's landward facing perimeter, and so on. But this is not sufficient. A presupposition is not an assumption. To have presupposed, the generals must have taken for granted that there would be no landward approach such that they never even made this judgment. Here too there may be evidence. There exist records of every meeting between the responsible generals during the preparation for the battle, none of which contain mention of a possible attack by land. Or consider a case in the present. After learning the principal parts of the verbs walk, talk, and dress, a student of English attempts to provide them for swim. When she quickly and confidently says, "swim, swimmed, swimmed," it seems that she is presupposing that the pattern established by the other verbs will hold.

Such attribution of presupposing explains behavior by the unnoticed authority of tradition. Others who presuppose are in the grip of an interpretation that they cannot recognize as conditional because things have always conformed to it. It is because "everyone knows" that the city cannot be approached by land that the generals do not bother to think it. Similarly, because the student has only been exposed to one morphological pattern, she does not even judge that the next word will conform to it, but rather follows it as a matter of course. The others who presuppose are supposed to be in the grip of tradition at the moment of their presupposing, which is why the presupposition remains unrealized. The fact made prominent in attributing unrealized presuppositions to others is that they are embedded in traditions. The narrative and evaluative understanding of their condition is guided by this fact. For instance, seeing what others cannot because they are caught up in routines is the condition for appreciating certain forms of irony and tragedy. There is also the ethical problem of whether others are culpable for failing to realize what, from another perspective, seems realizable. There are certainly similarities between how I am concerned by others' "unrealized presuppositions" and how I am concerned by my own realized presuppositions. These similarities may even be due to a distinction, within myself, between I who realize and I who could have, but did not realize, my presupposition. However, as we will see, the realization of one's own presupposition introduces a dynamic of alienation and recovery far removed from an interpretive interest in how people are blinded by traditions.

Consider now a case of attributing unrealized presuppositions to oneself in the present. I am struggling to assemble a piece of furniture. I am confident that it has been manufactured correctly, and that all the required pieces are there. I have read and reread the instructions for assembly, and attempted to follow them, but to no avail. Surely, I say to myself, I must be missing something. Such situations justify the suspicion that I will, in the future, realize that I am now presupposing. This is because I know that what I am failing to accomplish is accomplishable, not only in principle, but for me. This knowledge relies upon a self-interpretation mediated by the idea of "the reasonable person." The task has been designed so that a person with certain capacities can complete it, and I am a person who has these capacities. In other cases, this mediating function is played by my past self. I have solved this problem or similar problems in the past, so the fact that I cannot find the solution might be due to my missing something. Some intervening standard for normal apprehension is necessary in order to conclude that I should be capable of what I am not. Suspicions that I am currently presupposing can be confirmed in realizations that reveal just what I was missing and inculpate me in having missed it. However, as soon as the suspicion turns out to be true, I employ a new way of understanding and evaluating the capacity I should have had. As we will see, this self-understanding dispenses with every intervening standard.

The repeated realization of presuppositions can motivate skeptical iterations of suspicion. For instance, an acquaintance with one's own intellectual development, or with that of broader communities, gives rise to the worry that one is probably missing the signs that one is probably missing something. In certain contexts, there is no check on this tendency, and the judgment that "one is always presupposing something" seems inevitable. However, this judgment is only an instrument of method. It is a watchword for the vigilant, not a piece of knowledge. The only knowledge of presupposing is the knowledge of having presupposed that occurs in self-concerned, pastward realizations and the reflections they entrain. Here, the subject of the presupposition is considered unable only as she possesses that very ability, blind only as she possesses sight. As we will see, the realizing subject is in the grip, not of tradition, but of the illuminative power of realization.

4. Awakening and Naïveté

If x is realized, x was not ready to be noticed. However, that x was not ready to be noticed is not the thematic focus of the original realization, which is first of all directed toward the suddenly dawning x. We call "awakening" the process of reflection within realization that focuses on the fact that x was not ready to be noticed and, in self-reflection, that I was not ready to notice it. These shifts of focus are *within* the realization because they are still explicating the way in which the subject has been affected by what she has realized. We may regard such reflections as developments of the realization itself, just as reflections within a memory fill out the past scene. The realization of having presupposed is a developed realization that has brought into focus, through awakening, the presuppositional content as unavailable to apprehension, and finally me myself as having been unable to attend to it. For example, suppose I am busy cooking dinner for friends. In the midst of wondering whether there are enough wine glasses, it suddenly dawns on me that my guests' children might be coming as well (level 1). On this original realization is founded the past-directed, self-reflexive realization in which the presupposition can become evident: "I have been presupposing that the children are not coming" (level 2). Finally, the full-fledged awakening takes as its object my own inability to have taken a position about the children's coming (level 3).

The process of awakening ends in a condition of wakefulness. Wakefulness is an enjoyment of the evident and the ability to attend to the evident. It is characterized by its self-authenticating nature (the wakeful subject is aware she is awake) and its relativity to a non-wakeful condition from which it has emerged (the wakeful subject is aware she was not always wakeful). What the non-wakeful condition really was is apparent only from the perspective of wakefulness, whereas wakefulness is apparent as wakeful for itself. Even awakening and the possibility of awakening are disclosed as what they are on this side of the transition to wakefulness. Plato's famous cave allegory illustrates this well. The steep way that leads to the world above is not a path the prisoner sets out upon and traverses under his own power. Indeed, he can only make proper use of his capacities once outside, and only understands the meaning of his ascent once he has oriented himself by the light of the sun.

Not all awakenings concern having presupposed. In fact, biological contingencies have conspired such that for human beings the most global and dramatic experience of awakening concerns having been asleep. Here, it is the world, the universe of realities, that dawns, and that the subject of awakening was unable to attend to. According to the above schema, the realizations implied in diurnal awakening may be spelled out: "the world is" (level 1), "I was asleep" (level 2), "I was incapable of attending to the world" (level 3). Being awake is certainly not reducible to the realization that one was asleep. Diurnal wakefulness is a general orientation toward the world in which having been asleep is but a single fact. Wakeful attention to facts, however, tends to obscure the essential relativity of wakefulness as such by understanding having been asleep as if it were just one fact among others. While it cannot help but see everything in the light of day, diurnal wakefulness is still inseparable from an awakening in which the very one now awake realizes that she was wholly lost to the world.[5] The true statement "I was asleep" simultaneously includes sleep in the world available to wakefulness and admits that this world was unavailable to the one who formulates it.

The experience of awakening from sleep has implications for the understanding of awakening from naïveté at every level. Awakening from sleep authorizes a concept of rationally innocent non-wakefulness. Although the awakened person posits her sleeping as an occurrence in the world given to wakefulness (I was really asleep), she does not hold herself responsible for having been unable to apprehend the world. Diurnally wakeful reflection on dream images or the dreamless oblivion does not rejoin an attempt to target what is. Awake, I may find that my dream images "match" reality, but never that they show it. Likewise, immersion in the dreamless oblivion does not reveal the dark silence of my "inner world" as does an exercise of sensory deprivation. While falling asleep may have been a mistake, the mental accomplishments of sleep itself are never corrected in wakeful judgments because the sleeper is not answerable to reality. Even if a master psychoanalyst were to pair every dream element with a referent in waking life, this would not diminish the original sense in which sleep experience, for the wakeful subject, was not world-directed.

The diurnally wakeful ego treats its directedness toward the world as the condition for its rational responsibility. Naïveté thereby appears as a non-wakeful condition that is not innocent precisely *because* it occurs within world-directedness. It seems, then, that the awakenings that realize presuppositions occur within the condition of diurnal wakefulness and its orientation toward reality. As animals that routinely wake up from sleep, human beings naturally understand all other awakenings as events within the global condition of wakefulness that has sleep as its counterpart. We will follow this tendency, but only in order later to point out its limitations, and its negative effects on certain philosophical reflections. For now, we can seize upon the essential feature of awakening from naïveté that emerges in its contrast with awakening from sleep. Having been naïve is like having been asleep because both become evident for a realization that I was incapable of attending to what is and what is true. In both cases, the awakened subject has emerged from a benighted condition, but not by fulfilling any possibilities discerned from within it. But naïveté is not rationally innocent like sleep. In awakening from naïveté, I realize that I, in my wakeful orientation, was incapable of noticing something that should have been noticeable. Naïveté is distinguished thereby, not only from sleep but also from simple ignorance of the unknown. This having been unnoticeable refers directly to my factual, subjective inability to notice, not yet to any conditions that had to be met in order for the objectively noticeable to have been noticed by me. Awakening from naïveté is disconcerting because it reveals a genuine inability.

Some distinctions can serve to indicate the kind of inability we have in mind. We use inability here as a practical concept. A genuine inability must threaten or prevent the fulfillment of an actual will. The list of everything it is impossible for one to do includes many pseudo-inabilities at which one arrives precisely by pretending to will. Among genuine inabilities, we distinguish between those due to a lack of capacity and those due to not being in a position to exercise an existing capacity. This distinction concerns the experience of inability, not just the explanation of why one was unable. In the first kind of case, the experience of inability either arises through the exhaustion of a capacity at its limit or else barely occurs because the underlying practical intention lacks any transition to fulfilling action, and will collapses into wish. In the second kind of case, one encounters a hindrance to an action that belongs to the repertoire of an "I can." The hindrance is thus an abnormal circumstance to which the inability is relative. One is aware that "under normal circumstances" one would be able. Among genuine inabilities relative to abnormal hindering circumstances, we can make a further distinction. On the one hand, abnormal circumstances may be environmental in a broad sense that includes factors both internal and external to the agent. For instance, the cognizance of abnormal perceptual circumstances (such as dim or artificial lighting) discounts as merely apparent certain apparent sense qualities of things and brings about an awareness of being unable to see them. Cognizance of physiological abnormalities in one's own perceptual system works in a similar way. On the other hand, there is the experience of negligence. Here, the abnormal hindering circumstance to which the inability is relative is not environmental, even in the broad sense, but rather lies in the self. It is among these experiences that we find the awareness of naïveté. In social life, negligence is measured against a standard of appropriate care with reference to the reasonable person. In the awakening to naïveté, negligence is always measured against a standard derived from nowhere other than the awakened subject. We are now left with the problem of specifying the will and capacity in terms of which naïveté counts as an abnormal, hindering circumstance. Our section on basic integrity will look into this issue.

For now, we take note of the interweaving of ability and inability in the awakening to naïveté. Awakening is a reflective process embedded in a realization. All reflection is a free stepping back in which the subject makes the implicit explicit through modulations of interest. These modulations are at the disposal of the subject on the basis of a history of understanding. Reflection is thus the exercise of an ability. Within an awakening, I am able to reflect on what I was unable to notice as well as on my having been unable to notice. These, too, are exercises of ability. But as developments of the initial realization, they explicate an original experience of inability. Awakening reflections are internal to the realization, rather than reflections *on* the realization, because they have not yet grasped the inability of the reflecting subject as a result of negligence, have not yet comprehended it as a fault for which responsibility can be wakefully assumed. It is necessary to safeguard this original encounter with one's own inability to have noticed, not only from a third-person perspective that identifies an objective possibility for having noticed but also from an appropriative tendency emanating from the awakening subject that claims this possibility as its own. We will consider this tendency in our section on appropriation.

We have now outlined the kind of experience in which having presupposed becomes evident. It is an awakening to my own naïveté built upon a pastward-looking realization of something I was unable to notice. The presupposition and its content become objects of direct attention in the response to an appropriative demand contained in the experience of realization outlined above. This response need not be immediate. Descartes, for instance, begins his *Meditations on First Philosophy* by reporting that a period of "several years" has intervened between the realization of his naïveté and the attempt to appropriate it. We will argue, though, that the realization of naïveté confronts the subject with a task uniquely its own.

5. The "I" Who Presupposed

We now examine how the awakened subject assumes responsibility for its naïveté as a deficient mode of its own wakeful life. We will begin by considering how the awakened subject responds to naïveté. Then, we will treat that response as a clue to the appropriative demand that prompts it. Finally, we will consider what kind of appropriation can meet that demand.

In taking responsibility for having presupposed, one often uses "presuppose" as a first-person, active verb that expresses either past time or completed action: "I have been presupposing ...," "I was presupposing ...," "I presupposed ...," and so on. These expressions raise two questions. Was presupposing an activity accomplished by the one who has awakened from naïveté? Is the subject of this presupposing appropriately described as an "I" or an "ego" at all? Grammatical conventions are not reliable guides to the structures of experience. In this case, the construal of presuppositional content as the object of a past egoic activity seems to conform to a broader pattern of usage that places an I-subject before verbs that do not designate activities that an I-subject accomplished, if indeed an I-subject ever accomplishes activities ("I forgot," "I mistook," etc.). Against this skepticism, we will attempt to discern in "I presupposed" the basic form of response by which the awakened subject initiates the reinterpretation of naïve life from the perspective of wakefulness.

To this point, our reflections have been intentionally vague in their characterization of the subject who realizes a presupposition. This has been out of deference to the difficult and contentious issue of whether, and in light of which philosophical interests, reflection can find an ego to which experiences belong. According to one classical conception, the ego in question here is neither an object of experience, nor an experience or stream of experiences, nor finally a separable subject that stands "behind" this stream and generates it. It is rather an identical source of attention that aims at objects through the experiences in which it currently lives, and to which all background experiences in *its* stream belong as potential targets of focus (*Ideas I* §§ 57, 80). Critical assessments of this purported ego range from denying its existence altogether (Sartre), to demoting it to an abstraction from a more primordial way of being a self (Heidegger), to emphasizing its minimality compared to what is assumed by substantial theories of the self (Zahavi), to treating it as a clue for such a substantial theory (Hart). Working out a position on this general issue is beyond the scope of this study. However, describing the involvement of the subject in the experience of awakening to naïveté lies squarely within it.

We will thus have recourse to the following argumentative strategy. Let us assume that two of Heidegger's contentions in § 25 of *Being and Time* are true. First, we assume that reflection on the kind of ego described above (the "I of acts") does not provide access to how one is for oneself in everyday life.[6] Second, we assume that who "I" am in everyday life "is precisely not I myself." Even on these assumptions, the experience of awakening to naïveté involves an original emergence of the ego. I do not awaken as one does. The awakening ego claims for itself a domain of responsibility such that naïve life, which it lived through in absorbed anonymity, becomes appropriable as *its own*. Even if the ego is not fundamental to experience, the appropriative tendency of the emergent ego would explain the illusion that it is. Expressions of the form "I presupposed" already announce this appropriative tendency, and prefigure a narrative understanding that accounts for the anonymous happenings of the naïve life-phase in terms of what the awakened ego can know and do. The awakened ego has the presupposition at its disposal. Did it somehow have it at its disposal during the naïve phase? There are many difficulties hidden in this question, which upcoming sections will begin to address. But our framework for handling these difficulties is as follows: how the ego emerges in awakening will determine in what sense presupposing was a past act of the one who awakens.

Let us return to the first problem posed by the common expressions for assuming responsibility for having presupposed. Their simple linguistic form seemed to conceal the fact that they cannot be true descriptions of one's own life. "Presupposing" cannot refer to any mental activity of which I was previously aware. We have already said why this is so. Presuppositions become evident only now for the first time in self-reflexive realizations. Because presupposing is impossible in the present, it is impossible as a past present. It is thus a matter of principle that "I presupposed" does not describe a past act directed toward what was presupposed. However, perhaps presupposing refers to ways of taking the obvious for granted. If this were right, the realization would indeed target a passive mental bearing toward the presuppositional content (still an act in the broad sense). It would show that, during the naïve life-phase, the ego was taking the presuppositional content for granted as obvious. Two ways of taking for granted as obvious that seem suited to this view are persisting in a conviction and passively expecting. We will briefly consider them in turn.

Imagine that at some point prior to preparing the meal for my dinner guests I judge that the children are not coming. Evident judgments hold from now on, unless something speaks against them. Being the one who judges this, and the world being as it is judged, do not require reconsidering the evidential support for the judgment. Being convinced means not having to confirm a judgment. Convictions thus have a tendency to become self-evident or obvious. In this mode, they can recede into the background and enable explicit apprehensions that build upon them. If, during my preparation of the meal, I begin to suspect that the children might be coming, I may become aware of my failure to have tested my previous judgment, which now appears insufficiently substantiated. We see that this is a different type of experience than the realization of a presupposition in our sense, which presents the presuppositional content as available for consideration for the first time. Having been convinced refers to a previous judgment that has sunk into the background, whereas what was presupposed was never entertained. The obviousness of the conviction is a degraded mode of evidence, whereas the missingness of the presupposition is an original inaccessibility suddenly manifest in the awakening. We thus distinguish between the passive abiding in one's convictions and genuine naïveté. We will later consider, however, whether it is appropriate to describe the naïve ego as living *as if* of a certain conviction.

Now imagine that during the months leading up to this dinner, I regularly entertained guests without children. The interpretation suggests itself that my oversight was due to the thoughtless expectation that, in this case too, there would be no children. We can use the term "presumption" to cover all passive expectations that arise from tradition. Routines of experience engender associations that organize current experience. I expect things to go together or to follow one another as they have in similar circumstances in the past. This process of colligation is automatic: it operates beneath the level of explicit thought and is sometimes impervious to the will. It is true that presumption can explain how a presupposition came about. Nevertheless, "I presupposed" does not describe the passive activity of presuming. Although presumptions configure experience automatically, under normal circumstances one can freely advert to them in reflection, which is not to say undo them (e.g., I can consider my indefeasible, tradition-bound expectation that the summer will bring warmer weather). This is precisely what I was incapable of during the naïve stretch of life. The realization of naïveté directly confronts me with an unnoticeable feature of my situation, and, reflexively, my inability to have noticed it. Having presumed, on the other hand, is simply to have been in an intelligible situation at all.

Having been convinced and having presumed do not capture what is meant in "I presupposed" because this latter redescribes a phase of life from a perspective inaccessible to it. The awakened ego views the naïve life-phase in light of what was inaccessible to the naïve ego. This is where Danto's model of narrative sentences proves helpful. It encourages us to think of "I presupposed" as the product of historical self-knowledge. One hallmark of historical knowledge is that it goes beyond "the simple understanding of the meaning immanent to … action" (1985, 182). Rather than trying to recapture the past as it was originally lived through, historical thinking often takes advantage of one's distance from the past in order to make true statements about it. These statements can take the form of narrative sentences, which bring past events under descriptions that were unavailable to their witnesses or participants because they involve a later event as a necessary condition for their truth. One of Danto's favorite examples is the description "anticipated," as in "Augustine anticipated Descartes' discovery of the cogito." Although the statement is true, it describes Augustine's activity as Augustine or his contemporaries could not have. To what extent can we understand "presupposed" along these lines?

Danto's basic intuition about historical retrospect readily translates into an autobiographical register. Life stories contain true claims about how earlier activities or attitudes "anticipated" later ones. People often recount their "ill-fated" adventures, "fateful" decisions, and "lucky" accidents in narrative sentences that provide past actions with descriptions under which they were not intentional, but which highlight their biographical significance. In each case, the description depends upon knowledge of some event posterior to the event so described. When both events function as part of a larger configuration that is developing in the present, the descriptions lose their finality. But so long as the later event determines the perspective on the prior event, they are as true, and as alien to the immanent sense of the past they describe, as narrative descriptions at the historical level. According to this schema, the awakening realization is the posterior event that warrants the redescription of a preceding life-phase as "presupposing *x*."

However, upon closer examination, "I presupposed" reveals distinctive features. First, while the awakening realization is necessarily posterior to the presupposition it discovers, its posteriority is insufficient to account for its superior perspective on the naïve life-phase. Retrospective description can transcend the immanent sense of the past present just by filling in what was indeterminate in it. Tomorrow, I can utter a true narrative sentence that determines my current risky behavior as ill-fated or lucky, depending upon how things turn out. But when things turn out well or badly they actualize a potential held in the purview of my risk. The awakening to naïveté, by contrast, transcends the immanent sense of the life-phase it determines without actualizing any of the latter's potential. Thinking myself wakeful, I do not know that things will be missing for me in the way they are when I turn out to have been naïve. What is missing is not an indeterminacy that gets filled in. Awakened subjectivity has broken free of the non-wakeful ways of seeing more and has its retrospect from a perspective that sees better. Diurnal wakefulness can determine what sleep phenomena really were, not because it follows sleep, but because its ways of making evident have access to a sleep world that had no way of access to it.[7] The awakening to having presupposed finds itself similarly positioned beyond every future vaguely foretold within naïve life.

Here is a second difference. The naïve ego could have noticed the presupposition were it not hindered by naïveté. Within Danto's framework, this capacity to have noticed already indicates that we are no longer dealing with the "distinctively historical ignorance" of which narrative sentences take advantage (1985, 351). Danto's opposing category is tragic ignorance, "where what we know in fact was available then, without any claim on the … future" (351). But here we notice something striking. The wakeful judgment that the naïve ego had a capacity to notice does not depend, as it does in tragic ignorance, upon an assessment that "all the facts were in place, so to speak" (350). Instead, it follows simply from the awakened ego having this capacity. The awakened ego is the standard in light of which the naïve ego counts as negligent. This is possible because the awakened ego subsumes the naïve ego within itself as a moment. Just as the person who is diurnally awake inevitably considers sleep a real condition in the world available to wakefulness, and her waking self to have been asleep, so does the awakened ego consider its naïveté a benighted phase of *its* life. The "I" in "I presupposed" refers to the wakeful ego in its assumption of responsibility for not having noticed. This attribution of capacity and assumption of responsibility are illegitimate not only in cases of historical ignorance where historian and subject are different people but also in autobiographical reflection that employs knowledge unavailable to the past self.

"I presupposed" is neither a description of a past act nor a judgment of historical retrospect. It is rather an assertion of responsibility whereby the awakened ego installs itself as the negligent agent of naïve life. This installation is not an illusion brought about by accidents of grammar. It is an actual installation. Wakefulness realizes an inalienable standard of appropriate care that it projects backward into naïve life. Thus, the formula for wakeful responsibility for naïveté runs: *though I was factually unable, I was in principle able just because I am now able*. Naïve life is "based" on presupposition in the sense that the awakened ego asserts its constant negligence with respect to the life-phase during which the ground was maintained. The dependence of the ground upon its presupposition expresses an egological as well as a formal relation: the subsumption of naïve by wakeful life. The awakened I is the concrete I. When, after affirming himself as cogito, Descartes asks himself "what then did I use to think I was?" (1993, 18), must he not interpret the I who used to think as the cogito thinking of itself, naively, as a man?

The "I" in "I presupposed" is not the agent of the past situation in which the action of the verb took place. It is the emergent ego of the present awakening, an ego that, projecting its capacity for apprehension into the past, asserts that the failure to have exercised it was self-incurred. Winning evidence for this assertion is a matter of interpretation, both discovering and creative. This interpretation is anything but objective. It is a process of appropriation in which a wakeful I intervenes in *its* history—claiming it as *its* history through this very intervention—and reconstructs it—and thereby itself—according to the wakeful demands of self-responsibility. Nothing is more alien to awakening than just appreciating the power of tradition. The awakened ego has the task of remaking this tradition in its own image so that it can understand itself in it. We now explore this intervention and its program of self-transformation.

6. The Devaluation of Naïve Life

Awakening reflection reveals not only that I could have noticed what I presupposed but also that I should have. The appropriation of naïve life responds to something bad about having been naïve. We will advance the position that there is an inherent disvalue in having presupposed that is distinct from those disvalues associated with incorrectness. We begin by rehearsing two basic points. First, having presupposed and having been incorrect are logically independent. The fact of having presupposed decides nothing about the truth of the presupposition. In particular, having presupposed x does not exclude that x is the case. Second, in a concrete episode of reasoning, the realization of having presupposed x can precede or follow a determination about x being true or false. The first case has already appeared in our examples. The second involves the discovery of a fact that prompts the self-reflexive, past-directed realization that I have presupposed things to be so or to be otherwise.

Consider a sequence of the first sort, in which the realization of having presupposed precedes any determination about the presupposition's truth. During the phase before this determination, there is no awareness of incorrect judgment. But there can already be a negative valuation directed toward my naïveté, my inability to have considered the position now realized as presuppositional content. Nonetheless, it is still possible that the disvalue of naïveté is essentially connected to incorrect judgment. To have presupposed that the children were not coming was to inhibit any informed consideration of the matter. I was unable to achieve an optimal understanding of those factors that had to be understood in order to ensure that my course of action was appropriate. On this view, it is the inability to test what matters for correctness that accounts for the disvalue of naïveté as it appears to realization. Restated in a more practical register: naïveté is bad because it compromises the reliability of the ground. We cannot separate the disvalue of naïveté from the disvalue of incorrectness by finding experiences in which devaluation occurs without awareness of incorrectness. Being naïve might be bad because it increases the likelihood of incorrect judgment.

Consider, then, a sequence of the second sort, in which the determination of truth precedes the realization of the presupposition, and let the presupposition be correct. For example, I find out that the children are not coming, and then realize that I have been presupposing this. In this case, the possibility of error is ruled out before the presupposition becomes evident. There can still be a devaluation directed toward my having presupposed, despite the fact that my naïveté cannot destabilize the ground. Again, this does not dissociate the badness of naïveté from incorrectness. Simply because presupposing did not lead to incorrect judgment in this case, it might be bad because it often does.

Finally, let us distinguish between an intrinsic and an extrinsic value to having presupposed, where the latter tracks every consequence and implication of having presupposed not identical with having presupposed itself. Now we imagine a case in which this extrinsic value is maximized. We assume, first of all, that the presupposition was correct. But there are other factors. For instance, presupposing often saves time. So we imagine a situation in which it saved time crucial to the solution of some practical or theoretical problem. Presupposing can also help secure the truth of the presupposition. Suppose that, had I not presupposed that the children weren't coming, the only way to look into the matter would have been to contact my friend, who, knowing what I know about him, would have interpreted my question as a desire that he bring his children. Suppose, too, that I desire that the children not come. My presupposing has fulfilled this desire. Even if all such extrinsic factors are maximized, is there not a counterweight that reduces the overall worth of having presupposed, one attached to naïveté itself? Again, an affirmative answer does not rule out an essential connection to incorrectness, which would trace the disvalue of naïveté to the disvalue of one of its potential consequences.

We find similar results when we approach the problem from the other side: the positive value of the realization itself. Why is it better to have realized my naïveté than to have persisted in it? Is it simply because it allows for testing the reliability of the ground? Consider a realization where the truth of the presupposition is already decided, or where it is practically impossible to test the ground. Is the realization of naïveté not still good? Or consider a case where the extrinsic value of having realized is maximally negative—a truly devastating awakening that leaves no way forward to a totally disoriented subject. Can we not detect a positive value, even here, in having awakened to naïveté? One can answer these questions affirmatively while identifying the value of wakefulness with vigilance against error. One simply argues that realizing naïveté is better than persisting in it because, in general, it puts one in a position to minimize error. Even if the devastating awakening is bad, wakefulness in general is good precisely because it prevents one from building enormous edifices upon unstable grounds. This is analogous to the fact that strenuous exercise is healthy for a healthy body, though not for a body that has become obese. Strenuous exercise would have prevented strenuous exercise from becoming unhealthy.

There is a legitimate connection between naïveté and the disvalues of incorrectness, exposure to error, and the instability of the ground. The connection is forged by an interest in making determinations about the world of realities. The truth of every worldly statement and the appropriateness and viability of every worldly action depend upon circumstances that are not immediately evident. To be wakeful in the world is to be able to take notice of and test these dependencies, so as to avoid the reversal of positions to which one is committed. The claim that the axiological connection between naïveté and incorrectness is inessential is thus tied to the claim, which we will make, that interest in the world of realities does not exhaust the scope of wakefulness, or that wakefulness is not finally the opposite of sleep. This will turn our inquiry away from the Cartesian ideal of wakefulness in an important respect. The goal of establishing something firm and lasting about the world guides Descartes' interpretation even of the appropriative abilities of the realized cogito. For this reason, he remains preoccupied with decisively distinguishing waking life from sleep, with proving that the world is not a dream.

7. Basic Integrity

The varied scenarios of the preceding section have helped frame our position about the inherent disvalue of naïveté and the corresponding value of wakefulness. They have not, however, said anything in its favor. We will now try to show how the inability to test what matters for correctness manifests a deeper deficiency at the heart of naïve life. Similarly, wakeful life's vigilance in testing the ground is the expression of a value that more properly defines its superiority over naïve life. It is by considering this pair of value and disvalue as they become evident in the experience of awakening that we can understand the most original sources of the demand to wakefully appropriate naïve life.

Without deciding whether or how reflection can discover an ego at the center of pre-reflective life, it is possible to recognize the sense of being-mine that pervades this life. Here, it is helpful to follow Zahavi's strategy of focusing on a "minimalist notion" of self that is "an integral part of our conscious life with an immediate experiential reality" (2005, 106). Mineness is not dependent on private or unique contents of experience, but instead characterizes the experiences themselves, which have the "experiential property" of being first-personally given (122). In other words, access to things, which are essentially public, is in each case my access. Any identifying marker one might nominate for the function of according life its first-personality depends upon this first-personality as a condition of its manifestation. Although Zahavi calls this pre-reflective sense of mineness the "ego-centricity" of experience (124), the kind of subject indicated by the possessive adjective can remain indeterminate. Initially and for the most part, the subject of the life that is mine may be best described, not as the ego that has its acts, but as *das Man*, the one caught up in everyday concerns, or as lived body, the sentient matrix of feeling and movement.

Regardless of whether the ego is a fundamental or a derivative feature of experience, its stance toward first-personal life is crucial for our account of the value of wakefulness and the disvalue of naïveté. The awakened ego never confronts the alternative of being awake or naïve. So the question of the value of wakefulness is not posed for a deliberation about whether I should be awake, but rather for an ego that is already awakened. Insofar as I live as a wakeful ego, I believe that I can occupy my entire subjective life as *my* accomplishment or undergoing, even where this occupation is hindered by the factual limits of my mental powers. The ego thus stands under a form of responsibility that concerns it simply qua ego: it is on call to attend to its life. We call "basic integrity" the ability to carry out this egoic occupation of what is mine as mine. Our proposal is that basic integrity is an egological value, and that naïveté exposes a fault in basic integrity.

Occupation in general refers to how the ego owns its experiences. We may distinguish between two forms of occupation: inhabitation and appropriation. Inhabitation refers to how I settle into my experience with attention. I am not engaged in most of my life. I can, though, turn toward my experience and "live myself into it." The experience thereby takes on an egoic character it previously lacked, which is precisely the engagement of my self in my life.[8] Attentive experience not only provides its objects with a certain distinctness and manipulability; it is also lived through as an experience in which I am present. The ego is, to varying degrees, present or absent in its experiences. This presence is often the prerequisite for cognitive activities that take charge of the original experience and articulate its object. However, inhabitation itself need not be intellectually creative. I can, for instance, turn toward a perception and begin to live through it attentively without explicating its content. In an extended sense, spontaneous acts, in which I am involved in the experience as its performer, are inhabitations of the passive experiences on which they build, though the passive experiences themselves may be insusceptible to direct inhabitation or active performance. In inhabiting experience, the ego need not attend to itself. Attentive experience can mean losing oneself in what one attends to. However, even this being lost involves an implicit sense of engagement that peripheral experiencing lacks. This sense often becomes increasingly explicit in resisting the tendency of peripheral experiences to capture attention.

Appropriation is occupation that makes the mineness of my life into a theme. The ego is here occupied with itself. For instance, autobiographical memory is an appropriative experience because the remembering ego has its past egocentricity as part of its object. But appropriation also includes more complex forms of self-reflection and narration that aim at understanding oneself as the subject of one's life. Here, the appropriating ego has a tendency to assert its own perspective, not simply revisiting its egocentricity, as in simple memory, but interpreting it in light of its own concerns. Appropriation also encompasses socially constituted ways of taking responsibility that link my action to its consequences or to the actions of others (such as accepting blame or acknowledging participation). However, it is always a claiming of my first-personal accomplishments, and thus excludes what Sokolowski describes as the "informational" use of the first-person (2008, 10–12). For instance, picking myself out as "the one" who meets a certain description is not an appropriation of my life as mine, whereas thereby acknowledging that it was I who committed the deed is.

These provisional definitions allow us to address some questions. Is it really the case that the wakeful ego lives in the conviction that it can occupy its entire life? Can it "actually" do this? And if it cannot, does this mean that the stream of experiences does not "actually" belong to an ego? Remembering one's past aims to represent that past as it actually was. It is perhaps the simplest form of appropriation in that it need not involve complex narrative formations and targets the subject matter, my past life, to which such formations refer. Let us take autobiographical memory, then, as a test of our claim that the wakeful ego has its entire life as open to occupation. Can the wakeful I appropriate its entire life in memory?

We can take the first step toward a positive answer by considering an extreme form of skepticism according to which memory might not appropriate any past experience at all. G. Strawson seems to advance this view by arguing that whether the remembering ego discovers remembered experience as its own is a contingent matter of "temporal temperament" (2004, 431). While "diachronic" individuals may find themselves in their memories, "episodic" individuals do not. The episodic person would claim that, in remembering, he does not experience the past experience as his. He would say, for example, "it's clear to me that events in my remoter past didn't happen to me [the one now reflecting]" (433). The "my" in "my remoter past" relies on an assignment of experience to a particular person on the basis of objective evidence. One's handwriting, perhaps, is on the document. When the episodic person claims to know perfectly well that "I have a past, like any human being" and also to "remember some of my past experiences 'from the inside', as philosophers say" (433), the possessive relation to the past expressed by the terms "have" and "my" is achieved, *ex hypothesi*, independently of memory, via facts about human beings in general, and about one human being in particular. The problem with this view is that there would be no person there at all, whatever his temperament, if "I was there" did not guide memory in its very aiming at the past.

Strawson claims, as an episodic person, to remember having fallen out of a boat. But this is not just to have in the mind's eye a perspectival scene of "the water rushing up to meet me" (2004, 434). It is to target the *experience* of the fall as having actually been originally lived through, whether this turns out to be accurate or not. The relevant philosophical sense of "from the inside" refers to the condition failing which there would be no subjectivity or intersubjectivity: the only experiences with which I am possibly acquainted as originally lived through are precisely mine. The very conviction of "having" a past life depends on the availability of a retained field of *my* past presents, and cannot be accounted for in terms of facts about human beings (who, *ex hypothesi*, can be there without having "insides" to their lifetimes). When the remembering ego intends its own remembered life, it does not match itself to a self it finds in the middle of the past; it moves, from the beginning, in the possession of its originally lived-through experience.

Given that the remembering ego can appropriate some experience, we turn to the more difficult claim that it can appropriate all its experiences. The difficulty is clear. A normal adult, for instance, is practically amnesic with respect to her childhood. It is a phase of life perhaps symbolized by a few questionable memories, and testified to by documents, stories, and photographs. One has to ask, given the tenuous character of such evidence, what justifies the conviction of having lived through childhood at all. The conviction, at any rate, would seem to survive the annulment of the available evidence. If I should discover that the documents have been forged and the memories suggested, the childhood indicated by that evidence would now count as a fiction. However, I would still be convinced that I lived through my real childhood. The conviction is not the result of an inference to the best explanation for the available facts. To account for its rationality, one has to reverse the order of foundation. Documents and pictures provide putative information about what happened then, but the conviction that I was then to some degree present to my life draws upon a more basic intuition of my past that gives this information a reference.[9] This intuition renders superfluous any transcendental argument that invokes the ego as a unifying condition for experience. The ego, in the present, actually has its life as having been lived. Ströker captures this movement from argument to description: "An infinite past that is empty of intuition could not be the background for the awakening of an ego … To be sure this reservoir [of the lifeless past] is closed off to the ego. Nonetheless it is, in a very peculiar way, at the disposal of the ego" (1993, 155–6). The life now evident as mine is lived through as the surface of a deep, featureless past out of which may leap scenes and episodes that already lay claim to having been experienced *by me*. This claim is the other side of the ego's "very peculiar way" of having even the deepest past at its disposal. Being an ego, as Hart emphasizes, is synonymous with possessing a life that is mine in its very transcendence: "these elemental temporal havings are the extension, the spill-over, of the original upsurge that is inseparable from my original *I am*" (2009, 138). Even when I am not remembering my life, I have the indeterminate depth of the past beneath me and can judge with evidence that "I was there." This is already a first form of appropriation.

We can go further. The "I was there" implies an accessibility to remembering. This is an accessibility in principle that survives every factual inaccessibility, just as the outer reaches of the galaxy are accessible to my locomotion. Lived space and time are directional dimensions. This means that they exhaust my actual capacities of traversal but do so with reference to in-principle capacities of traversal, the denial of which would also deny the very remoteness whereby something in the dimension exceeds my actual grasp. Actual traversal of space moves in traversable directions looked into by perception. This traversal is also perceiving and so could have traversed farther in this direction, converting "there" into "here." Actual traversal encounters its limits *within* such directions, along which every real body is reachable by an extrapolated locomotion equal to the perception that (perhaps with the help of instruments and inferences) looked into a direction to find the body. Similarly, every recollection of a retained past present has directions of before and after open to recollective attention. The actual exercise of recollection indicates a more encompassing retained sphere into which it can range and within which it encounters its indefinite limits. Recollection is exhausted within a dimension of past life in which every "then" emptily referred to is convertible, in principle, into a past now by an extrapolated recollection that would reach farther into the retended directions. Only as such is it a "then" at all.[10] The dimension of lived time across which appropriations occur is egocentrically possessed in its very ego-transcendence. It is this possession that justifies the ineliminable confidence that psychological impediments to distant recollection are contingent obstructions to essential possibilities for appropriation. Analogously, the remote regions of the galaxy are unreachable because of facts about technology, nature, and so on. But they are reachable in principle insofar as they are there as remote.

Having had a childhood is a socially constituted experience. One may therefore suspect that my confidence that I too was a child depends upon syllogistic reasoning about human beings. The point we want to establish, however, concerns an ego as such. We can try to refrain from using anthropological concepts that figure in descriptions of life-phases, purifying the "I was there" so that it targets past life as such. But this method is not necessary. The point is simply that these concepts articulate rather than produce the mineness of my lifetime. I believe I was a "child" because I live in a certain sort of community, but I believe I was there when I was a child because of the in-principle availability of my life to my self. *Every imaginable ego is responsible to its whole life.* With this formula, we express the ability of the ego to take up its life in inhabitation or appropriation, an ability it possesses even when it cannot actually exercise it.

The claim for this universal power of occupation draws upon the distinction between inhabitation and appropriation. The powers of inhabitation seem limited not only in fact but also in principle. I cannot pay attention, in fact, to a vivid scene unfolding in phantasy or in memory while also attending to the visual field before my eyes. Instead, the attention I give to one, I take from the other. I cannot pay attention, in fact, to many associative links that tie together what is close in space, time, and content. Instead, it is the already linked elements that grab my attention. Neither can I, in fact, open up those unities into which complex episodes of long-past experience have congealed. Instead, they confront me as atomic events that I cannot explicate. Let us assume that it is not only difficult but impossible to conceive of an ego for whom some such facts do not hold. Granting that inhabitation faces essential limitations does not undermine the claim that the ego can in principle occupy its entire life. The appropriation that occupies my experiences need not enter into an attentive living or reliving of these experiences. The life of an ego may contain various dimensions that are inaccessible to attention. But even sighting these inaccessible dimensions in their retreat from attention is a form of appropriation. For example, it now occurs to me that because I was just engaged in semi-verbal thinking, I could not attend to the voices downstairs that I was nonetheless monitoring in the background. This very obliviousness to what was being said downstairs is thereby owned as my own.

According to the well-known Kantian view, for my representations to be mine at all, the "I think" must be capable of accompanying them. For Kant, this "must be capable" ultimately refers experience to one of its conditions of possibility. The ego that thinks is a kind of guarantor of experience, but is not given in experience itself. But, if we stick to what is available to self-reflection, the "must be capable" refers to an ability I am convinced I possess insofar as I am convinced that I am, a conviction more basic than my assent to the psychological facts that speak against its exercise. If the ego were the lord of the house of subjectivity, owning everything there by right, basic integrity would be an accomplished fact. Instead, it is an ability-in-principle, evidenced only in tasks that exercise but cannot exhaust it. The ego, then, is more like the butler, charged, as the central operator of the house, with attending to whatever might demand attention; taking care of one thing, it is already responsible for everything. Alterations are conceivable in the rules governing what the ego can inhabit when, such as those pertaining to the structure of perceptual fields or to the mutual exclusion of imagination and perception. But that the ego is the owner of a stream of experiences that exceeds its grasp is essential to any conceivable ego.

On the basis of this sketch, we can indicate what kind of value basic integrity is. Having basic integrity means being able to make good on a claim that the wakeful ego brings with it in its very being as ego. Broadly speaking, it is an excellence defined in terms of proper function. As soon as it is on the scene of experience, the ego is the identical owner of its life. Its basic integrity consists in having the capacity to exercise this ownership, and it "does well" insofar as it does so.[11] Having access to the whole subjective life that slips away is an egoic value that accompanies rational values of various sorts, but that is distinct from them. For example, an evident judgment that has become an obvious conviction can be reassembled in its original evidence. The sense of the conviction and the reassembled judgment is identical, but the rational value of the latter is superior (*Ideas I*, § 140). The reassembly is itself an exercise of basic integrity in the form of inhabitation. But it has its *own* value apart from the values of clarity and insight with which it is here associated. Similarly, basic integrity is often tied up with personal virtues from which it can be distinguished. For example, sincerity clearly requires, but is not the same as, the egoic occupation of experience. One can also raise Schopenhauerian concerns about the "curse" of being burdened with one's own life. Nevertheless, being able to attend to my experience constitutes a primitive form of the good life that orients subjectivity as such, however it may be intertwined with human flourishing and misery.

In particular, basic integrity is distinct from and more basic than the virtue of intellectual prudence. Only when I can occupy my positions as mine is it possible to be vigilant in testing them, and so to protect whatever depends upon them from cancellation. This protection is a beneficial outgrowth of basic integrity. But the latter can be dissociated from the former. The bringing to mind underlying testing is a concrete accomplishment on its own. There are also forms of egological occupation that simply have nothing to do with intellectual prudence. Consider, for instance, those exercises of appropriation that aim to recover or transform life's narrative coherence or those exercises of inhabitation that suspend practical-epistemic concerns in favor of attending to an unfolding sense experience. Basic integrity is not only dissociable from cognitive vigilance, but it is also inherently valuable apart from whatever knowledge it enables.

The awakening to naïveté reveals a fault in basic integrity. Basic integrity is an ability or power. Its opposite is a form of inability or impotence. To this point, we have emphasized how the basic "I can" of egological occupation survives every factual impediment to its exercise. The realization of naïveté does not compromise this "I can" either. An awareness of presently presupposing is absurd. The awakened ego is no longer presupposing and has the realized presupposition at its disposal. However, the presupposition, as realized only now for the first time, implies that it was not ready to be occupied, and the reflexive level of awakening makes explicit my inability to have done so. This is a fault in integrity, albeit a past fault. The appropriative posture of the awakened ego converts this "could not" into a "could in principle" by interpreting the naïve life-phase as the result of its own negligence. As soon as naïveté is manifest, it comes under the power of basic integrity and is material for a possible appropriation. An accomplished appropriation would integrate the stretch of naïve life into a unity of experience in which the wakeful ego can recognize its own activity.

Because there is no dilemma about whether to be naïve, a test of basic integrity can only be posed in the following way: Do I prefer to realize, in the future, that

I am now naïve without knowing it? Or do I prefer the apparent self-possession of a life that, for all I know, is wakeful? At the end of his first meditation, Descartes considers the vices of "laziness" and "fear" as they pertain to a potentially "toilsome wakefulness" (1993, 17). Awakening is laborious because it introduces new standards of evidence in light of which my accomplishments have to be reassessed. Even more importantly, it causes me to become, as we will see, a mystery to myself. The preference for future awakening requires the diligence and courage that seek out the work of appropriation. Perhaps this resolve could persist in the contemplation of a future awakening that would upend everything. It could then express itself in the formula: *I do not want to be naïve, but, if I am, I want to realize that I have been, no matter the consequences.*

8. Jeopardy

The realization of having presupposed destabilizes the ego. This destabilization is felt as a condition of being in jeopardy. This jeopardy is twofold. Its first aspect concerns how the ground of the realized presupposition comes to attention. The ground is a dependent moment of a new whole it forms with the realized presupposition. But the naïve ego was not aware of this dependence. The awakened ego is jeopardized because it has become newly dependent in its commitment to the ground.

The uprooting of the ground is also a change suffered in the ego. Although this change may leave undisturbed those narratives central to my self-conception, the realization of a presupposition implies that I may not be who I thought I was. Even where the ground is only relevant for a routine project I pursue as viable, its uprooting jeopardizes my self-understanding as its accomplisher. The awakened subject faces a predicament in which her objectives, interests, and thereby identity are at stake. There is gravity in being jeopardized by naïveté, a felt urgency to recover orientation. The genuine awakening to having presupposed is never a move in an intellectual game.

The problem is that many necessary conditions appear in retroactive realizations that lack this affective background. Consider two conditions for the success of the dinner as I am preparing it: (1) the children are not coming; (2) the floor will not collapse. Or consider these conditions for my trip overseas: (1) I can bring two bags on board; (2) the plane will not crash. Both fulfill the required formal relationships to the ground, and both may appear in retroactive realizations, but it is easy to imagine that the second conditions fail to jeopardize me. At first, it seems that we can fix criteria for jeopardy by focusing on how the presupposition is relevant to deliberations about the ground. For instance, it would be unreasonable to do anything to ensure that the second conditions obtain, and if they do not obtain, I cannot adjust my behavior so as to achieve my ends. In this sense, they are practically irrelevant. Or again, it is highly unlikely that the second conditions do not obtain. In this sense, they are theoretically irrelevant.

These criteria are plausible, but admit of exceptions. In any case, we do not understand the limits of jeopardy by looking for universal criteria that determine the relevance of a condition to the accomplishment that depends upon it. Instead, we should attend to how relevance and irrelevance factor in the realization itself. Jeopardy is absent when the realizing subject has not, or not yet, registered the importance of the unnoticed condition.

Let us define irrelevance and relevance as importance variables inherent in any practical situation. In the background of any engagement with things relevant to what I am accomplishing is a flow of experiences best characterized as a non-engagement with what need not be taken into account. This is not an overlooking of the irrelevant, but a regarding of the irrelevant as irrelevant that lets it persist in its non-salience. Except in cases of extreme concentration, the irrelevant is the object of ongoing explications that run their course in tandem with an attendance to what matters, and which often tease attention even in their impertinence. Much of what is necessary for what I am up to is originally irrelevant in this sense (e.g., breathing is necessary for changing a lightbulb, but I ordinarily regard it as irrelevant). The pseudo-presupposition given in a pseudo-awakening simply enters into this explication of the irrelevant.

Pseudo-awakenings are like genuine awakenings because they realize a condition for an activity in which I am involved. However, in a pseudo-awakening the presuppositional content pertains to an *obvious* setting condition for what I am accomplishing. These awakenings unfold in a contemplative mood that stands in contrast to the urgency that attends the realization of genuine presuppositions. There is no demand even to assess the viability of what is being accomplished on the basis of what went unnoticed. Even so, every pseudo-awakening can elicit a genuine awakening through a broadening of interest that reinterprets what I am, and have been, seeking to accomplish. This is because accomplishments themselves are variably important in a way that affects the practical salience of what is important for them. Often, what counts as an obvious setting condition for an accomplishment belongs to the practical field of a broader accomplishment that has itself fallen into unimportance. Genuine awakenings require a prior commitment that makes the uprooting of the ground a threat to my continuing to be who I am in doing what I do. The reinterpretation of what I am up to can discover this commitment. We will investigate this in our discussion of basic attitudes.

The realization of having presupposed jeopardizes the awakened ego by confronting it with a predicament in which its established interests are at stake. Regarding this aspect of jeopardy, we can classify awakenings according to their relative scope and centrality. Scope pertains to the magnitude of what is at stake in the predicament. There are various measurements to take here: the duration of the uprooted accomplishment, the number of logically distinct beliefs implicated in its viability, the number of distinct projects for which these beliefs function as premises, and so on. Centrality pertains to the degree to which I myself am at stake in the predicament because of my commitment to the uprooted accomplishment. We may speak of dedication and indifference as the maximal and minimal extremes. Awareness of jeopardy of some scope and centrality is not a phase subsequent to the realization of the presupposition. The presupposition is realized in the seriousness of my being in jeopardy.

We now turn briefly to the second aspect of jeopardy. The awakened subject is jeopardized in something she is committed to accomplishing. She faces a predicament because what she was doing and who she was in doing it depend upon things she sees only now for the first time. But the project uprooted in realization is uprooted *as naïve*. The predicament matters to the awakened subject, not only because it puts at stake something she cares about accomplishing but also because she herself is at stake as a wakeful subject. Facing the predicament, I am in jeopardy as the accomplisher of something, but also in my basic integrity. This second aspect of jeopardy is decisive for the task of appropriation posed in awakening. To rectify the situation bought on by jeopardy, the awakened ego has to assess the uprooted accomplishment in light of the continued pursuit of established goals. However, this assessment alone will not respond to the deeper disvalue of naïveté. To respond to the fault in basic integrity discovered in awakening, the ego has to reconstruct *its* naïve life, and thereby itself, according to the demands of wakeful self-responsibility. This means being able to understand my naïve life as something that I, the wakeful ego, lived through.

9. The Finality of Wakeful Life

Starting from the paradigmatic case of waking from sleep, we can discover a curious finality inherent in wakefulness. We will draw it out by pursuing a familiar speculation. Given that I routinely seem to wake up from a condition in which I was incapable of dealing with reality, is it not possible that I will wake up from what I now call wakefulness to realize that this entire alternation between sleeping and waking presents a merely apparent reality that will be globally annulled by a dawning true reality? The discovery of essential distinctions between dreaming and waking experience would not undermine this possibility. The dream speculation need not contest these distinctions, but suspects that their true place might lie within a broader reality to which I am now oblivious in the same global way that I am oblivious to my "reality" during "sleep." Let us examine the nature of this suspicion.

The dream speculation relies on the authority of wakeful life to determine the truth of non-wakeful life. Wakeful life, as I am now living it, takes interest in one unique world in which all phenomena, both "objective" and "subjective," have their true place. My stretches of sleeping life also have their true place in this world. That I was unconscious or dreaming or that my dreams have these aesthetic features or this psychic significance are determinations about how the world given in wakeful experience is, a world that dreams and the oblivion of sleep are themselves incapable of directly showing. As we said earlier (§ 4), diurnal wakeful life cannot help but see everything in the light of day. The sleep that is there for wakefulness counts as a worldly reality in connection with others. The question is whether all possible waking up will merely fill in the horizons of this unique world in which I, now apparently awake, am interested. An affirmative answer would imply that, having once awakened and understood the truth of sleep as a reality, I can be certain to have discovered the destination of all future awakenings. Certain particulars in what I now accept as reality might be cancelled or amended, but the new realities will assume their true place in the one world in which I now believe.

This, however, does not seem to be the case. The unique world that is there for wakeful life is not a logical placeholder for the sum total of everything that will finally be established as true. It is rather the concrete spatiotemporal universe of realities. Were a future awakening to reconnect me with a course of wakeful life for which my current "wakefulness" (and its correlative non-wakefulness) will have been a dream, this would not fill in the indeterminate horizons of the world I now inhabit. True, the significance that I now attribute to "world" and "wakefulness" is retained in any future awakening I can imagine as a meaningful possibility. In this sense, if I, the dream speculator, am dreaming, I hold the true belief that there is a real world. However, this conjectured real world is not the unique world in which I now believe. Upon awakening, this latter would suffer a global nullification, not a corrective enrichment. For the wakeful subject, nothing *shown* in the dream images belongs to the real world, not even their "true" colors or sounds. Husserl makes this case quite precisely. In an image consciousness, the sense contents are wholly used up displaying an unreality and cannot simultaneously make present a real quality (2005, 48–9).

But is it even possible to think about the real world in which I, the dream speculator, am now sleeping? Husserl argues in several places that the hypothetical assumption of realities beyond our spatiotemporal world is contradictory. His point is that the very sense of a transcendent reality includes its experienceability for some actual ego, and that every conceivable actual ego must stand in a relationship of possible communication with us, even if this possibility can only be realized in imagination (e.g., if I were on that planet, I could see what its alien inhabitants see). This possible communication is exactly what determines that these other egos belong to our world—even if to its remote past or distant reaches. This line of reasoning, however, does not demonstrate any contradiction in the speculation about a future awakening that would nullify the world to which I am now awake. The speculation envisions a scenario in which the things to be experienced as real are indeed connected to my current experience by an understandable chain of motivations between perspectives; it thus meets Husserl's criterion for sensible assertions about transcendent reality (*Ideas I* § 48, *Cartesian Meditations* § 7). The motivational connection posited here does in fact place the hypothesized realities in the same world as my current illusions. However, the interpretation that will decide the true place of my current illusions as real sleep phenomena in the world of realities will only be possible for the awakened I. In this sense, the hypothesized realities are nonetheless beyond the concrete validity "our world," even to its distant reaches.[12]

It is true that the dream speculation reveals a certain finality in my present wakefulness. This is evident in how the speculation relies on the concepts of dream and reality. Were the speculation to abandon these points of reference, it would become absurd by suspecting that, in reality, reality means something unfathomable. The very wakefulness I am now living determines what reality and non-reality can mean. It also determines the relationship between my true wakefulness and my current dream. Descartes sees this clearly in his first meditation when he points out that if I am now dreaming my dream must somehow be derived from reality. This is simply what it means to dream. That the true reality to which I may awaken will necessarily contain sources from which my current "reality" derives does not imply, however, that the horizons of my current world will expand in the awakening. Once awake, I will negate this world as world, and understand it as the phantasy of a real sleeper in the real world. (Just how I, the speculator, can identify myself with the I that will awaken is a problem we cannot yet investigate). Having once awakened from sleep, diurnal wakefulness can never be certain that the nullification it exercises over sleeping life will not be visited upon it. The subject of wakeful life is jeopardized by this lack of certainty only when pursuing extremely unnatural interests. Ordinarily, the presupposition that this unique world is the final frontier for wakefulness is entertained in a pseudo-awakening, an intellectual game that uncovers an obvious condition for anything that I can meaningfully accomplish.

Turning now to the awakening from naïveté, we discover that it enjoys similar privileges. We can summarize them in terms of two co-functioning principles: the principle of epistemic authority—wakefulness always has the power to determine the truth of naïveté—and the principle of maturity—wakefulness is always better than naïveté from the standpoint of integrity. The awakening that devalues the stretch of naïve life is also the discovery of the truth of this life as naïve and is thus a rational accomplishment. My past naïveté is itself a fact in the universe of facts available to wakefulness. Further, because I am responding to the value of integrity, it is better to have realized my naïveté than not. The awakened ego makes progress in realizing it has presupposed. Progress here simply means to have come into a position where seeing and understanding my naïveté is now first of all possible.

However, the problem of relativization emerges here as well. The progress won in the realization of the presupposition depends upon its being true that I presupposed, and that the uprooted ground has the scope and centrality I accord to it in awakening reflection. But if these are uncertain, wakefulness seems to require the anticipation of its own relativity. Once again, however, awakening can only relativize itself with reference to its own power to establish true progress. If I am naïve about my own awakening, this will become clear only in another awakening that will once again represent the height of my maturity. In view of this problem, we can classify awakenings, and their correlative presuppositions, as amendable or irrevocable according to whether the very fact of their occurrence as well as the centrality and scope of the uprooted ground are fixed.

It seems that all awakenings to naïveté are amendable. Not only does the uprooted ground always seem to lie within a developing history that continuously alters its significance, but, because each awakening to naïveté occurs within the general state of wakefulness, its very existence also seems exposed to the possible nullification of the world as a mere dream. The childlike speculation that life is but a dream and the sophisticated conviction that life always has more to teach both point to the same truth. To be mature is to recognize every wakeful apprehension of what is as only provisionally wakeful. To be mature is to be skeptical about maturity. Let us grant, provisionally, the equation of historical sensibility with the conviction that the meaning of everything that happens in the world is provisional.[13] Let us also suppose the cogency of a future nullification of the world as a mere dream, despite its difficulties. Neither of these considerations rules out the possibility of an irrevocable awakening.

To see why, we have to recall a limitation we placed on our reflections. To this point, we have followed the natural tendency to treat awakening to naïveté as a local development within a general world-directed wakefulness that is the opposite of sleep. What if the progressive overcoming of naïveté were to reverse this relationship? If progress in wakefulness leads beyond its self-understanding as an attendance to reality that is the opposite of sleep, it will no longer be compromised at its core by the threat of a world-nullifying awakening, nor even by the continuous unfolding of reality in experience. The opposition sleep/wakefulness would then belong to a naïve understanding of wakefulness itself. By considering this possibility, we are anticipating the phenomenological attitude, which opens up a "completely different sort of waking life" (Husserl 1970, 144/147). We mention it here only to invoke the idea of an irrevocable awakening.

10. Appropriative Reflection

The awakened ego is jeopardized by having presupposed. The condition of jeopardy determines the goals of an appropriative reflection that aims to resolve it. Jeopardy is a twofold condition. Accordingly, its resolution is a twofold task. Appropriative reflection seeks, first, a critical assessment of the uprooted ground to which the naïve ego was committed. Second, this critical assessment must also achieve a reclamation of the naïve life-phase as a lapse for which the awakened ego can assume responsibility. Appropriative reflection is reflective in that it returns to the naïve life-phase in light of the presupposition first made available by the realization. It is appropriative in that it thereby owns the naïveté as *mine*. We conclude our outline of the general structures of having presupposed with a description of this reflection according to the tasks set before it in awakening.

Appropriative reflection reconsiders the ground in light of the realized presupposition. As an exercise in practical-epistemic vigilance, it is concerned with the truth of the presupposition, its scope and centrality, and whether and how the fulfillment of interests at stake in the ground might be resumed. Even in this first dimension, the reflection concerns what I have been accomplishing, not positions that could belong to anyone. I am jeopardized precisely because the realized presupposition uproots the ground in which established interests of mine are at stake. Jeopardy always involves an identity crisis, the seriousness of which depends upon the scope and centrality of the awakening. Appropriative reflection addresses itself, not just to what remains true and viable in light of the presupposition, but also to whether I can still be who I thought I was. Among its possible results are the reaffirmation, reformation, and giving up of self-conceptions tied to the commitments and projects of the naïve ego.

The awakened ego finds itself jeopardized in its commitments and projects. For a narrow success-mindedness, the question of whether I can now wakefully accomplish what I was then naively aiming to accomplish is answered simply by determining the truth of the presupposition, and making any necessary adjustments. But there is a difference in sense between what was naively aimed at and what is now aimed at wakefully. The naïve aiming failed to attend to some feature of what now constitutes success, even if this failure did not happen to hinder success. It thereby also failed to attend to the way to success, even if it happened to travel that way. The failure to aim wakefully has to be understood as a failure. This means reclaiming what I naively accomplished as a partial fulfillment of, or deviation from, the project of which I now take myself to be the wakeful subject. We call this reclamation "teleological reconstruction."

This reconstruction aims to reclaim naïve life as a part of the life that I, as wakeful ego, can occupy as mine. We have seen how the expression "I presupposed" already contains the basic form of this reclamation. The wakeful ego subsumes the naïve ego by asserting *its* responsibility for having presupposed. This can only occur in the form of a historical narrative in the minimal sense that it transcends the immanent meaning of past activity in order to discover something true about that activity. We have also seen, though, that the wakeful appropriation of naïveté is not merely retrospective. Naïve life has to be divested of its naïve self-understanding. *Appropriative reflection exhausts what naïve life was like in terms of the new evidence and ways of making evident first won in awakening.*

The awakened ego can attend to the presupposition whereas the naïve ego could not (in fact). Appropriation accounts for this inability in terms of a pathological form of attention to which it was captive during the naïve life-phase. The primary explanatory concept of appropriative reflection is "consuming interest." This describes a preoccupation with something such that the monitoring of its implications and the context they afford is replaced by automatic functions born by tradition. The consuming interest fixes upon some feature of what I am accomplishing such that I cannot (in fact) freely advert to the overall accomplishment from which this feature derives its meaning. Appropriation explains naïveté by establishing that, had it not been for the consuming interest, I would have attended to what I can now formulate as presuppositional content.

The explanation of naïveté in terms of consuming interest demotes to a mere occasion the proximate motive for the realization of having presupposed. This proximate motive is sometimes detectable in the grip of the dawning realization itself, sometimes in subsequent reflection, sometimes not at all. Sometimes its power to break the spell of naïveté is explicable in terms of a chain of associations that provoke the thought of the presupposition. Sometimes its power remains obscure. However it stands with this proximate motive, appropriative reflection renders it incidental by explaining awakening as the overcoming of my own negligence. I would have attended to the presupposition were it not for my consuming interest. The occasion of awakening releases the naïve ego from the bonds of its consuming interest, but, precisely because the interest was consuming, the occasion was not necessary for the awakening.

The greatest difficulty for an account of appropriative reflection is the extent to which explanations in terms of consuming interest are also descriptions. The presupposition was implied in the naïve life-phase, but could not become an object of attention. Did this implication exist for the naïve ego? If so, how was it there? There are two obvious mistakes to avoid here. The first mistake is to describe the implication as something previously given to the naïve ego. By claiming to find the presupposition within the naïve ego's purview, as something noticeable for it through a mere redirection of attention, the appropriative reflection would deny the realization to which it, as reflection, owes its genesis. The second mistake is to derive the implication from the wakeful consideration of the logic of the naïve situation (concluding, for instance, that someone who only purchases alcoholic beverages must have been convinced no children were coming to dinner). The problem here is that the assignment of a phantom mental activity does not allow for an appropriative understanding of the naïve life-phase as my own. I can only conclude that everything happened "as if" I were convinced of the presuppositional content.

In avoiding these mistakes, it is tempting to characterize appropriative reflection as a form of recounting that mixes inference and description.

Philosophers of history have identified several strategies for reconstructing the past that forge middle ways between retrodiction and direct representation.[14] Mandelbaum (1977) has emphasized that theoretical generalizations are often necessary supplements to direct description in historical accounts. While obviously insufficient on its own, knowledge of "general factors that affect the behavior of individuals," such as the fact that emotions can influence judgment, is a useful instrument, not only when documentary evidence is lacking but also in the interpretation of that evidence and the assessment of its reliability (120–1). The historian's aim is not, of course, to develop or test such generalizations, but to account for what happened in a particular sequence of events to which they may apply: "once he has obtained guidance from a generalization he can look for further evidence either to support or modify his use of it in the case at hand" (123). Danto has shown how "conceptual evidence" about how types of people behave in different sorts of situations not only helps distinguish plausible from implausible narratives but also guides the attempt to construct original true narratives: "An imaginative appeal to our general concepts will fairly soon get us a narrative of some sort which we might use as a guide for further research, seeing whether some further but independent evidence might be found for our narrative" (1985, 123).

Dray's notion of "rational explanation" might also seem to provide a description of how appropriative reflection appropriates. Dray points out that satisfying historical explanations of actions are often reconstructions of the calculation an agent undertook in his situation. This is a *reconstruction* because the agent need not have actually carried out the explicit process of calculation attributed to him. It is nonetheless accurate because "in so far as we say an action is purposeful at all … there is a calculation which could be constructed for it: the one the agent would have gone through if he had not seen what to do in a flash, if he had been called upon to account for what he did after the event" (1957, 123). Dray even extends this form of explanation to self-reflection: "if the agent is to understand his *own* actions, i.e. after the event, he may have to do so in exactly the same way, although at the time he recited no propositions to himself" (ibid.). The reasons for having done something need not have been noticed *as* reasons. The explanation succeeds, not when it provides an account of what the agent might remember having thought, but when it makes understandable how the action was "appropriate" to the situation as the agent conceived it: "Rational explanation may be regarded as an attempt to reach a kind of logical equilibrium at which point the action is *matched* with a calculation" (125).

Let us consider what these models yield when applied to the explanation of naïveté in terms of tradition and consuming interest. In historical research, the use of generalizations and conceptual evidence is meant to guide the attainment and interpretation of artifacts that directly testify to the past. In the case of appropriative reflection, there would seem to be a parallel reference of indirect to direct testimony. Generalizations about how a certain type of preoccupation blinds one to certain types of consideration would seem to define a window through which to look for direct recollections of being so blinded. But because no such recollections are here possible, the object of this "looking" is really a plausible scenario that I, knowing what I now know, let stand as a depiction of my past. The model of rational explanation makes this explicit. The presupposition is here the assumption I would have entertained were it not for my consuming interest. The "match" between this calculation and what I actually lived through works with reference to a hypothetical scenario in which the naïve ego enjoyed better conditions for explicit reflection (e.g., in which I had more time, less distractions, etc.).

These models are suggestive, but are surrogates for the immediate way that the appropriative reflection annexes the naïve life-phase as it was lived. The wakefully reflecting ego does not match a rational reconstruction with what it recalls from the naïve life-phase. It rather *recognizes* that the naïve ego was already acquainted with what it presupposed, and that the presupposition was, in this sense, eligible for admission into its purview. The presupposition was there to be seen, but missed. It was missed in that it was actually implied in the purview of the naïve ego according to the very meanings it relied upon. The failure to follow the implication, and therefore to have anything as implied, is now detectable in a fixation upon some element of the accomplishment that is only what it is (as it was fixed upon) in light of the unrealized presupposition. For example, the choice of beverages, the table setting, and so on all bear the implied meaning that the prepared dinner is not for children, a meaning that the wakeful ego cannot help but find in every action of the naïve ego *as a meaning with which it was acquainted* but to which it could not attend. A preoccupation with selecting a good wine, for instance, let blindly function the traditionally established associations that link wine to a certain type of evening with a certain type of guest.

The way appropriative reflection recognizes the implication in the naïve life-phase has its closest analogue not in historical research but in historical seeing. Although most of Danto's analyses work at the linguistic level, he briefly considers what we might call historical or narrative perception. A visitor to the house in which Newton was born in 1642, who knows that Newton was born there, "will see it as the birthspot and early dwelling of one of the great scientists of all ages" (1985, 158). As Danto points out, this is not to transport ourselves back to the seventeenth century, but to be "sensitive to the significance" that events posterior to that period bestowed upon the house (ibid.). Narrative seeing does not, we emphasize, impose an artificial lens over our perception. The "sensitivity" Danto invokes simply registers properties of the house that have accrued to it through the temporal development in which it stands for contemporary observers. Carr has explored how these sorts of temporal configurations already populate the pre-reflective life of the individual. For instance, when a melody takes a "surprising turn" the past notes "are now part of a different whole: what they are 'heard as' is revised retroactively" (1986, 29).

Narrative perception does not assign to a past event a description only available in the present; it has before it a historically developed thing in which it cannot help but see the properties it exhibits as a consequence of its development. In this sense, it is like the wakeful recognition of what was implied in naïve life. However, the historical sensitivity characteristic of narrative perception differs from the wakeful understanding of naïve life in an important respect. Let us pursue Carr's example further. Imagine hearing two phases of a melody, *a* followed by *b*. Upon hearing *b*, *a* is now heard as part of the whole *ab*, for example, as the calm before the storm. This retroactive revision is automatic, not the product of an explicit reinterpretation. Now imagine a subsequent reflection upon, or even a replaying of, *a*. I can now explicitly consider *a* alone in light of the whole *ab* and understand it as the calm before the storm. However, I am also free to modulate my reflective attitude so that I try to recapture an "innocent" hearing of *a* as it was first heard. This may occur in memory, or in a sympathetic listening along with someone who has never heard it before. In fact, an appreciation of the melody's own qualities seems to require that this "innocent" hearing of *a* remain accessible against the overriding understanding that it is the prelude to *b*. Similarly, an historically appreciative perception of the house of Newton's birth seems to require, in addition to the appropriate knowledge about Newton, an innocent interpretation of the house as the birthspot of a boy with an uncertain future. What we want to underline is that retroactive revision though a developing temporal whole leaves intact the unrevised, "innocent" phase, which can become an object of reflection oriented toward the full significance of the whole. The "innocent" *a* is not cancelled as a result of its becoming part of *ab*.

By contrast, the wakeful understanding of naïve life radically severs the "innocent" interpretation from the true significance of the whole. Even where there is no motive to doubt the presupposition, the wakeful ego cannot enhance its understanding by recapturing what it was like from the naïve perspective. Recapturing the past moment in its innocence of the present remains instructive for the present precisely because the present moment was not already present in the past. Wakeful understanding, however, receives no instruction by recapturing naïveté because it recognizes what it has realized as already having been there in naïveté, but missing. Whereas recapturing the innocent past highlights how the present fulfilled what was only potential in the past, wakeful understanding cannot find in naïve life any such potential. This is because wakefulness does not emerge by fulfilling potentialities projected in naïve life.

The appropriative reflection is "historical" in that it transcends the immanent sense of past action in order to discern what really happened. But this discernment occurs through a peculiar annexation of the naïve life-phase to the present of the awakened ego. What the awakened ego can know and do the naïve ego could in principle have known and done, though it factually could not. In appropriative reflection, the awakened ego recognizes itself as having undergone "motives" that explain its past naïveté. There is descriptive power in the concepts of passivity and tradition ("associations," "habits," etc.) that explain how leaving things to function as usual made me factually unable to notice. However, this power is inherently ambiguous. Such concepts do not simply capture things as they were. They rather effect the subsumption whereby an awakened ego occupies *its* naïve life on its own terms. Were it not for its consuming interest, the naïve ego would not have been blinded by tradition. The awakened ego thereby determines naïveté as a deficient mode of living in the same world that is now available to wakefulness, and the naïve ego as an ego alienated from its own capacities. According to the self-understanding of the awakened ego, the realization of its naïveté is not just the discovery of something new, but the recovery of itself from a kind of self-estrangement.

11. Illusions

We conclude by identifying illusions to which appropriative reflection itself can give rise. Appropriative reflection tends to construe the naïveté of naïve life as both inevitable and inexcusable. The explanation by way of passivity and tradition shows why the unnoticeable could not be noticed, and yet it should have been noticed, and could have been noticed in principle. This tension stems from the assumption of responsibility by which the awakened ego asserts itself as the subject of having presupposed. From the moment of awakening, the reasons for naïveté explicated in reflection are already projected within the range of my powers of attention. By carrying out this egological occupation now, I understand what I was naively undergoing then. This critique interprets the presuppositional content as what had to be but should not have been taken for granted on the basis of tradition. It can afford original, if paradoxical, evidence for the necessity of having presupposed. It provides no evidence, however, for judgments that would generalize this necessity and assert that it holds in the present (e.g., "we are always presupposing something"). One can conceive a possible future awakening to one's present naïveté without contradiction, but this possible awakening cannot find supporting evidence in the present without destroying the naïveté it would claim to discover. We might call the pretended recognition of a present-tense naïveté the illusion of false modesty.

The appropriative reflection determines the truth of the naïve life-phase (principle of epistemic authority) as an inferior or deficient moment of the awakened ego's own development (principle of maturity). However, it falls prey to illusion if it attempts to assume responsibility for the event of awakening itself. Nobody wakes herself up, neither from sleep nor naïveté. From what center would this waking up occur? Was the wakeful ego somehow already monitoring naïve life, perhaps lurking "in the shadows" or "behind the scenes"? This intuition is probably derived from the observation of sleeping or hibernating organisms, the vital functions of which are reduced, but maintained. The reflection on the experience of awakening yields no such intuition. The awakened ego rather owes its appropriative powers to an event of awakening from which it is born. Awakening does not fulfill expectations set up in naïve life, but neither is it a sovereign accomplishment of wakeful life. One sign of this is the role of the occasion for awakening, from which the naïve ego benefits in its transition to wakefulness, even though the wakeful ego, making itself negligent, renders the occasion incidental. The interpretation of naïve life according to the capacities of the awakened ego, and of wakefulness as a kind of self-recovery, cannot go so far as to forget that it is an *appropriation* necessitated by the awakening that first generates the wakeful ego. "I woke up" does not attribute an action to a subject, but describes the materialization of that subject for itself. In honor of Plato's myth, we might call the illusion of recollection this conviction that in awakening the wakeful ego calls itself back to itself.

Appropriative reflection responds to a destabilization that accompanies awakening to naïveté. The awakened ego is in jeopardy both as the accomplisher of what is at stake in the uprooted ground and in its very wakefulness as ego. Considering appropriative reflection as a whole, this second aspect has priority.

The reconsideration of the uprooted ground in light of the presupposition is a moment of the attempt to recover my wakeful life. To the extent that the reflection is able to recognize and understand my past naïveté, I have achieved an absolute maturation. This achievement stands even if the presupposition turns out to be false, and even if I am thereby forced to abandon a project to which I have dedicated myself. Alternatively, if the presupposition turns out to be true, the disvalue of the life-phase based upon it will not be diminished. In either case, the point of the entire reflection is to reestablish myself as the wakeful accomplisher of what was interrupted by the realization of naïveté. Insofar as I am oriented by basic integrity, what I am doing needs to be transformed into something to which I am awake, not just something accomplishable. The proper telos of critical reflection on presuppositions is the recovery of basic integrity, not success understood in abstraction from the inner nature of the accomplishment that succeeds. To forget this is to fall prey to the pragmatic illusion.

This fundamental aim also has priority over any concern with theoretical certainty. At a particular level of awakening, it may be that appropriative reflection has access to indubitable evidence. However, this is not a universal feature of appropriative reflection. The kind of evidence available depends upon the nature of the elements that constitute the predicament. In many spheres of activity, every aspect of the predicament faced in awakening admits of only probabilistic determination. I can be optimally awake to what I was naively accomplishing without enjoying indubitable evidence. We should bear in mind, however, that just as a reinterpretation of what one was really accomplishing can transform an intellectual game into a genuine awakening, so can it transform the kind of evidence proper to the appropriation of naïveté. To subordinate, in advance, the appropriation of naïve life to the interest in securing the certainty of unshakable grounds is to fall prey to the epistemic illusion.

This completes our structural outline of having presupposed. Underlying any explicit consideration of presuppositional content is an experience of awakening, jeopardy, and appropriation, itself traceable to the exertions of an ego compromised in its basic integrity. This dynamic is at work in various ways in accordance with the various interests that guide experience and thinking. The next division examines the modifications these interests introduce into the structures of awakening and appropriation as well as the possible transitions between these interests in the life of an ego.

Division B

Levels of Awakening and Appropriation

The analyses of this division specify the description of having presupposed in terms of three basic attitudes relevant to phenomenological reflection. By attitude, we mean a general orientation of interest that prefigures what is noticed. By basic attitude, we mean an attitude that prefigures how wakefulness and naïveté themselves come to attention. A basic attitude affords a kind of awakening peculiar to that attitude. The awakening to a new basic attitude is a meta-awakening that reinterprets wakefulness and naïveté in light of a new form of wakefulness and its ways of making evident. An original distinction between basic attitudes thus occurs in a realization of naïveté, not in a reflection. These attitudes are essentially ordered. Each is the historical and structural prerequisite for the next, which realizes the presupposition upon which its predecessor was based. The value of wakefulness justifies describing subsequent attitudes as higher-level attitudes, and someone capable of adopting them as more mature—*with respect to her basic integrity*—than someone who is not.

At the same time, each basic attitude has its own endless tasks of appropriation that higher attitudes cannot usurp. This introduces ambiguity into the rank order of basic attitudes. The tasks of appropriation that define the "lower" attitude are neither renounced nor subsumed through reflections in the "higher" attitude. Each basic attitude thus retains a final legitimacy for a life wakefully lived. We will pay special attention to this insufficiency of any attitude to the ideal of wakefulness. It will ultimately justify the synthesis of concerns that constitute the crisis problematic in transcendental philosophy.

1. Awakening and Reality: The Mundane Attitude

As far as possible, our general reflections presented an account of awakening that holds across attitudes. We will now revisit that account and assign to a particular attitude a certain understanding of its elements. Because this attitude is that of the everyday life of human beings, its particularity is elusive. By highlighting what is particular to awakening in the mundane attitude, we safeguard the generality of the general analysis. We also identify those appropriative tasks that a higher, phenomenological attitude cannot advance but in light of which it must justify itself if it is to guide the human practice called philosophy.

Mundane awakening is shaped by a fundamental interest in the real world, a realm of true being opposed to merely subjective appearances. The opposition between objective reality and merely subjective appearances is a central accomplishment of diurnal wakeful life. We have already indicated how it informs the understanding of wakefulness as the opposite of sleep. Whatever appears in dream experience is understood upon waking up to have been really a mere appearance. The representation of the dream as a past event, the determination of when and why it occurred, the understanding of its meaning—these wakeful acts concern the reality of the mere appearance construed as dependent upon the real sleeping of a real sleeper. Sophisticated reflection in this mode will, for instance, treat dreaming as a product of the chemistry of the sleeping brain.[1] What was dreamed, however, was itself a mere appearance, which means that it does not count for a wakeful person as having afforded a view of the way things really were. The dreamed objects cannot explain the occurrence of the dream, even if they are images of the real objects that do. If I dream about how my brain is producing this very dream, this dreamed brain still explains nothing. Likewise, dreamless sleep is retroactively understood as a mere illusion of absence. The oblivion of dreamless sleep was not an actual eclipse of reality, but, like the dream, is placed in reality as a mere subjective state dependent upon the real sleeping of a real sleeper. The wakefulness opposite sleep is, for itself, an enjoyment of reality *rather than* the mere appearances that take place in reality, but do not show it.

Reality is the setting of the wakeful life that contrasts itself with sleep. Within this form of wakeful life, reality can also become a theme and target. Here, again, it stands opposed to what is merely subjective. Reality becomes a target when the engagement with reality falters in a way that brings this engagement into focus. The mundane attitude thus has reality as an explicit concern in the context of a critique of experience as potentially alienated from it. The claim to contact reality implicit in experience becomes explicit as a claim in becoming problematic. The problematic character of the claim is traceable to subjectivity in a number of familiar ways. First, the perceptual basis of experience is tied to a spatiotemporal perspective. Second, all experience is the experience of a particular organism.

Third, judgments not only form on the basis of a perspectival, biologically framed experience but also reflect preferences, passions, and moods that have developed in the psychological history of a particular individual. In these and other dimensions, the critique of experience distinguishes between normal subjective conditions, which conduce to things being the way they seem, and abnormal subjective conditions, which conduce to a distinction between how things seem and how they are. These normal and abnormal conditions are themselves determined in normal experience that shows reality as it is. This critical understanding of subjectivity as having a problematic claim on reality while simultaneously belonging to it is a feature of ordinary mundane reflection. It underlies and continues to animate scientific theories that postulate a reality beyond both normal and abnormal seemings.

In the mundane attitude, the realization of having presupposed is one way of exposing subjectivity in this problematic relationship to reality. Typically, presupposition and ground are expressible as empirical claims. In these cases, it is easy to see how one's own experiencing is brought into view as accountable to, but potentially estranged from, reality. Occasionally, however, presupposition and ground have directly to do with formal subject matter such as algebraic equations or logical proofs. In these cases, reality is not directly at issue. However, the basic relationship between seeming and subjectivity remains in force, as becomes clear in worries about mistakes. Further, the subject engages these formal domains only intermittently against the backdrop of world-directed interests. For herself, the thinker is a real person now and again occupied with formal subject matter.

In the self-reflexive moments of awakening, the subjectivity that becomes thematic as negligent is itself, in its own manner, a reality. The appropriative reflection ultimately concerns my naïve life, which falls within the world-interest characterizing the mundane attitude. That and why I was naïve are psychological matters in the broad sense that they pertain to the mental states of a particular human organism at a particular time and place. The awakened, appropriating ego is thus interested in the same reality as was the naïve ego. This identity of concern is what accounts for the critical import of awakenings to naïveté in the mundane attitude. The awakened ego is capable of determining the reality of the naïve ego.

It is worth emphasizing the obvious fact that in all mundane consideration of itself, the ego finds itself and its activities in the middle of reality. I am located in a particular space and time from which I stage any activity I can possibly accomplish. When I consider my present activity of perception, for instance, it is rooted in my body such that I know that it is happening here, as is evident when I blink my eyes or change my position. More broadly, it is taking place in the vicinity of its surroundings, not in some far-off place. The perception of the room takes place in the room. I also know that this perceptual activity is simultaneous with the scene it takes in. My perception of the sunrise takes place in the morning, and if I happen to perceive a clock, I can mark the time of the perception more precisely. With regard to where and when my experience happens, it also makes sense to trust trustworthy others, who can provide true information about these matters. In general, when I direct my attention to myself, I consider the same person available to others, who sometimes have a better perspective on what I am doing than I myself do. Only because of this obvious inherence of experience in reality can subjectivity become a theme for critical reflections that assess whether it accesses things as they are.

2. Reality and World

The awakened ego is interested in the same reality as the naïve life it critiques. From the perspective of the awakening, the core of this reality is the predicament, a new practical situation brought into view by the realization. Some presupposed circumstance is relevant to the wakeful resumption of the uprooted accomplishment. However, this object of attention is encompassed by the single world of realities that orients all wakeful experience and judgment in the mundane attitude. This encompassment accounts for the provisional character of the awakening and everything established by the appropriative reflection.

Belief in the world is a defining characteristic of the mundane attitude. This belief is foundational for all beliefs about inner-worldly realities (things, animals, people, etc.) and may prove so inseparable from pre-reflective life that "belief" seems an inappropriate term. Nonetheless, we may ask in what exactly this uniquely foundational belief believes. What is added to the content of beliefs about realities by the fact that these realities are taken to be in the world? In addressing this question, we will focus on the "natural concept" of the world that frames experience before it is reframed by epistemic or scientific interests. Those who pursue such interests do so in the world that is obviously already there and in which the "worlds" of scientists and philosophers are special contexts.[2]

We will point out three ways the world shapes the experience of real things and judgments about them. We can express them in the formula: the world is the pre-given, open, universe of realities. According to a useful schema employed by Husserl in *Ideas I*, whatever is real lies either in the scene of direct experience or else in a surround from which it can be brought to direct experience, or finally in an indeterminate horizon out of which it can be discovered. Scene, surround, and horizon are there at once, together, in terms of one another. There is nothing beyond them; they are the infrastructure of beyondness. The world is a universe in the sense that any real thing points to the unique spatiotemporal configuration of reality in which it is situated. The configuration, though it itself cannot appear sensibly, is there intuitively for experiencing "each waking moment" (2014b, 49/49–50). Real things indicate to any actual experience further possible experiences in which they also are, or could be, appearing. These further experiences cannot discover just anything. They must deepen and enrich what appears and has appeared in actual experience. Even conflicts and reversals must fit within a broader harmonious development. This presumption that experienced reality harmonizes with the experienceable reality it indicates is already at work in any inductive procedure that would claim it as its result. It is how one has the world as *universe*, as cosmos, as "order of things."[3] The world is *open* because the network of experience to which it is correlated is infinite. I presume that I live in the one world, not an enclosed sector of it. This means that it, as the one world, has an open horizon. The world itself is there in my immediate scene and its surroundings by already including them and every indication that points beyond them. The world is *pre-given* because of this "already." There are orderings of things that result from attentive activities. But these activities order within the world-horizon. As Husserl points out, because of the openness and pre-givenness of the world, all judgments that determine it are relative to unknown "causal and spiritual dependencies" (2008a, 711, 715). These unknown circumstances render provisional all world-directed judgments, including those that supplement or correct previous judgments.

But this is just to say that mundane wakefulness has the whole world implied in its purview. So long as it maintains belief in the world, it has as potential whatever can become actual. Whatever is real out there is experienceable, in principle and in however mediated a way, beginning from the here and now. The world-horizon is not populated with random logical possibilities, but with possibilities for the most general ways of being real. It is determinable so as to incorporate what is already determined into a coherent whole that has variously changed and endured. The basic integrity of the subject who finds herself and her experience in the middle of reality is legible in this comprehensive coherence of the world-order. The directional dimensions across which her life spans are mundane dimensions. She appropriates who she is in terms of possibilities for living opened by the world. We will later consider a thought experiment that highlights this world-order by imagining an experience in which it collapses. The experiment requires a philosophical perspective for which the world does not contain experience and experience does not guarantee the world. This perspective cannot be reached in the course of world-directed life.

3. Provinciality and Worldliness

Mundane naïveté is neglect of the comprehensiveness of the world. In its wakeful course, world-directed life regularly reinterprets realities as parts of new wholes that expose the confinement of prior understanding. Mundane naïveté misses the implications that should have prompted such a reinterpretation. Where this missing is due to a fixation on what is local, we call naïveté "provinciality" and "worldliness" the ideal of wakefulness opposed to it. This section sketches some features of provinciality, partly to prepare the claim that the equation between naïveté and provinciality is particular to the mundane attitude, partly to prepare the claim that overcoming provinciality is an endless task.

To be local is not already to be provincial. The former is a necessary feature of life in the mundane attitude. To be local in one's understanding is simply to have orientation in the world. The world orients insofar as scene, surround, and horizon provide the setting for actual and possible actions. The oriented "I can" is a practical agency correlated to results, not a mere bodily agency correlated to changes in what appears. To be oriented in the world is to have at one's disposal the means to fulfill practical intentions and to be sensitive to opportunities to form such intentions. Reorientation, accordingly, is the process of discovering bearings in response to disruptions that affect the formation and fulfillment of practical intentions. Local understanding is essentially open to such disruption.

Locality is implicated in the very spatiotemporal form of the world. Every "here" is a "there" in relation to perspectives beyond those already within one's surround. The discovery of these perspectives reconfigures the spatial order. The exploration of distant places incorporates the place from which one disembarked into a revised landscape. Even places within familiar terrains are constantly acquiring new positions in relation to a changing or more closely determined environment. Every orientation in mundane space thus utilizes local points of reference open to being resituated. Similarly, phases of world-experience do not replace, but rather build upon one another such that a longer experience experiences more just by being longer. At every moment there is a mundane future and past that situate the present in a more comprehensive development that alters its narrative qualities. Every enduring experience is thus limited in its temporal surround with respect to an experience that outlives or precedes it. This limitation is clearest in cases where further experience prompts revisions, but even the basic connections of before and after expose the limits of temporal perspective.

Concretely, one does not merely move and endure in the world, but acts and ages there. The things that provide orientation for local understanding are pragmata, legible in terms of the opportunities for use they afford or fail to afford. Arrangements of useful things solicit or lie in wait for "things to do," activities accommodated by the local world, for which there are means, time, and space. Things to do are themselves arrayed into systems of alternatives, as are the things with which one does them. At every level of generality, this field of action engages practical interest in realizing something worthwhile, up to the goal of a satisfying life. The others with, for, and against whom one acts all have a share in this same orientation, however they vary otherwise. They are part of the "everyone" with whom one lives. The subject of local understanding forms self-conceptions from within this orientation. What goes right and wrong concerns her as a bearer of the projects, roles, and relationships through which she participates in the life of the local world. No less than spatiotemporal location, so is this personal location open to reorientation. Everything in the local world orients only provisionally because its orientating function is relative to that endless network of causal and spiritual dependencies emphasized by Husserl. A change in circumstance, actual or possible, means an actual or possible change in orientation. Certain dependencies can be reckoned with explicitly, others, vaguely indicated as to type, are revealed only with the occurrence of the change itself. As the change or possibility of change is registered by local understanding, established ways of doing things stand out in their contingency. The local world could have been and can be otherwise; it is essentially situated within a broader realm of possibilities for living. Attention to this contingency is the source of reflective postures, like appreciation and critique, that address the local world in its very locality.

Provinciality can arise from locality because of the tendency to everydayness. Everydayness is an outcome of life in the mundane attitude, not its form. It originates in the routinization achievable in an equilibrium between the formation and fulfillment of practical intentions and the orienting world. Things, such as they are, are reliable, even reliably novel or aggravating, and it is generally clear what they are relevant or irrelevant for, adequate or inadequate for, and whom they concern. Practical intelligence looks toward what has already been rendered intelligible, takes up this type of thing, is ready for this type of activity, reckons with these types of alternatives. Oriented in this manner, everyday understanding neglects those emergent circumstances that might prompt reorientation. We can speak of provinciality whenever the tendency to everydayness has allowed a closed, fabricated, world-context to stand in for the open, pre-given universe of realities.

Welton's account of the lifeworld-horizon as an "interplay of context and background" is helpful here (2000, 344). For Welton, "background" means the nexus of sense that guides and is shaped by experiential and actional involvement with things, "context" means the socially constructed framework in which possibilities for involvement are already delineated according to established conceptual schemes. Context determines the types of variability that matter in a given domain as well as the paths of approach that lead to the specification of variables, but every such context refers to the open background of experience and action in which it was originally established, through which it might be altered, and in light of which it serves certain ends. In Welton's view, "average" world understanding emerges when "background recedes and context dominates, i.e. allows background to come into play only to the extent that actions already conform to acceptable types" (2000, 366). What one is doing counts as "acceptable," we emphasize, in a way that forecloses attention to contestable standards that might render it such.

In this same spirit, Steinbock shows how the standard philosophical use of "everydayness" is a symptom of everydayness itself. The problem Steinbock identifies with this "quasi-phenomenological, quasi-existentialist locution" is that it often denotes the usualness, typicality, or reliability of the practical world in isolation from the history of discriminating experience that has carved out certain ways of acting and living as preferable or optimal (1995, 164). By conceiving the normal as typical apart from the normal as optimal "one conceals the very precariousness of norms' coming into being, and the acquired resilience and stability that norms so readily exhibit" (161). To treat "everydayness" as an essential feature of world-experience is to overlook the normative generation, regeneration, and potential transformation of the average. This is in line with Welton's criticism of structuralist theories that view contexts as explanations rather than observable outcomes understandable in terms of acts and actions (2000, 385). At the same time, the philosophical use of everydayness as a transcendental framework for experience gives direct voice to the phenomenon itself. The tendency to everydayness lets sink into oblivion the link between orienting things and the open history of striving that continues to win orientation through them. Contexts correlated to routines of experience and patterns of action crowd out the dependencies that make local contexts local. The one world, and the *infinite* course of experience to which it is correlated, becomes perfectly irrelevant to the practical attitude of everyday life. Husserl coins a formula for understanding this process when he writes that praxis "finitizes the infinities" (2008a, 698). The ongoing fulfillment of practical interests establishes a "continual reign of concordance" and a "homogeneous certainty" of the world (674). World-belief involves the presumption that order encompasses disorder at infinity. For an interest consumed in everydayness, the finite order of the local world disappears as it takes over this encompassing function.

The encounter with the alien has a unique power to illuminate the provenance, limits, and prospects of the local community and its world. For Husserl, these encounters are simultaneously encounters with the local world as the product of a "history" and "culture" (1973a, 216). They result in a localization of the orienting world that exposes its contingency. Steinbock and Waldenfels have pursued this theme in great depth. We will draw on only a few basic insights about the alien encounter in order to outline how provinciality becomes appropriable as a form of naïveté.

Negatively, the phenomenology of the alien has highlighted why a comparative interest in differences or a communicative interest in reciprocal exchange lack the power to localize orienting contexts. A system of typical differences and an ethos of mutual understanding are constitutive of the user-friendliness in which the locality of the surrounding world is concealed. Waldenfels highlights how familiar discourses posit a "reversibility of positions" between self and other as diverse manifestations of the same genus: "Asians are not Europeans, just like Europeans are not Asians ... No matter how different Europeans and Asians are, they are undoubtedly human." That it is "Europeans who speak about Europeans and non-Europeans" remains unnoticed: "one side of the difference is clearly marked, but the other is not" (2011, 73). Facts about ways of life in the long past, in foreign cultures, in subcultures, and so on, are already available for everyday understanding. Even the divergent perspectives of the others who live otherwise are understandable because the ways they are different refer to these well-known facts. The alien cannot be pointed out within such a system of differences. It is best to define it provisionally according to its function, as whatever brings locality to prominence.

Positively, the phenomenology of the alien has described the distinct way that liminal encounters make the local world appropriable. Steinbock draws attention to disruptions in which the alien, rather than registering a typical difference, indicates an alien world in which it belongs. The initial incomprehensibility of the anomalous "reaches deeper into an incomprehensibility that has the integrity of another normativity, one that cannot be overcome through a simple appropriation" (1995, 242). The alien is here the bearer of "an alien normativity and generative density that is not my own" (242). This generative density refers to the matrix of traditions into which the anomalous fits as a feature of normal life. For Steinbock, the inaccessibility and integrity of the alien imply one another. The alien has another world in which she is at home, and which I cannot readily make my own. The encounter with this inaccessibility and integrity, however, brings the home-character of my own world into relief: "rather than losing the home in the encounter, we gain the home *as* home, as constituted for us in a more intimate mode of accessibility" (245). What especially becomes accessible is the limitedness of my world, not in the sense of its deficiency, but rather its determinacy as a unique historical formation for which my community is responsible: "transgression crosses over the limits and thus brings an explicit experience of the limits into being" (249). The homeworld is now critically appropriable in its discovered limits. Because this appropriation of home possibilities emerges from the encounter, Steinbock describes it as "an implicit way of responding to the alien" (256). The critical perspectives that emerge at home unfold out of an encounter to which they owe their genesis.

If we accept the critique of comparison and reciprocity, then it is a peculiar synthesis that grasps the own and the alien together. Home and alien ways of life do not enter into an empirical generality, such that the experience of A and B shapes a single type that contains them. Nor are they instantiations of an invariant *eidos*. Instead, the alien-typical is given in its inaccessibility along with the own-typical made strange in the fact that it is inalienably own. This particular inalienability is connected to that particular inaccessibility. This leaves intact the evidence that supports empirical generalizations and essential insights about culture. Indeed, such evidence must be operative in the very detection of alien normativity (these intelligent beings are living in their environment, etc.). When Waldenfels claims that "there can be no culturalism which regards the own culture and the alien culture as one among others" (2011, 70), this ought not imply anything to the contrary. Instead, when ownness and alienness stand out in the encounter, the empirical types and universal characteristics of culture are not at issue. At issue is the appropriation of one's own orientation in the world in its provenance, limits, and prospects. The strange fact that one lives the way one does gives way, in appropriation, to the reclamation of serious life in which one intends to live in some way.

We can distinguish those appropriations of local life that have to do with naïveté by looking at what is owed to the encounter. The alien encounter has the power to illuminate the locality of my world. The question is whether what it illuminates could have been noticed but for consumption in everydayness, or whether it is delivered by the particular relation to the alien established in the encounter. It seems that the particular encounter always brings to notice features of the local that could not have been noticed otherwise. It is in tandem with *this* foreign tradition that my own stands out as particular in these definite ways. In general, the encounter always determines which features of my world are thrown into relief and shapes the space of possibility that governs their appropriation. However, the very contingency of everything in my local world is implied in local understanding as such. It is the missing of this contingency that is realized in the awakening to provinciality. Provincial presuppositions are expressible as necessary judgments. I was presupposing that things in my world *had* to be the way they happen to be or are presumed to be. This is perhaps what Husserl's "homogeneous certainty" describes. While the encounter with the alien can enrich my local world in unforeseeable ways, it cannot have been required for me to apprehend its locality with reference to an indeterminate "outside" that sustains the distinction between my world and the world (Steinbock 1995, 180). The world awakened subject has this reference in her purview, a reference missed because of consumption in everydayness. The encounter with the alien is only the occasion for the awakening to provinciality.

If we understand alienness broadly as the strange self-possession by which anything transcends its function in a context, then the alien is at work in the occasioning of all mundane awakening to naïveté. Even the most ordinary things can become alien to everyday activity just because they originally belong to the openness of the world. For instance, instruments in a context of routine action leave room for a dawning realization by outflanking the practical intention that addresses them. To do so, they need not break, go missing, or prove unsuitable. All that is required is an encounter with the integrity and inaccessibility of the thing. The thing has a depth of significance that resists incorporation into the narrow framework of the action. In the encounter, the thing is not objectively present as a bearer of properties, but as a conduit to its own world. To return to our example: in checking whether there are enough wine glasses, it dawns on me that my friend's children might be coming. I initially address the glasses only regarding their number. There is a readiness for there being too few, or enough. Everything else is irrelevant. But the glasses themselves refer to beverages and drinkers of a certain sort as opposed to others. The disorientation that attends the dawning realization is connected to the alienness of the glasses. They become strangely incomprehensible in this moment, as a challenge to the routine action through which they are approached. One wants to say that they are trying to tell me something. The alien demand, for Waldenfels, "does not have sense and does not follow rule," but "interrupts the familiar formation of sense and rule" (2011, 36). It is through this slight hint of uncanniness that the action falls out of sync with its instruments and first becomes accessible to itself in light of its blind necessity.

The critique of provinciality faces ambiguities. First there is the problem of hypocrisy. The putative realization of provinciality is actually a reflection that engages a closed, everyday context in which "everyone" already knows what is acceptable. The evils of over-specialization and partisanship, for instance, are identifiable with reference to broader routines of work and politics that remain concealed in their contingency. The appropriation of provinciality is genuine only where it is occasioned by the disorienting encounter with alienness. But there is a second problem that emerges even here. As Steinbock points out, the appropriation is from its beginning "embedded" in the norms and traditions that constitute the integrity of the home world. The wakeful appropriation of provinciality has the orienting world in its contingency, but remains oriented by it. Steinbock emphasizes that the possibilities "freed up" for critical appropriation by the encounter are not entertained by an autonomous or unconstrained reason. It is instead a matter of "evaluating [these possibilities] as they are historically emerging" (1995, 207–8). They emerge, that is, for the members of a home world stable enough to support the critique of everydayness. But everydayness is a tendency in any world stable enough to support its critique.

In awakenings to provinciality I am jeopardized *as* someone shaped by the projects, roles, and relationships of my local world. It is in terms of this self-conception that the awakening can have any centrality for me to begin with. The provincial presupposition is false by virtue of its modality. So the awakening always involves confronting new possibilities that appropriative reflection seeks to integrate. Throughout the appropriation, however, the "practical identity"[4] of the awakened subject retains its guiding function as the source of possibilities that count as mine. To evaluate what is relevant or irrelevant, appropriate or inappropriate, viable or unviable with respect to these possibilities is to make sense of things within the fit between patterns of action and reliable world-contexts that gives orientational power to any historically developed world.

Local world understanding can never discover a sign that it is not provincial. The ideal of worldliness can only demand a sensitivity to alien encounters and a readiness to pursue them. This disposition is a kind of uncertainty that allows for a suspension of judgments that might be rooted in the homogeneous certainty of provinciality, which already understands the anomalous in everyday terms. One important expression of this uncertainty, we want to suggest, is curiosity.

The curiosity we have in mind is an attitude toward the arbitrary, toward what is freely variable within the parameters of a given context. In an action, perception has a grip on certain features of orienting things. These gripped features function as points of reliance for the action in its unfolding. They cannot be otherwise, or can only be this way or those ways, if the action is to continue harmoniously. In such practical focus, arbitrariness is a species of irrelevance. The arbitrary is whatever can be otherwise without consequence for the action. Both Husserl and Heidegger link the emergence of curiosity to the dropping of serious life interests and their governing frames of relevance. To speak in Heidegger's terms, when Dasein rests, the circumspection that guides its taking care becomes free; it no longer has to bring near what is at hand in the context of action. Circumspection continues to attend to things, but now "lets itself be intrigued just by the outward appearance of the world" (1996, 161). Heidegger is right that the practical essence of things lies in the grip they afford action, and that, in comparison with this essence, what interests freed circumspection is mere appearance. However, by addressing curiosity as *Neugier*, a distractible tendency to "just see," he perhaps overlooks a dimension of this comportment connected to a genuine worldliness and even, as we will see in a later discussion of Husserl (II B § 7), the emergence of philosophical wonderment.[5]

Focused practical perception discovers the arbitrary as the irrelevant. When this focus is relaxed, the arbitrary becomes discoverable as curious. By curious in this sense, we mean the strangeness *that* it is this way, though it could just as well be otherwise. The arbitrary becomes a theme in its own right once it is released from the practical focus that holds it at the fringes of attention. But once practical focus is relaxed, the scope of the arbitrary expands to include the relevant as well as the irrelevant. What previously had to be a certain way for the maintenance of an action now stands clear of that practical context and can become curios. Curiosity about the curios is not a distractible *Neugier*, but a careful yet playful attentiveness to the strange fact that things are, and are how they are. Where it is pure, curiosity does not desire explanations at all, and where it is persistent, it can include every explanatory factor in its theme. Wondering at is not already wondering why. Given wide berth by curiosity, the arbitrary can spread into every facet of the orienting world: what there is to do; how one does it; the roles, projects, and relationships rooted therein; and so on. Whereas Heideggerian *Neugier* tends to flee what is nearest at hand "for a distant and strange world" (1996, 161), this mode of curiosity tends to alienate the familiar world. As a disposition opposed to provinciality, curiosity is called upon in any alien encounter that prompts localization. The alien perspective unsettles local understanding only if local understanding is prepared to find its own world strange.

Worldliness does not require abandoning the familiar in favor of something foreign, only the readiness to appreciate, understand, or justify the familiar within the endless nexus of dependencies in which it stands, and thereby to make it one's own. But even this readiness entails the paradoxical attitude toward maturity outlined in our general reflections. There is no final world-wakefulness by which one overcomes provinciality. The worldly person can only anticipate that she is insufficiently worldly. This applies especially to those "central" accomplishments to which one has dedicated oneself. Where I would be most jeopardized by naïveté, there must I be most open to its realization. And yet, there is no world-orientation apart from a local understanding and the contexts fabricated within it. One can only live in light of this understanding, affirmed and reformed through available forms of appreciation and critique. Attitudes of false modesty cannot absolve one of the serious business of taking up one's orientation in the world. An ironic orientation is no less local than a sincere one.

4. The Ideal of Reclaiming the World

We can imagine mundane realizations that uproot grounds of ever greater scope in personal and interpersonal life. No matter how massive these configurations, the appropriation that attends to them is oriented by the world in which they have their place. The appropriative reflection is thus provisional or perspectival in all of its determinations. But this raises the question of whether someone living in the mundane attitude can ever wakefully appropriate her life as a whole, an ability implied in being an ego at all. To do so would mean no longer to have the world naively as ground, but to have realized a presupposition of *universal scope* in terms of which to appropriate the world as a ground. The awakening that could reclaim the world in this way would be irrevocable because it would realize a presupposition seen to underlie *any* and *all* mundane accomplishments. From the perspective of the worldliness opposed to provinciality, this possibility can only arise by neglecting the inexhaustible world-horizon in favor of the illusory sanctuary of an interior. But the ideal of reclaiming the world has more to offer than this retreat. Instead of closing oneself off from the world, the irrevocably awakened subject would appropriate the very acceptance of the world as the open framework for life. We will outline two different ways of conceiving this appropriation from within the mundane attitude, both of which help define the limits of mundane wakefulness.

The first approach tries to posit belief in the world as a universal presupposition. The I who has this presupposition at its disposal becomes responsible, not for local possibilities within the world but for being taken in by the world at all. The whole of world-directed life counts as naïve insofar as it failed to appropriate the fundamental conviction that the world is there. We will see that the understanding of naïveté and wakefulness operative in the mundane attitude prevents this appropriation. To realize belief in the world as a presupposition, the subject of mundane wakefulness would have to realize a dimension of its own egoic being that does not lie within the world-horizon. Within the framework of mundane self-reflection, the idea of this realization is only a speculative gesture. Even as such, it destabilizes the connection between wakefulness and world-directedness, a connection that a new basic attitude will finally break.

Cartesian doubt is the classic strategy for occasioning the realization that I have been presupposing that the world is. Descartes' first two meditations are instructive because they actually show that this strategy only works if the mundane attitude has already been suspended. Otherwise, the scenarios Descartes entertains are contradictory. This will not be fully clear until we have examined the phenomenological attitude. For now, we will follow the mundane attitude to its limit by showing that it cannot comprehend Descartes' attempt to appropriate the universal naïveté of world-directed life.

There are two thought experiments in the first meditation that conceive the non-existence of what mundane experience takes to be the one true world: (1) the appeal to a possible awakening that will determine everything now available to wakeful experience as a mere dream world; (2) the appeal to an omnipotent "evil genius" who has duped me into falsely holding for true all my beliefs about the world as well as my basic belief that the world is. As is well known, these two experiments serve different functions in Descartes' method, and he thinks he can doubt something by means of the second that he cannot by means of the first. We can forego these issues here. We merely pose a simple question to the thought-experimenter, who as yet knows nothing of the cogito. To the first experimenter we ask: who is dreaming? To the second experimenter we ask: who is being deceived? In neither case can the experimenter answer that it is she.

Let us grant the premises of the Cartesian dreaming experiment and rid it of the problematic, unnecessary claim that there are no discernable differences between what is called wakeful and dream experience. Should wakeful reflection discover an essential difference between waking experience and dreaming experience, this would justify my confidence that I, who am reflecting, am not doing what I now call dreaming.[6] I would no longer grant Cartesian premises about the similarity between actions in what I now call waking and dreaming life. However, this would not immunize my "waking" life against a cancellation of its convictions (including those regarding essential differences between dreaming and waking experience) in some future awakening that will reveal that I, who am now reflecting, will have been dreaming. In fact, Descartes' "dizziness" seems to arise from his contemplation of such a future awakening (1993, 14). Within the framework of methodological doubt, his subsequent assumption that he is now dreaming would have sufficient motivation in this possibility.

The experimenter assumes she is now "dreaming" in the minimal sense of believing in a world that is an all-encompassing illusion just as what she now calls a vivid dream world is an all-encompassing illusion when she *apparently* wakes from it. The Blumenfelds (1978) rightly concede Moore's objection that the doubt is incoherent if it relies on the premise that the doubter has actually had dreams. The posture of doubt, as Descartes himself emphasizes, affects everything "my deceitful memory represents" (1993, 17). However, they are also right to conclude that the doubter requires only the "concept" of dreaming, not the fact of his having dreamed (1978, 240). The core of the concept is the complete annulment of the dream world in light of the real world that contains the sleeping dreamer. This means that the wakeful understanding of the current dream will completely annul the world that now captivates the experimenter rather than enrich or correct it. No parts of the current dream will count as successful manifestations of reality, even if wakeful judgment discerns that they match up with it or unlock its significance.

The experiment is impossible in the mundane attitude because of the material contradiction it implies in the sense of "I." The problem is of the same order as trying to intuit a round square. On the assumption that I am dreaming, the "I" in my current dream is not the dreamer, but merely a figment for the dreamer. This cancellation of myself is total. It extends from socially constituted roles and self-conceptions to the basic sense of myself as a psychosomatic individual. Even if wakeful experience can "match" the dreamer and me in various ways (as real colors to dreamed colors), I who now say "I" am merely dreamed. Because, in the mundane attitude, I and my experience are in the world that I experience, the assumption that "I am now dreaming," which annuls this world, leaves no place for the dreaming I. As the experimenter, I can only assume that the world I now experience is the dream of someone else. This means, though, that it is not I that am dreaming.

The evil genius experiment collapses in a similar way. Mundane reflection finds my world-directed beliefs at the center of the world they are about. The theory that true world-directed beliefs are caused by their objects builds upon the more basic reflection that they occur in their spatiotemporal vicinity. But false beliefs also occur at the center of the world they target. This is most evident in the enjoyment of true beliefs about these false beliefs, which situate them in mundane space–time. For instance, my false belief that my friend was sitting in that restaurant was formed just as I was walking past its front window. Now assume that an evil genius has arranged things so that my basic belief in the world is as false as that about my friend in the restaurant. Entertaining this assumption, I now say with Descartes "I believe the world exists, but I am being deceived." I treat "I am being deceived" as a possibly true belief about my belief that the world exists. But where and when is this event of being deceived? If it is not taking place here and now, in the vicinity of the realities in which I believe, if it is not a mental event intimately connected with my body (or some other body I could get into from here), then it is not mine in any sense available to me in the mundane attitude. I cannot identify myself with the person upon whom the evil genius exerts his influence. But then I am not being deceived.

The mundane attitude is incapable of doubting that "I am living in the world" by extending familiar forms of falsification so that they might cover this exceptional case (such is Descartes' method). The ordinary ways of motivating doubts about inner-worldly realities become paradoxical when applied to the being of the world itself. However, not being able to doubt that the world exists does not preclude its discovery as a necessary condition of my experience in a mundane realization. Generally speaking, presuppositions need not be dubitable, nor must they be dubitable to warrant attention. If we momentarily abandon the Cartesian approach, we will see that the belief that the world exists is discoverable without contradiction. However, a new problem will emerge. We resolve the contradiction only by reducing the awakening in which the belief appears to a pseudo-awakening. There is thus no presupposition in the strict sense.

Let us entertain the "presupposition" that the world exists. Its scope is universal in that it conditions every ground that incorporates inner-worldly realities. Expressing this universality, I might say: "In everything I have known and done in my life, I have been presupposing that I am in the midst of the real world." The fact that, in saying this, I continue to presume that the world exists does not prevent the realization of the presumption. In appropriative reflection, I can now recognize and affirm a certain "realism" to which I naively stood committed and may even explicate it as a transcendental argument. Life, such as we live it, is possible only given a real world. In fact, this world-wakefulness seems irrevocable because it is safe from any disruption brought on by the realization of my own provinciality. However, there is no genuine awakening because there can be no definite accomplishment uprooted by the realization that it has the world as its necessary condition. The world is simply the obvious setting for anything that can matter in the mundane attitude.

There is no definite accomplishment for which it can matter that the world exists because life in the mundane attitude is essentially life in the world. The universal scope of the presupposition undermines its ability to jeopardize. While this seems contradictory, an inverse relationship between scope and affective power is already discernable in certain inner-worldly realizations. It is a characteristic of provinciality that necessary conditions for the broadest spheres of practice become irrelevant. For instance, it might occur to me that making a deposit at the bank presupposes the continued functioning of the financial system. But the broad scope of the presupposition diminishes its affective force. The ground includes such wide-ranging patterns of activity that a reinterpretation of any definite actions in light of the presupposition seems unnecessary. In reflection, the continued functioning of the financial system appears as a setting for accomplishments without itself entering into their practical field. It is a condition of my life without significance for it. Of course, this is only a provincial illusion. The presupposition underlies a world-context that, as a correlate of routines, stands in for the world. In such cases, there is a possible realization that would localize everyday life in the world-horizon and enable its appropriation as local. However, so long as I am in the mundane attitude, I can truthfully say of the presupposition "the world is" that it is coextensive with my life. Even for the worldliest of mundane attitudes, it is a condition of life without significance for it. The existence of the world enters squarely into all of my possible accomplishments and so does not provoke the reconsideration of any of them, or of myself as their accomplisher.

It is for this same reason that Cartesian world doubt cannot succeed in the mundane attitude. The experiments of the first meditation try to conceive experiences as my own that are not situated in the world. The mundane attitude cannot think such thoughts coherently. Once wakefulness is understood as the capacity for reality as opposed to subjective illusion, it is contradictory that an awakening should require the appropriation of reality itself. We can spell this out in an argument that employs concepts of "I" and "wakefulness" inescapable for world-directed life. Either I am awake or I am not. If I am awake, this means that I have the real world before me. If I am not awake, and this is not the real world before me, then neither am I myself. It therefore matters neither that the world is nor that it is not. If it is not, then I have no access to anyone whom this concerns. If it is, this is synonymous with my having concerns at all. The upshot of this argument is that the being there of the world, for any reflection anchored in the mundane attitude, is inherently uninteresting. This lack of interest becomes militant in philosophy that protests against the impropriety of the Cartesian world-question.

The second approach to an irrevocable world-wakefulness seizes upon something profound in this fact that the world itself is uninteresting. Belief in the world cannot be appropriated in the mundane attitude because wakeful life in this attitude always has to do with the world. Insofar as anything matters at all, it matters for my life in the world. Rather than trying to take epistemic responsibility for belief in the world, the second, "existential," approach sees the universal presupposition of the mundane attitude in anything mattering in the first place. In existential awakening, the mattering of anything becomes appropriable within the mundane attitude via a disorienting suspension of importance that attends confrontation with my life in the world as a whole.

Every way to be myself in the mundane attitude lies in roles, relationships, and projects of the orienting world. If I am jeopardized as the subject of an accomplishment, it is with reference to those amendable "practical identities" through which these accomplishments have any importance. The existential strategy for occasioning an irrevocable awakening is to pursue those ways of encountering one's life that decenter these self-understandings and jeopardize me as responsible for importance itself. In light of the presupposition that anything should be important for me, the importance of any project, role, or relationship becomes appropriable from the immovable perspective of having to be myself.

The philosophical accounts of existential responsibility are legion. Our concern is only to indicate the universality of the awakening to this responsibility. Let us return to our earlier claim (A § 8) that it is possible to convert pseudo-awakenings into genuine awakenings through a broadened interpretation of what one is doing. A pseudo-awakening discovers a previously unnoticeable necessary condition for some accomplishment, but it does not motivate an appropriative reflection because what it discovers belongs to an irrelevant background that need not be taken into account. We mentioned examples such as realizing that my dinner preparations have presupposed that the floor will not collapse. The conversion succeeds when I discover how the initial accomplishment is contained in a broader accomplishment of which I am the naïve subject. This occurs through an original expansion of interest that incorporates peripheral elements into the practical field and thereby enriches the sense of the accomplishment itself. One expresses this enrichment by saying, for example, that *in* preparing the dinner I was living in a well-constructed building. For a genuine awakening to transpire, this broader accomplishment must become salient in its importance; I must discern in it a commitment the uprooting of which jeopardizes me in being who I am through doing what I do. I can then reflect upon genuine presuppositions to which I failed to attend because of my consuming interest in a routinized world-context.

This method of reframing works by situating local accomplishments in broader accomplishments that explicate them. It yields radically different results, however, if it embraces the broadest accomplishment of the world-directed ego, its life in the world as such. The path to this broadest accomplishment is accessible from every definite mundane accomplishment. However, it is seldom traveled because it leads nowhere in particular. Realizing that *in* doing something I have been living my life in the world demands appropriative reflections fundamentally different from any others in the mundane attitude. This is because of peculiar features of my life in the world that usually seem trivial but can suddenly become strangely disconcerting.

Unlike all my definite accomplishments, there is nothing that I can do in addition to living my life in the world. When I deliberate in the mundane attitude, every definite action has an alternative, but not living my life in the world. Ending my life, as a limit case, is also something I do in my life. My life is inevitable. Connected to this is the fact that I can willfully suspend and come back to definite actions at some later time. My life cannot be suspended and resumed like this. In this sense, my life in the world is wholly encompassing. At the same time, it is finite. My life is an irreversible position taking in worldly space and time. I was, and forever will have been, born on that date, in that place, to these parents, and so on. Likewise, in the practical and theoretical realms, every position I adopt will have always been adopted by me. I may abandon the position, but I cannot undo the fact that I adopted it. Further, while my life is one among others, there is no possibility of exchange. Surrounded by various lives and by examples of various types of life, I cannot take over the life of another. This highlights the feature of life in the world emphasized by Heidegger in his own idiom: while I am free to pass off or cooperate in other accomplishments, no matter their centrality, I am not free to pass off or cooperate in the living of my life in the world. My life is inalienable.

It is impossible to consider my life in the world for itself, apart from particular things I am doing. However, it is possible for anything I am doing to present itself as a moment of my life in the world, taken in its original inevitability, encompassment, finitude, and inalienability. When this occurs, the definite accomplishment undergoes a strange modification in its relevance. Receptivity to my life as such requires a disengagement from every self-conception according to which I am the agent of this particular accomplishment in a space of alternatives. No matter what I do, I am living my life. Whatever is explicated from this perspective thus shares in a unique unimportance. Normally, unimportance is relative to a concern with what is important in terms of a particular interest. My life in the world is not unimportant in this way. In fact, it is the one accomplishment that can never become unimportant in this way. On the other hand, neither is it important. The attempt to treat it as central always miscarries because it is impossible to objectify within a space of alternative undertakings.

While framing accomplishments in this way adds nothing to their sense, it can occasion an awakening to the presupposition that any definite accomplishment has importance. This is a meta-awakening in that it renders undefined the universal variable of centrality, the extent to which any accomplishment is *mine*. Ordinarily, mundane awakenings are already rooted in self-conceptions relative to definite accomplishments that guide the understanding of centrality. Existential awakening uproots these self-conceptions so that this understanding becomes unguided and falls to a self that encounters its freedom in its *having* to confront these self-conceptions. Living in existential naïveté, certain possibilities were already mine because of my place in the world. The only support I now have for mundane self-understanding are commitments that I make mine starting from the inalienable fact of my life. Facing my life as a unique project that is beyond relevance and irrelevance, I discover the need for an original stance about what and how things matter.

The task of appropriating the presupposition that anything is important invites nihilistic attitudes about the meaningless character of life in the world. It also invites a mania that denies the pre-givenness of the world and pretends to invent orientation in an arbitrary choice.[7] These are ways of groping around in the void left by the existentially naïve sense of mineness. But existential appropriation ultimately aims at a dedication to definite accomplishments reclaimed as authentically my own. Crowell's formulation of Heideggerian authenticity is helpful here: "To be authentic is to have a certain stance toward the reasons provided by my practical identity ... I am not responsible for their existence; their existence comes from *das Man*. But in being authentic I make them *my* reasons by taking responsibility for endorsing them. They are *at stake* in what I do" (2013, 300). Exposing oneself to the hazards of existential awakening is the most extreme exercise of basic integrity possible in the mundane attitude. Even if only in strange glimpses, it uproots life in the world, not in favor of a more comprehensive life and world, but as a total project, already underway, in terms of which I have to reassess anything to which I have committed myself. Here as elsewhere, awakened subjectivity is concrete but posterior. The total project of my life was always lived by me, the one responsible for having neglected it.

No higher-level attitude can undo this peculiar antecedence of life in the world. Everything undertaken in a higher attitude remains responsible to the question of its importance for life, its *Lebensbedeutsamkeit*, to use Husserl's term. This is because my egoic life, however transfigured through the realization and appropriation of its own naïveté, will have always begun as life in the world. It did not have to so begin, but it did in fact, and this fact is irreversible. A higher-level attitude, in turn, is necessarily conditioned by its factical emergence from the mundane attitude. Philosophers may do their thinking in an attitude that knows itself to have overcome the naïveté of mundane life. However, being a philosopher is a practical identity and stands in need of existential appropriation. Anticipating the role of this appropriation in the *Crisis*, Husserl writes, in his *Prague Letter* of 1934, that genuine philosophers "have taken over this task [of philosophy] in existential resoluteness as their ownmost life-task, absolutely inseparable from their personal existence [*persönlichen Dasein*]" (1989, 243).

5. Transition to the Phenomenological Level

The preceding reflections have described dimensions of awakening within world-directed life. We will now consider how this life is dominated by a universal presupposition. To do so, we will have to outline a higher-level attitude based on the awakening to a naïveté that characterizes wakefulness as such within the confines of the mundane attitude. Exploring what is revealed in this awakening will lead us to specify the mundane attitude as the natural attitude, and the attitude awake to its defining naïveté as the phenomenological attitude. The following sections examine this new attitude in light of its originating experience of awakening, always with an eye toward developing our general analysis. We do not already assume that the phenomenological attitude is in the service of philosophical interests. We will eventually account for these interests beginning from the examination of phenomenological awakening.

This approach will emphasize a dimension of the phenomenological attitude anterior to phenomenology as a theoretical program. Phenomenology, Husserl writes, "moves entirely in acts of reflection" (2014b, 139/162). We will argue that the availability of phenomenological subject matter to reflection depends upon an awakening realization. This realization confronts the phenomenologically awakened ego with the naïveté of its own life in the natural attitude, which is to say with the prior unavailability of what is only now available for the first time. The in-principle availability of phenomenological subject matter is the result of the appropriative tendency exercised by the awakening ego. Just as diurnal wakefulness sees everything, including sleep, in the light of day, so does phenomenological wakefulness see in its own light the natural-attitude life from which it has awakened. It owes this seeing to an awakening.

The primary object of phenomenological awakening is the same as the primary object of phenomenological theory: transcendental life. But the subject of the former is a jeopardized, not a spectating ego. This difference is apparent in how each encounters the natural attitude. For phenomenology proper, the methods that make transcendental life thematic (epoché and reduction) are meant to secure access to a field for theoretical experience and judgment. Once the field is established, it can become the object of an abiding transcendental-theoretical interest. For someone who regularly exercises this interest, the natural attitude functions in two ways: as neutralized and as transcendentally apperceived.[8] The natural attitude functions as neutralized when, in carrying out phenomenological reflections, one runs through episodes of natural life with the intent of investigating them transcendentally. It functions as transcendentally apperceived when, no longer actively exploring phenomenological themes, one returns to natural life in the conviction that it is now a possible theme of transcendental investigations. For phenomenological awakening, on the other hand, it is my inability to have noticed transcendental life that takes center stage. Life in the natural attitude is therefore salient as a past naïveté to which I can never fully return, but that I am responsible for appropriating precisely as naïve. Transcendental life is salient as the universal presupposition of my past life. Although theoretical reflection can serve appropriation, appropriation has more than the phenomenological field in view. It keeps the fact of pre-phenomenological naïveté in focus and mobilizes the phenomenological perspective in order to integrate natural-attitude life into a developmental whole through which I can wakefully take over what had been naively intended.

These remarks anticipate complications arising from the availability of phenomenological theory as an employment for the phenomenological attitude. Our first task, though, is to describe the awakening that institutes this attitude. The following section will introduce the rudiments of this description. Succeeding sections will then clarify how the awakening to transcendental life is different from awakenings in the mundane attitude and how it brings about a transformation in the relationship between wakefulness and naïveté themselves. We will bring out this transformation through an assessment of the finality and centrality of phenomenological awakening, which will finally pose special problems for the possibility of an appropriative reflection.

6. The Consuming Interest of the Natural Attitude

Life in the mundane attitude is fundamentally interested in the world of realities. If this interest is consuming, critical reflection will be able to show that it prevents the apprehension of the overall accomplishment within which the world of realities lies. This seems impossible, however, because it is rather the world that contains all possible accomplishments. Interest in the world is thus a consuming interest only if the world does not actually contain all possible accomplishments. The awakening to the defining presupposition of the mundane attitude shows that this condition is satisfied. The awakening ego here realizes that its world-interested life has been based on an accomplishment that is not in the world, but in and through which the world itself is there. This accomplishment is its own transcendental life. If we bring this presupposed accomplishment into focus, the consuming nature of world-interest will become clear.

Let us introduce the term "mundane being" for any entity bound to the spatiotemporal world. An ontology that simply tracks what can be pointed out in ordinary life will discover, beyond reality, a system of reality that includes every ontic dimension held in reality's orbit. At its core are the corporeal things that allow for the identification of any particular event, process, or quality.⁹ But other sorts of entities besides bare corporeal things are identifiable. For instance, some corporeal things grow, move themselves, and behave. They are then not just material realities but animals in the broadest sense. Other corporeal things matter for communities of intelligent animals according to their use in actions and significance for ways of life. They are then cultural things in the broadest sense. Sentient and culturally significant entities are founded in the corporeal reality by virtue of which they are immediately apparent and identifiable, but they are their own kinds of individual entities. One abstracts from a horse, a piece of clothing, or a word by focusing only on its material basis. This roughest of ontologies, then, teaches that there are material, animal, and cultural things, all of which depend upon the materiality that provides them with definite location. Fictitious or otherwise false things also fall into these categories of mundane being. The Loch Ness monster is a real cultural thing and a purported animal thing, for example. Life in the mundane attitude is concerned with mundane beings. In its critical forms, it establishes distinctions between and hierarchies of realities, searches for things that have not been discovered, and finds ways to distinguish between purported and actual reality. Its awakenings to naïveté all partake in this interest. In their paradigmatic form, they problematize reality claims while adverting to the world-horizon in which realities are determinable.

We may notice the universal role appearing plays in this interest. Appearing and possible appearing is how mundane being makes a claim, legitimate or not, on world-directed subjectivity, immediately, through the appearing of things themselves, or mediately, through the appearing of signs, images, and traces. This is why three-dimensional bodies, which can directly appear for the senses, occupy a basic position in the implicit ontology of the mundane attitude and in any philosophy content to explicate it. The system of reality is centered on my surroundings, in some orientation to my own body. Despite this ubiquity of appearing, interest in mundane being ordinarily pays no attention to it, occupying itself rather with what appears. What appears is primarily what is identified and talked about. The awakening to transcendental life can be occasioned by modulating this interest in reality so that the appearing of what appears becomes thematic.

There is no method for awakening of any kind. The methods for reflecting on what has become noticeable in an awakening are not themselves means of awakening. Husserl recognizes this when he writes that "the epoché, as an explicit basic methodological requirement, could be a matter of subsequent reflection only of one who, with a certain naïveté and through a historical situation, was already pulled into the epoché, so to speak" (1970, 243/246). Although there are no methods for awakening to transcendental life, there are reflections that court awakenings. Reflections that make thematic the appearing of what appears, such as those Husserl presents in *Crisis III*, can function in this way. They create a situation that prepares the realization of one's own transcendental life, and the subsequent awakening to the naïveté of the mundane attitude. Their pedagogical efficacy, however, ultimately requires a dawning in the reflecting subject that the instruments of method can only occasion.

Normally, the mundane attitude gains access to what appears by way of an appearing in which it takes no interest. However, the appearing of what appears is not entirely unavailable. When something appears otherwise than expected, when there are disputes about the way things appear, or when an idle experimental interest plays with the alteration of appearances, the mundane attitude attends to what appears in light of how it appears. It would seem to be within the capacity of a world-directed ego to constrain its interest consistently in this way and to reflect on what appears *entirely* in light of how it appears. For example, leaning forward, I attend to how an object of unchanging size appears through an ordered system of spatial displays of the front side that increase their share of the visual field in tandem with this definite way of moving my own body. Similarly, rotating an object in my hand, I attend to how the object itself, as a whole, appears now from this side, now from that. Or again, I attend to how the unchanging colors of the room appear one way in the afternoon light, another way at dusk, and never appear apart from some particular illuminative atmosphere.

However, the mundane attitude cannot actually universalize this shift of focus from what appears to how it appears. Instead, appearing and ways of appearing are situated within what appears, within the system of reality. This happens because the mundane attitude already understands the familiar ways in which seeming is dependent upon what is. For example, changes in the apparent size and perspective of material things depend upon the changing position of my body in space relative to the position of the thing that appears. Apparent surface colors depend upon the position and quality of illuminating bodies. In general, all changes in how things *really look* indicate the changes in real things that cause them. If there is a change in appearance that does not count as a real change (a mere seeming), this is because I know it is caused by disturbances that affect the perceptual systems in that particular real thing I call my body.[10] Unreality is an effect brought about within reality. Finally, that there are appearances at all depends upon the organic functioning, whether normal or abnormal, of this same body. On the basis of this dependency of material appearance upon material reality, higher-level dependencies that link variations in emotional, practical, and cultural significance to facts about human beings are also readily available. Because of such facts, the same thing appears as tool or as art object, the same gesture as affront or as good humor, the same event as omen or as accident.

The consistent focus upon how things appear thus has the sense of an abstraction. One leaves behind the concrete reality in which appearing occurs to attend to appearing and the apparent as such. It is within this abstraction that subjective life and its ego become thematic for the mundane attitude. Dropping the interest in reality, one focuses merely on how reality appears to the subject for whom it appears. Empathetic listening can suspend what the listener knows to be real in order to discover how reality seems to another. Similarly, introspection can attend, not to how my opinions match up with reality, but simply to their content, how they influence my actions, and so on. A life of interpretation, of "taking as," thereby comes into view for the mundane attitude. But, as P. F. Strawson has pointed out, even to identify whose life of interpretation this is, one must give up the abstraction and index the subjective life of seeming to a concrete psychophysical person inhabiting the spatiotemporal world of realities. To talk of a consciousness that has things according to their appearance is always to assign this consciousness to some particular conscious being that appears.[11]

So long as the subjective life of "taking as" becomes thematic by way of an abstraction, it is absurd to treat this life as a transcendental accomplishment in and through which reality is first of all there. Of course, in focusing on subjective life, reality also belongs to the theme. But it does so under an important restriction. Reality is under consideration strictly according to how it seems to the subjectivity involved. In introspection, in empathetic listening, in various forms of sociological and psychological research, it is always the view of some animal or person, or community of animals or people that is at stake. To make reality *itself* first of all dependent upon subjectivity would be to forget that subjectivity is first of all identifiable in reality. The initial identification that selects some subjectivity as foundational looks around in the spatiotemporal horizons of the real world. The logical contradiction that bothers subjective relativism regarding the truth of its own claims about relativity emerges from the fact that psychophysical entities experience the world in a relativity of perspectives.

The reflection on how reality appears can occasion the transcendence of the mundane attitude only when the variation in manners of appearing indicates a life of "taking as" that is not itself anchored in some appearing entity. The life that originally has what appears in and through its appearing does not itself appear, either directly or indirectly. Descartes already drew attention to this by observing that the cogito "does not fall within the imagination" (1993, 21). Mundane skepticism will assert that this primordial life of subjectivity is nowhere to be found. This is because mundane finding seizes upon what appears on some sensuous basis. But transcendental life is not accessible to the senses. Refinements of sensibility, an aesthetic attunement to the shadow and sheen that everyday perception overlooks, are no help here. There is no feeling for this life, no way to catch it out of the corner of one's eye. This is not because transcendental life is something elsewhere, beyond the senses. It is because sensibility is not the object of a sense.

Rather than a squinty eye or a sensitive soul, what is required for the perception of transcendental life is to let lapse entirely the interest in what appears while attending to the event of its appearing. "Event" is here a placeholder for a happening that has no location within the world-horizon. Every locatable event would appear through the primal event that dawns in phenomenological awakening. Where do I find, for instance, the focusing through which a privileged sector of my surroundings stands out? There is a felt tension, here, in the part of my body I call my eyeball. Should I locate the focusing there? But this felt tension is clearly an accompaniment of the focusing in its accomplishment. It registers a body-space quite different from the space occupied by the three-dimensional things held in focus, but not a location from which focusing itself emanates. If I follow my interest in the felt tension, it motivates a tactile focusing on my eye. Where, then, is this "following of interest" or the "focusing" through which my eye captures my attention? One is tempted to say that the event occurs, at any rate, here at the center of my appearing surroundings. However, indulging this temptation restores the interest in what appears. One must rather ask about the event through which my surroundings appear as surroundings, through which my body appears as mine. The primal event, then, is a flow of manifestation that has no position in what is manifested.

To risk an inadequate analogy, we might say that mundane being is to transcendental life as the figures on a movie screen are to the rolling of the film. The rolling of the film has no place on the screen, but this happening is the event through which everything directly and indirectly appears there. The limited utility of a comparison like this is that it drives home the universal dependence of mundane being, actual or possible, on the event of appearing. The whole movie world, what it shows and implies, exists only through the rolling of the film. Further, there can be no real dependency relation between the rolling of the film and the filmic world it enables. The activity of projection simply does not belong to the spatiotemporal dimension inhabited by the characters on screen. Similarly, the primal event of appearing does not *really* underlie what appears. It is nowhere next to it or before it as its cause or support. Instead, it is operative in the very "there it is" of every mundane being and connection between mundane beings.

The analogy is misleading, not only because it reifies transcendental life but also because it separates the event of manifestation from me myself. I myself am involved or potentially involved in the showing of everything that appears through the event of appearing. "I," of course, can no longer mean "this person who appears," but rather the grantor or tender of what appears. In the mundane attitude, life in its active and passive modes is attributed to those appearing beings called animals and persons. In the new attitude, my own activity and passivity tend the appearing of mundane being itself. The unbroken mode of this involvement, which I can find at work in every manifestation to which I now direct my attention, is the passive granting of the world of what appears and can appear. My believing acceptance of the world, persisting through every doubt and negation based upon it, is the event in and through which the world is first of all "there." We can take over Husserl's term "constitution" to refer to this transcendental function of granting or tending. It is the accomplishment in and through which mundane being occurs.

The primal event of constitution-manifestation enters into the history of the mundane attitude as a mundane event that serves as the occasion for its own realization. In relation to the appearing of particular mundane beings under particular circumstances, one is suddenly "pulled into" one's own life as a living for, rather than in, the world. As occasion, the event fits into the motivational nexus of my life in the world. As realization, the event is the exposure of a dimension of manifestation encompassing every mundane motivation. The lifting of transcendental naïveté is explainable neither with reference to the mundane situation that happens to motivate it nor to the fact, apparent for the awakened ego, that transcendental life was always there, though not ready to be apprehended. The event of this lifting is therefore "gratuitous."[12]

This dawning of my own transcendental life can motivate a self-reflexive awakening that takes its previously unnoticeable character as a theme. We are familiar with the formula that expresses this presupposition in all its universality: "All my wakeful life, I have been presupposing my belief in the world." The mundane attitude understands this presupposition as a problematic reality claim and confronts the paradoxical task of deciding whether, in reality,

reality exists. Phenomenological awakening, however, does not advert to the world-horizon as does the mundane attitude. Instead, it makes world-belief thematic as the manifold accomplishment through which mundane being is first of all there in its manifold ways. The phenomenological realization that my entire wakeful life has presupposed my world-belief does not imply that I have been unable to take a position on the reality or non-reality of the world, but that I have been unable to take a position on the various ways of constitution through which the world first of all counts as being there. We can take over Husserl's term "epoché" to describe how phenomenological awakening draws attention to our universal world-belief in complete abeyance from any assessment of its truth. The truth here realized is rather: this world-constitution, in and through which the world appears, *is*.

The phenomenological awakening can only be genuine if it is of universal scope. Were it to concern only particular beliefs in particular mundane beings, the defining interest of the mundane attitude would continue to advert to the world-horizon in a way that already determines the belief as a psychological event in the world. But the psychological, just like the physical and the cultural, is a kind of mundane being, while constitution is the accomplishment of mundane being itself.[13] Every kind of mundane being, including the human being in its physical, psychic, and cultural dimensions, depends upon definite forms of transcendental constitution. Not only must the phenomenological awakening be universal in scope, but it must also become aware of this universality to be achieved at all. It uproots in a synoptic way the entire egoic life that has taken place on the ground of world-interest. Wherever I should turn my attention, I will find previously unnoticeable accomplishments of constitution in and through which mundane being occupied my attention: the perceiving event through which the material thing was first of all there, the introspecting or empathizing event through which the psyche was first of all there, the understanding event through which the cultural meaning was first of all there, and so on. This life is now in need of appropriation and is already being appropriated in the awakened ego's assertion: "I have been presupposing my own transcendental life." We will soon attend to the ambiguities contained in this assertion.

The consuming character of the pre-phenomenological interest in mundane being can now be made clear. A consuming interest appears in critical reflection as preventing me from having noticed what was unnoticeable in a stretch of life based upon a presupposition. In phenomenological awakening, I realize that I was unable to notice the life of constitution that accomplishes the being there of mundane being. It is easy to see why this accomplishment is inherently uninteresting for an attitude fundamentally concerned with the system of reality. For any engagement in the world, my flowing life of world-belief, in its various forms, constantly *is*. Compared to any discoverable physical reality, this life is unshakable. It does not move or depart with the moved or departed thing, but gives it as moved or departed. Compared to any discoverable mental reality, this life is unimpeachable. Because it is for itself correspondence or non-correspondence with reality, it cannot be held up to reality as a measure. Compared to any discoverable cultural reality, this life is uninterpretable. It has the context as context through every recontextualization, and so cannot be localized. Just because it is unshakable, unimpeachable, and uninterpretable, my transcendental life is inherently uninteresting for an attitude concerned to sort out reality and non-reality. So long as I persisted in the mundane attitude, I could not turn my attention toward this life. Preoccupation with realities prevented me from noticing the overall accomplishment in which these realities show up.

Parmenides was probably the first to diagnose this "two-headed" form of human negligence. Mortals go astray because they see no necessity in naming the continuous being that encompasses the doxic distinction between presence and absence. Guided by their senses and language, they are consumed by an interest in establishing reality against non-reality and evolve a commonsense ontology that equates these with being and not being. To awaken to the fundamental belonging together of being and noesis means also to appreciate that knowledge conditioned by light and reality—being as presence *opposed* to absence—is unthinking.[14] Husserl writes in *Crisis III*: "Since this [transcendental life] is to be a matter of spiritual functions which exercise their accomplishments in all experiencing and thinking ... it would certainly be understandable that all objective sciences would lack precisely the knowledge of what is most fundamental" (1970, 119/121).

The ego awake to the universal presupposition of the mundane attitude is in a position to identify the uniformity that characterized its previous life. Even in its awakenings and critical reflections, this life was always directed toward the world. This means that the life of the ego could only become an object of interest as psychological experience, as something happening in the world, though not always faithful to it. Even the general condition of wakefulness was understood as a factual complement to sleep in a diurnal creature. This basic outlook on life and the world was simply grown into by the ego; it was not the product of a conversion or decision. It is thereby recognizable as "natural." We can take over Husserl's term "natural attitude" with the following emphasis. Whereas "mundane attitude" merely describes the usual way of living in the world, "natural attitude" includes a reference to its naïveté, and thereby to its suspension in an awakening.

We note here a striking difference between the way in which mundane life as a whole becomes thematic in the existential and phenomenological awakenings. For the former, life in the world is the inalienable, inevitable project that jeopardizes every alienable, optional project in terms of its *Lebensbedeutsamkeit*. For the latter, the interest in the world itself has been suspended and therewith the concern for *Lebensbedeutsamkeit*. This difference foreshadows a problem of synthesis that will arise for a higher-level attitude that, existentially and phenomenologically attuned, has in its purview both the naïveté of natural-attitude life as well as the *Lebensbedeutsamkeit* of accomplishments in the phenomenological attitude.

7. Naïve World-Belief as a Transcendental Accomplishment

We have said that the ego in the natural attitude is naïve because it is unable to notice the world-constituting accomplishments in and through which mundane being occurs. However, we must always assess descriptions like this within the dynamic of appropriation at work in the awakenings that disclose presuppositions. We then see that they are not simple descriptions. To describe the natural attitude in terms of an unnoticeable world-belief, itself a constitutive accomplishment, is to express the results of the appropriating initiative of the phenomenologically awakened ego. A full account has to describe the initiative itself.

In *Ideas I*, we find this problem at work between the lines. Husserl there introduces the phenomenological perspective by subjecting to epoché the "general thesis" of the natural attitude, which he carefully distinguishes from discrete judgments about things in the world. The general thesis is that "by virtue of which we are constantly conscious of the real environment (not merely in keeping with apprehension in general but as an 'actuality' *that is there*)" (2014b, 53/62). Through this thesis, "everything from the natural world of which we are conscious experientially and prior to thinking, bears ... the character of [being] 'there', 'on hand'" (ibid.). This "by virtue of which" (*vermöge deren*) shows that Husserl ascribes to the thesis a transcendental function. Such ascription is only possible if the natural attitude has already been suspended. While the natural attitude can recognize the general thesis as explicating an unthought conviction, it cannot find evidence of this "by virtue of which." The thesis instead expresses a trivially true belief about things in general, which are obviously "there" whether I believe in them or not. The belief itself, mundanely construed, is the mental state of a human animal. As Husserl himself points out, it thus occurs in "the same natural actuality" affirmed by the general thesis (57/67).

The general thesis, as Husserl characterizes it, is essentially different from the other examples he uses to demonstrate the delicate posture of epoché, not only because of its generality and latency but also because it has a sense unrecognizable to the natural attitude. Husserl derives his other illustrations from the attempt to doubt a particular state of affairs that we have evidently judged to be the case. Here, it truly is a matter of suspending "the thesis that we have posited" which "remains in itself as it is" and is "still here as before," only set out of action (2014b, 54/63). But from what perspective is it true that I have before posited the real environment through the general thesis? Husserl's definition of natural-attitude life as that which "lives naively in the implementation of the general thesis" (103/120) clearly makes use of evidence available only to phenomenological wakefulness. This kind of imposition is inevitable for the wakeful attempt to state what naïve life truly is. It certainly risks circularity as an attempt to solicit the suspension of the natural attitude. Does it do justice to the discovery and appropriation of my own transcendental naïveté?

Husserl is not guilty of accounting for the entry into the phenomenological attitude by assuming its attainment. Instead, he explicitly postpones the epoché of the general thesis and returns to the perspective of natural experience. The observations that follow mimic naïveté in that they treat experience as a "psychological" domain of being alongside reality. Here, as Husserl writes, "we do not trouble ourselves with any phenomenological epoché" (2014b, 59/69). At the same time, this revisiting of naïve life is strategically oriented toward its overcoming. The overall import of Husserl's analyses in this mode is to show that experience as such, particularly sense perception, bears within itself a reference to appearing reality, and that any other reality that one would place beyond this reference is nonsensical. The domain of reality alongside which experience stood will henceforth count as nothing. At the same time, a rational form of the general thesis has been identified with the constitutive function of experience (the irrational forms stem from higher-order "realist" interpretations). Reflection on the thesis under the suspension of its implementation now means to perceive one's own natural experience in its orientation toward reality without adopting this orientation oneself.

To secure this possibility, Husserl emphasizes the *in-principle availability of unreflected experience to reflection*. Unreflected experiences are like things in the periphery of the visual field just in the sense that they are "intrinsically ready to be perceived" because "we are conscious of them in a certain way already, namely, as something that we have not paid attention to" (2014b, 81/95). Things and experiences meet conditions of readiness in different ways. Peripheral things must have already appeared. The unreflected experience, however, which cannot appear, "always fulfills those conditions merely through its manner of existing and, indeed, does so for the very ego to which it belongs and whose pure focus may live 'in' it" (ibid.). Since the availability of pure experience to itself is included in the availability of naturalistically apperceived experience to itself, it becomes apparent that my accomplishment of the general thesis was in the "background" of my world-directed life. It was in principle available as an unreflected experience, though all my previous reflections leaped over it by situating it in the world it originally delivers. Returning now to the exercise of epoché upon the general thesis, one is supposed to be able to recognize the thesis as an experience: "We can also say: the thesis is an experience, *but we make no use of it*" (54/63).

In the guise of an eidetic psychology, this procedure wrestles with the ambiguities of appropriation outlined in our general analysis. The phenomenologically awakened ego says to itself, as it were, "I was all along constituting the world, but was unable to attend to this constitution." But this reference to past constitution finds no fulfillment in simple recollection. When I was naively perceiving something before, I did not then perform acts of constitution that I now reactivate, trying to represent them as they were before. The thing was simply there to look at; it was not given as the product of accomplishments. Similarly, my looking was available to reflection as a real event here at the center of my surroundings; it was not constitutive of these surroundings. Careful attention to "what it was like" in natural-attitude life is a virtue of descriptions possible in the natural attitude. These descriptions can never turn up transcendental life. Investing such descriptions with phenomenological concepts poetizes natural experience rather than appropriating it through a new form of self-responsibility. Phenomenological description cannot capture what the natural attitude was like because it exercises epistemic authority over the naïveté of the latter.

At the same time, the appropriation of naïveté is not based on the logical inference that I must have been performing acts of world-constitution in order for things to be there at all. If constitution were merely a principle deduced from the givens of natural-attitude life, I could never recognize it as *my life* of constitution, nor could I appropriate it as my presupposition. The "I" in "I presupposed" would be merely informational in Sokolowski's sense. One of Husserl's complaints about a deductive approach to transcendental philosophy (which he associates with Kant) is that it prohibits genuine appropriation. The awakening ego, then, does not discover its life of constitution as always having been at work in the natural attitude, as if it merely needed to be reminded of it, nor does it construct accomplishments that must have happened although they can have no meaning for me as my accomplishments.

Husserl's middle way is to interpret constitution as an unseen background of natural life. There are many formulations of this. We have just considered his procedure of suspending a transcendentally construed thesis of existence that he finds in natural consciousness itself. In other places,[15] Husserl claims that world-constitution constantly goes on in the natural attitude, but remains concealed. Luft (2011) supplies the fitting analogy for this approach when he writes that the general thesis of existence "lasts continuously" throughout the natural attitude, "like a constant sound that the ear blocks out" (59). Such descriptions are true. They simply do not focus on the dynamic of awakening and appropriation that makes them true. The descriptions are not about (nor are they meant to be about) how we "find ourselves" in the natural attitude; they rather assert the truth about the natural attitude as seen from the perspective of what was unavailable to it. When Husserl insists in *Cartesian Meditations* § 62 that phenomenological reflection only uncovers, but never alters, the sense the world already has prior to all philosophy, he means to emphasize that it does not construct the world through speculative concepts. The reflection does, however, determine the intrinsic readiness of experience to be immanently perceived by making use of a kind of evidence unavailable in the natural attitude. It is always an appropriation of naïveté. It thus employs the epistemic authority of the awakened ego. To ask whether I "actually" constituted reality in the natural attitude without considering this authority of the awakened ego is nonsensical. What is actual is everywhere tied to the wakeful capacity for evidence.

In an approach like that of *Ideas I*, this epistemic authority is so silently invoked that it at least invites the illusion of recollection (A § 10).[16] This is Merleau-Ponty's concern in *The Visible and the Invisible* when he critiques aspects of Cartesian, Kantian, and Husserlian thought under the heading "philosophies of reflection." It is characteristic of the philosophy of reflection "that it bring us back, this side of our *de facto* situation, to a center of things from which we proceeded, but from which we were decentered, that it retravel this time starting from us a route already traced out from that center to us" (1969, 33). He then adds in a note: "Idea of return—of the latent: idea of the reflection coming back over the traces of a constitution" (ibid.). And finally: "the illusion of illusions it to think now that to tell the truth we have never been certain of anything but our own acts" (37). Merleau-Ponty's problem with such attempts to return to ourselves as world-constituters is twofold. First, they cannot account for the reflection itself as an act of recovery; they do not help us "comprehend our own obscurity" (39). Second, by remaking the world as a spiritual product, they "forego comprehending the effective world" (36). As an alternative, Merleau-Ponty proposes a "hyper-reflection" that takes into account how reflection transforms our relation to the effective world by making use of powers (such as motility and linguistic expression) that originate there. This direction of thought eventually leads him away from the framework of transcendental constitution.

One advantage of foregrounding the awakening and appropriative moments of the phenomenological attitude is that it allows for a "comprehension of our obscurity" within the framework of constitution made authoritative by phenomenological reflection proper. The ego awakening to universal world-constitution discovers a new dimension in which I am now responsible for my life. Holding myself responsible in this dimension in accordance with the task of basic integrity, I now claim as *my* naïveté the life *I* lived in the natural attitude. In other words, natural-attitude life, not yet neutralized or transcendentally apperceived, was a blind accomplishment of the subjectivity currently there for me in phenomenologically wakeful perception.[17] This assertion is provisionally made good in a kind of synoptic grasp of my natural biography. It is historical in that it is orientated toward the divergence between the immanent sense of natural-attitude life and its current sense, while simultaneously exercising that power of annexation discussed in our general reflections. Cashed out in particular appropriations, this annexation will always lead to the *identification* of any episode of natural-attitude life with accomplishments of world-constitution.

In this, phenomenology departs from the Cartesian model. Like Husserl, Descartes attempts to clarify the meaning of his meditative stance by orchestrating a controlled return to the perspective of naïve life. However, Descartes identifies his newly discovered subjectivity with a *particular* aspect of the self-conception he enjoyed in the natural attitude, that is, mind as opposed to body, or thinking as opposed to corporeally dependent capacities. When he then reactivates his naïve attitude, he purports to unmask what *seemed* to be a perception as a confused mode of thinking, or "inspection on the part of the mind alone" (1993, 22). Phenomenological appropriation does not find transcendental life as a special faculty among those of the naturally living human being. Transcendental life is instead the previously unnoticed depth of all of these activities. Perception, transcendentally understood, is simply perception. Likewise, in being recognized as correlates of world-constitution, the mundane beings of the natural attitude retain their look (*eidos*), rather than being stripped, as Descartes has it, of their "external forms" (23). The mundane beings and the activities that show them in the natural attitude are left alone. This is what is meant by the "phenomenological reduction." It is the leading back of mundane being to the constitutive sources through which it is what it is. It is never anything other than my naïve life as it was that the phenomenologically awakened ego identifies as its own anonymous functioning. The true assertion that phenomenology reveals natural-attitude life and its system of reality as it always was simply must be qualified in the following way: it expresses the appropriation of naïveté through the epistemic authority of the wakeful ego, not the return to a lost origin.

The potential for the recollective illusion arises once the phenomenological attitude has become available as a perspective from which to view life in the natural attitude. Once someone has established the phenomenological attitude, whatever she finds in natural-attitude life indicates its possible reconsideration in light of the life of world-constitution with which she is already directly acquainted. Through the exercise of a familiar ability, she can bring about this reflective reconsideration through the same rhythm of suspension and engagement by which she modulates how she is interested in things within the natural attitude. Phenomenological reflection in the strict sense has then become possible. It is misleading, though, to assert as a fact about natural-attitude life that it has constituting life within its purview, at its "margins" or in its "background," ready to be perceived in reflections. This is a semblance achieved through a history of switching between attitudes. But the distinction between the natural and phenomenological attitudes is first achieved in an awakening. The freedom to reflect on the constitutive accomplishments indicated in natural-attitude life is dependent on an original awakening to the dimension of world-constitution as something *missing for* the natural attitude. In the *Prague Lecture*, Husserl expresses this clearly when he claims that the "inner" perception of pure consciousness "is so far from being something immediate and everyday that *it was not even possible before* the introduction of the phenomenological method of epoché" (1993, 129; my emphasis). In the *Crisis*, Husserl finds a metaphorical idiom preferable to that of "background" and "margin." He borrows Helmholtz's vision of planar beings who are oblivious to the depth dimension that includes their world. In explaining the inaccessibility of transcendental life to the philosophical tradition, he writes: "It is *not* the case that this is a matter of merely turning our gaze toward a sphere which up to now has simply not been noticed but which is accessible without further effort to theoretical experience and experiential knowledge. Everything experienceable in this way is the object and domain of possible positive knowledge; it lies on the 'plane'" (1970, 120/122).

To shift between established attitudes is to exercise one's ability.[18] To awaken to a basic attitude through realization is to discover one's ability, and so to be changed. Husserl once remarked that the discovery of the phenomenological attitude effects a transformation in personal life comparable to a religious conversion. The comparison is fitting because the conversion concerns the nature and source of truths that count as ultimate, and also because it makes the unconverted self appear blind. It is noteworthy, though, that Husserl explicitly restricts the comparison to the effect that the phenomenological attitude has "in the beginning," when it is "at first" discovered (1970, 137/140). The phenomenological awakening makes available a depth of meaning in the natural attitude that will, with repeated phenomenological reflection, sediment into a feature of that attitude itself. It then becomes possible, as Husserl says in an appendix to *Basic Problems*, to judge about pure consciousness "almost as if in natural reflection" (2006, 120/110).

The breakthrough to the phenomenological attitude is an awakening for the ego. It thus accrues an appropriative responsibility with respect to its previous life. This life was naïve in the strong sense of having in fact been unable to attend to what, from the perspective of wakefulness, could have in principle been attended to. My own life of transcendental constitution is here evident as the universal presupposition of natural-attitude life. As in the case of natural-attitude awakenings, the installation of the wakeful ego, according to its capacities of attention, into the course of naïve history (the "I was presupposing") is founded upon the present assertion of responsibility that claims naïveté as a deficient mode of the awakened ego's own life (the "I have presupposed"). There is nothing in the experience of phenomenological awakening and appropriation to support the idea of a return to an original source of constitution that had been covered over or forgotten. We rather discover a process of maturation in which the ego expands by a new dimension the life for which it holds itself responsible.

8. Self-Reflection, Self-Creation, Self-Realization

We may now state in condensed form the results of the two previous sections regarding the transition from the natural to the phenomenological attitude.

Through this transition, what I lived through as my mundane life comes to count as my transcendental life and the ego of this life as a transcendental ego. Because there is no way of transit into transcendental life that proceeds from natural interests, one has to account for the possibility of the transition by means of transcendental life. This procedure is unavoidable and indeed legitimate from a certain perspective. However, the nature of the transition itself is obscured when the dynamic of self-reflection or self-creation replaces that of the self-realization proper to the awakening to naïveté.

Self-reflection begins by employing the freedom of the transcendental ego to modify its interest so that it notices its own accomplishments. This freedom is absolute in that it is guaranteed by the nature of the accomplishments themselves. The life of the self has always been intrinsically available to itself. The free exercise of transcendental self-reflection uncovers an underlying life of accomplishment to which I previously did not attend. But this "I" who did not attend was I myself, the transcendental ego. If the appropriative element of this identification is overlooked, the transcendental ego is posited as a previously existing subject that somehow concealed itself from itself, but that now reflects on itself. This also means that the transcendental ego must have somehow brought about the transition from the natural into the phenomenological attitude. Fink ends up at this position: "transcendental subjectivity, concealed in its self-objectification as man, reflectively thinks about itself, beginning *seemingly* as man, annulling itself as man, and taking itself down as man all the way to the ground, namely, to the ground of its life" (1995, 32–3).

Self-reflection has its mirror image in self-creation, which first wins the transcendental perspective by spontaneously bringing myself into being as a transcendental ego. Instead of thinking of objects, I think of thinking, and this having of my thought in its productivity is just what the self is. This interpretation of the transition between attitudes has the advantage of purging the mundane of any transcendental embellishment. Transcendental reflection generates its own subject matter. This is Schelling's view of how philosophy begins: "The self simply *has no existence, prior* to that act whereby thinking becomes its own object" (1978, 25). But the philosopher now confronts the mundane as an alien domain that has to be accounted for via the self's own creativity on pain of reinstating the natural attitude.[19] From the transcendental perspective, I infer that the freely initiated act that accomplishes the self matches the original free activity of the self that creates its own limit in the mundane. This, though, is to rejoin self-reflection by another route. The transition to the transcendental perspective is the coming to consciousness of an unconscious activity:

But the question now arises as to how the philosopher assures himself of this original act, or knows about it. He obviously does not do so immediately, but only by inference. I discover, that is, through philosophy, that only through such an act am I generated for myself at every instant, and conclude, therefore, that only through such an act can I likewise have come into being in the first place. (47–8)

Self-realization describes the transition that results in the understanding of mundane life in terms of transcendental life and the transcendental ego as a recovered ego. Life in the world is not intrinsically available to itself as transcendental life. Like everything else, life has to appear, directly or indirectly, in order to make a claim on being. The freedom employed by transcendental self-reflection does not yet exist. Before this freedom can become a capacity, transcendental life must *dawn* on the mundane ego in a captive realization (A § 4). This is what Husserl describes as being "pulled into the epoché." The I dawns on itself, we say with Husserl, "with a certain naïveté and through a historical situation." It does not posit or create itself spontaneously. Instead, it emerges through the implications of a definite occasion, suddenly and as something altogether obvious but *missed*. The original transcendental reflection is the reflection within realization we have called awakening. Its object is the transcendental ego, but precisely in its negligence, in its failure to notice its own life of accomplishment. The in-principle ability to reflect on transcendental life is only constituted along with the consuming interest that divests the occasion of its motivational force. The awakened ego, who can reflect on its life through spontaneous acts, is now achieved.

9. The Finality of Phenomenological Wakefulness

For the natural attitude, wakefulness is a real condition of the ego that has its complement in a real condition of sleep that cuts the ego off from reality. To be wakeful, the diurnal ego has to be in the presence of the real world. Because certainty regarding its presence is unattainable, this wakefulness can never be sure that it is, in fact, wakeful. The phenomenological awakening introduces the ego to a form of wakefulness the opposite of which is no longer sleep. We can now reassess whether a mode of wakefulness can verify its own finality.[20]

Let us return to the Cartesian thought experiment that misfired in the natural attitude. We recall that it was impossible to make sense of the assumption that I, who think I am awake, am actually dreaming. The cancellation of the spatiotemporal world of realities also cancelled the only ego with whom I can identify, which made it impossible that "I" am dreaming. If we now claim that the experiment can succeed on the basis of phenomenological awakening, this is not to introduce motives for doubting the world, but to render intelligible those motives toyed with in natural-attitude speculation. The exercise of rendering them intelligible simultaneously establishes a sense of "I" and of "wakefulness" immune to all such doubts. In this light, the natural-attitude speculation that life is but a dream will look like a presentiment that a wakefulness tethered to reality implies a broader dimension of being to which it is oblivious.

Everything depends upon the possible truth of the statement: "Even though I am now sleeping, I am." Contemplating this possibility, I naturally imagine the true reality in which my true self is now doing something analogous to what I call, in my current dream, "sleeping." Descartes' observation that the cogito is beyond imagination is a warning against going along with this tendency. The initial problem is to clarify the unimaginable egoic life that enables me, independently of any mundane connection, to identify with whatever sleeper I might imagine. Phenomenologically awake, I consider myself not as an appearing being in the world but as the grantor or tender of what appears and can appear. This granting-of-what-appears makes no claim to be real. For instance, I bring to phenomenological attention an ongoing visual perception of this real object. The object of my current attention, the perceiving and its perceived, is, but it is not real. As Husserl provocatively points out, the appearing of wood in this perception, the wood in its appearance to consciousness, is not made of wood, and so cannot burn (1993, 128; 2014b, 177/184). Suppose now that nothing I regard as real in this or my other perceptions is real. The perceiving attention to the perceived retains its being, as do I as its agent, now altering its course in this way and that. Responding to the challenge that an ego might have only phantasies in its stream of experience, Husserl writes: "What I have in mind may be a mere figment, but the [act itself of] having it in mind, the fictionalizing consciousness, is not itself fictionalized, and the possibility of a reflection that perceives it and apprehends the absolute existence of it belongs essentially to it, as it does to any experience" (2014b, 82–3/97). The challenge does not affect the evidence of the phenomenological realization: "I *am*, this life is, I live: *cogito*" (82/97). The phenomenologist is awake in his attendance to this life that is, whether the world be real or not.

Working with this sense of the "I am," understanding the claim "Even though I am now sleeping, I am" is a matter of thinking through a possible experience of waking up that I, who am dreaming, can envision as my own. The Cartesian experiment rightly requires an analogy between, on the one hand, waking from dreaming within the dream world and, on the other, waking from dreaming out of the dream world. In the real world, there is something like dreaming. Like Descartes, we can focus the analogy on the fact that dream images are somehow derived from reality. Because Descartes is interested in maximizing doubt, he assumes that all complex things in the current (dream) world have no originals in the real world. This assumption, though, is not necessary to the experiment. The world I currently inhabit can be a more or less bizarre dream. Its "reality" may be a mashup of a reality that it closely resembles in many respects. The essential thing is that my current "reality" will suffer a complete nullification upon my waking up. Even if my dream can be matched with the real world in various ways from a wakeful perspective, it has not allowed the real world to appear in any of its features.

This means, most importantly, that my real self has not appeared to me in any of the experiences to which I currently have access. I have never—in this dream world—seen myself or heard my own voice. I have never felt the true position of my own body. Can I still meaningfully claim that the life I wake up to will be mine, that it is I that am now dreaming? The transcendental life of which I perceive myself to be the subject in the phenomenological attitude allows for an affirmative answer to this question. Not only does my current experiencing lay claim to being regardless of whether the world is real, the pure ego of this experiencing projects a sense of mineness that consists in the granting and having of what appears, and is thus in principle independent of any particular mundane beings. If the entire appearing world is suddenly supplanted by another order of appearances, I may not have the body, the personal characteristics, the memories, or social roles that I now think I have. However, I can coherently anticipate that their real counterparts will be mine in that they will appear in the same stream of manifestation to which I am now responsible. I can thus imagine undergoing a universal nullification of everything I could possibly call "mine" in the natural attitude. I, the bearer of everything that counts as existing, possibly existing or not existing, would still have this nullification as mine and would be the subject of its appropriation. Phenomenological wakefulness can fathom a coherence of life that cuts across even a total incoherence in what appears.

If this speculation now succeeds, it does not secure some reality against the threat of cancellation. On the contrary, it demonstrates that such security is absurd. It rather secures a form of wakefulness that no longer needs security against illusion. This runs counter to Cartesian reflection, which subordinates even the cogito to the interests of diurnal wakefulness. This is especially plain in the *Discourse*, where, after saving a few crucial convictions from his hyperbolic doubt, Descartes concludes that the thoughts "we have while [diurnally] awake" must have "some foundation in truth" (1998, 22). Phenomenological wakefulness simply leaves the evidence of reality as it is. This wakefulness is not the opposite of sleep; it is not directed toward a reality that contains merely subjective appearances. It is rather the opposite of naïveté pure and simple. Come what may, egoic attention can occupy as mine everything I have done or will have done in discovering and not discovering reality. In this sense, phenomenological wakefulness is final (which does not imply that the exercise of its epistemic authority in judgments is flawless).

To test the claim that the dream experiment can now succeed, let us consider again those objections Husserl seems to raise against it. In *Ideas I* § 48, Husserl concludes that "the formal logical possibility of realities outside the world, the *one* spatiotemporal world that is *established* through our *current* experience, proves itself to be, materially, an absurdity" (2014b, 88/103). His reasoning is that every real thing must be able to appear, which means that it "is part of the indeterminate but *determinable* horizon of my respective, current experience" (87/101). This determinability refers to a possible experience of the thing that is motivationally connected to, or prefigured in, the character of actual experience. Where real things are beyond empirically possible determinations of this horizon, there are nonetheless essentially possible determinations in which they would appear. Imagining aliens on distant planets, Husserl points to "possibilities for the factually separated worlds of experience to fuse (through connections among current experiences) into a single intersubjective world" (87–8/102–3). Husserl thus demonstrates the absurdity of multiple worlds or a world without connection to current experience. But is this an argument against the possible dissolution of this world into the dream of a real sleeper in the real world?

The answer is negative if we can identify the kind of motivational connection that links my current "world" experience to the hypothetical experience that would realize it as dream experience. Husserl requires that any possible reality beyond current experience be experienceable through such a connection: "Every current experience points beyond itself to possible experiences that point themselves to new possible experiences … And all that happens according to forms of rules and to kinds that are essentially determined" (2014b, 87/102). In this case, the kind of connection that annuls presumed reality as a mere dream has already been instantiated in diurnal life. The problem of multiple worlds does not emerge here because the awakened ego inserts the dream into the one true world it has before it. The actual ego that will experience the real things currently unavailable will be *I myself* in communication with actual others of whom I am now ignorant. There will be no fusion between the dream world and the real world, nor an expansion of community between dream and real persons, but rather the familiar kind annexation of the mere dream to the real. Because of this familiarity, which is necessary for the Cartesian experiment to run at all, one might think that the one world established through current experience, because it includes the "dream apperception," already contains all realities that would be experienced upon waking up. But that would be to ignore the difference between the determination of the world-horizon through local cancellation and its annulment through its subsumption as mere dream into the real world. The availability of the dream apperception to the dream speculator means that her current dream is transcendentally lucid, not that the current dream world is the real world after all. Though Husserl shies away from it, the experiment of thinking through this world annulment is uniquely suited to clarify the finality of the new form of wakefulness attained in the phenomenological attitude.

Husserl himself actually goes further, experimenting with world destruction in the form of total annihilation. This experiment highlights an aspect of phenomenological wakefulness that secures its finality absolutely. Let us rehearse some general points. In an awakening to naïveté, the uprooted ground is always a contingency within a broader range of possibility governed by the presupposition. The presupposition is a necessary condition for the ground, but not a sufficient condition. Because the awakened subject is concerned with the presupposition for the sake of the ground, he first traces a relationship of conditioning (the presupposition must be in order for the ground to be) that, if the presupposition *is*, can obscure the contingency of the ground (just because the presupposition is, the ground need not be). At the phenomenological level, our own language of "transcendental life" is a symptom of this insofar as it implies that phenomenological experience is essentially the complement of any possible real world.[21] This reflects the order of realization. The ego that realizes itself as a subject of transcendental life looks into its life in order to understand world-constitution. But included in the sense of the world is that it is a fulfillment of possibility within the broader range governed by transcendental life. Ontologically, the presupposition is always potentially independent from the whole it forms with the ground.

The naïveté of natural life consists not in its belief in the world but in the consuming world-interest that prevents it from attending to the experience in and through which the world appears. Part of this naïveté, though, is that its reflective judgments about experience inevitably place experience in the world as an event relative to the position and interaction of real things. The realization that the life of consciousness is potentially independent of the world it has as its correlate thus effects a radical reversal in perspective. In the reflective posture of *Ideas I*, Husserl describes this reversal as a case of the *ordo et connexio idearum* running against the *ordo et connexio rerum* (§ 50). In a text from 1926, he dramatically characterizes it in its original reorientation as a *kopernikanische Umwendung* (2002, 55). In truth, this reversal is as thoroughgoing and sudden as the reversal achieved by diurnal awakening when it naturalistically interprets the vast dreamscape by stuffing it inside the sleeping head of the real sleeper. In pursuit of certain theoretical interests, the scope of phenomenological wakefulness is restricted to the clarification of what seemed self-evident in natural life (I undertake an action; I express a judgment; I see a thing, an animal, a person; I value something; I imagine a fiction, etc.). Here, the language of surface and depth is appropriate. However, phenomenological wakefulness has its origin in an awakening that turns reality and experience upside down. It is only on the basis of this inversion that appropriations of the naively lived world are truly wakeful.

To see this, one has to effect the annihilation of the world in thought. The literary execution of this exercise requires a Kafka, not a Husserl. Nevertheless, Husserl's sparse suggestions at least identify the motivational bridge between experience as the correlate of the world and experience conceived as the correlate of no world. It is the familiar phenomenon of irresolvable conflict. Husserl, beginning from the world as it is, imagines a loss of coherence such that conflicts that initially seem irresolvable prove radically irresolvable, eventually undermining confidence in an order of real things. One place to start the experiment would be conflicts in the spatial distribution of things. Opening the front door, I am surprised to find, instead of the street, the backyard. Next, we let incoherence break out in the form of dissonance between kinesthetic sensations and the perceptual field. I feel myself turn around to the left to reenter the house, but the perceptual scene scrolls to the left, not the right. If this "situation" continues, its elements will become unstable. The yard, the house, the body that I turn around, will have lost the layer of objectivity corresponding to their recognizability. Now we destroy coherence between vision and touch so that their fields no longer overlap, first in "objects" and then even in the "body" I feel from within. Objective space has broken down. Finally, we volatize the unities appearing in any given field. My attention is drawn, now to this, now to that patch of color and shape, what I used to see as sides of things, but they are now like hypnagogic images, so protean and ephemeral they no longer sustain such seeing. In the natural attitude, I might ask what is wrong with my body. But in phenomenological experimentation, I have lost access precisely to identifiable things such as bodies, let alone the medical establishment I might wish to consult about my condition. (The experiment naturally goes nowhere if we assume the world throughout: "imagine that I suffer from a disorder caused by a brain lesion ….") Perhaps, though, I still remember normal, world-directed life. Let us then turn to the destruction and convolution of memories, which already has a firm guide in actually existing human ailments.[22]

The experiment is complete upon winning the conviction that "it is conceivable that the connectedness of experience loses the fixed, regulated order of profiles, construals, appearances—that there is no longer a world" (2014b, 88/103). Throughout this loss, though, the flowing life of experience continues. There is still a detecting, not of things but perhaps of "rough formations of unity [that] still come to be constituted to some extent" (88/103–4), and I, though unable to claim existence as a human being in the world, am the subject of this detecting as it unfolds. Breaking off the experiment, but remaining in the phenomenological attitude, the world in which I continue to believe stands there in a new light. Its being is synonymous with the fact that experience has had a coordination and regularity not required by the nature of experience itself. The phenomenologically awake ego is called to appropriate the naïve life in which the world was simply there, but its sphere of possible experience extends beyond this survey of world-directed life. It even comprehends the absence of world as such.

The demands of mundane maturity suggest a psychological critique of this exercise. Is it not an attempt to escape from the open vistas of the world into a pretended sphere of self-containment protected from all jeopardy? Correctly understood, however, it is a way of ensuring precisely the autonomy of the world and worldly being. The formal relations between ground and presupposition are enough to indicate this. Phenomenologically awake, I realize that the necessary condition for the being there of the world is transcendental life. If it were also a sufficient condition for the being there of the world, the world would simply follow from the functioning of transcendental life as such. By showing that it is only a necessary but not a sufficient condition, the world annihilation emphasizes that the world is the correlate of a genuine discovering process. Experience discloses a world that is not the necessary result of "hard-wired" faculties in the subject, but which is the fact of an organization that interests subjectivity from the start, from its response to simple perceptual patterns up to its formation of sophisticated empirical generalizations. The structures of the world belong to the world, not to the nature of the consciousness that reveals them. Phenomenological wakefulness is capable of something diurnal wakefulness, for all its devotion to the world, is not: it can find genuinely curious the very fact that there is a world, for example, that pursuing connections of events into the deep past should be possible at all.

When I, phenomenologically awake, attempt to clarify what my perspective on mundane space and time actually is, I attend to a coordination between my experiencing, my body, and the world accomplished in acts of perception and judgment that are situated in the order they reveal only through a psychological apperception that is itself a transcendental accomplishment. The facts that stand as a correlate of these accomplishments place human beings and animals in a world-time that passes them by and a world-space that encompasses their viewpoints. But the original *having* of this perspective has no place in mundane space and time. There is nowhere to lay the end of the measuring stick that would mark the distance between the immanent now of consciousness and its spatiotemporal surround. This is why the past, present, and future of the world are not relative to the existence of any given human being or human community. To say, for instance, that the pre-anthropological past is given *as past* to consciousness does not, as Meillassoux fears, construe the "deep meaning" of that past as "its being retrojected on the basis of a human present that is itself historically situated" (2015, 122–3).[23]

The awakening to my transcendental life is irrevocable because no larger context can annul or modify it. The exercises of world subsumption and annihilation provide an anticipatory intuition of this irrevocability. The domain of wakeful interest "my transcendental life" includes not only the world that is there for the natural attitude but also all of its possible transformations, including even its collapse. The scope of this presupposition encompasses all world-directed life. This poses the problem of whether it is now possible to be naïve with respect to constitutive accomplishments in my return to the natural attitude. We have claimed throughout that "I am now presupposing" is incoherent. But if I am implicitly aware that my current episode of natural-attitude life is appropriable in phenomenological reflection, does not such a judgment become possible? The most satisfying solution to this problem is the one Husserl embraces: if the implications of phenomenological attitude have been grasped, I never fully return to natural naïveté again (1970, 247/250; 1993, 136). This is best understood, not as my always having, as it were, one foot in the reduction, but as my holding for true the results of an irrevocable awakening (A

§ 9). Once the transcendental relativity of the world has become clear, the ego that lives on mundane ground is essentially an ego of the past: "We have it only as *past* natural ego" (2002, 59). The "naïve absolutization of the world" is "given up irrevocably [*endgültig*]" (59–60). As indicated in our general reflections (A § 5), this maturation is equally an enfolding of the naïve ego into the wakeful ego as a moment of the latter: "As a concrete ego, I cease to be a natural ego; I lose my naïveté" (85).

10. Complete Maturation

Phenomenological awakening achieves an irreversible progress over the naïveté of the natural attitude. Phenomenologically awake, I anticipate that I will in principle be able to recognize my world-constituting accomplishments in anything that has happened or will have happened in the world. I am free to speculate on every imaginable deception and reversal. None of them can decenter the ultimate dimension of responsibility and appropriation of which I now perceive myself the subject.

This complete maturation must be qualified in two ways. First, phenomenological wakefulness has attained this maturity strictly with respect to the basic integrity of the ego. It has not advanced in any way toward the ideals of mundane maturation as they bear upon the person; it has not become more worldly and less provincial. This is a consequence of the fact that phenomenological wakefulness cannot pursue those specific hidden dependencies, natural and spiritual, that determine the contexts of routine life. It leaps over all local prejudices by indexing them with respect to a universal presupposition. I have been presupposing the transcendental life of constitution equally in every naïve implementation of the world thesis, however worldly or provincial this implementation was. Even the transcendental clarification of my natural orientation toward greater world comprehension does not itself enhance this comprehension. In the realization of transcendental life, there is simply no new mundane information that could localize my situation in the world.

It is actually an abnegation of responsibility to pass off phenomenological maturation as worldly maturation. The discovery of transcendental naïveté does not vitiate the demands of integrity as they function on the mundane level, demands that phenomenological reflection (at least alone) cannot satisfy. There are then two vectors of maturation. Within natural-attitude life, it points to the dissolution and reconfiguration of contexts through the discovery of the world they suppress. Within phenomenologically wakeful life, it points to the annexation of world-directed life from the perspective of transcendental constitution. Both forms of maturation are endless, but the latter is complete because the awakening upon which it is based discovers a presupposition of universal scope; ontologically expressed: transcendental subjectivity includes all possible objects of interest, mundane and transcendental. However, only the epistemic illusion could make it seem that the discovery of transcendental life overcomes provinciality, as if encounters with the foreign, abnormal, past, or otherwise hidden dimensions of my surrounding world had nothing to teach me. A formula for counteracting this illusion is found in a felicitous phrase of Sokolowski: "philosophy does not correct ordinary experience, better ordinary experience does that" (1974, 193).

Neither does having awakened to transcendental naïveté discharge my existential responsibility for my life in the world. This latter requires, not better or more experience, but a responsiveness to being affected by the whole of my world life as an inalienable project in light of which every alienable project finally attains or loses its importance. Phenomenological interest temporarily suspends this responsiveness. Phenomenological awakening has my past, natural-attitude life in view. But it grasps it, not as a moment of my life in the world as a whole, but as a naïve phase of world-constituting transcendental life. Phenomenological reflection in the strict sense does not concern human accomplishments at all. It does not doubt that human beings and the human world are there. It simply accounts for how they are there in terms of constitutive accomplishments that are themselves neither psychological nor anthropological. However, the transcendental apperception underlying the return to natural-attitude life leaves intact the whole gravity of this life as an irreversible course of positions in a space of physical, mental, and cultural possibilities. Having phenomenological interests does not alter the fact that my life in the world provides the ultimate perspective for decisions about what matters to me, about what I am called to do.

However, it is also wrong to interpret the phenomenological stance as an evasion of the tasks of mundane maturation. Perhaps the interpretation accounts for the psychological motives of certain phenomenologists. And such an interpretation is even interesting if it deals with the unique non-worldliness achieved in the phenomenological epoché and reduction, rather than repeating the age-old accusations brought against every idealist philosophy. For the non-worldliness of phenomenology is distinguished by the fact that it does not subordinate "the sensible world" to "the intelligible world" or "the body" to "the mind" but rather gives up the whole world, in all of its dimensions, in order to view it in terms of a manifestation that is of the world (objective genitive) and yet not of the world (subjective genitive). But the phenomenological stance is essentially an evasion only if the world really is the framework in which every experience occurs and in terms of which it can be known. Can the determination of what the world is ignore what becomes evident in phenomenological awakening simply because one was not *initially* awake? Even Heidegger is careful to accord the "formal phenomenology of consciousness" its proper domain, which does not depend upon that of an existential analytic that captures everyday being in the world (1996, 109). Phenomenology is obviously derivative in the sense that its domain is factually discovered on the basis of everyday life. But what becomes evident in this discovery is precisely that what is factually derivative is ontologically absolute.[24]

The second qualification is that complete egoic maturation does not imply the exhaustive transcendental appropriation of natural-attitude life. Completeness just means that I have discovered a perspective from which my power to presuppose is in principle equaled by my power to appropriate. Husserl describes transcendental subjectivity as the "apodictic presupposition" of "everything which conceivably has being for me" (1970, 78/80). This is a nice formulation because it characterizes phenomenology's "presuppositionlessness," not as having already overcome all presuppositions, but as having discovered a final presupposition in terms of which to conduct the endless appropriation of naïveté.

11. The Devaluation of Natural-Attitude Life

Every awakening to having presupposed involves the devaluation of naïve life. However, the natural attitude frames what is ordinarily meant by the devaluation of an attitude such that the devaluation of the natural attitude itself is hard to recognize. In the phenomenological awakening, the natural attitude is devalued otherwise than attitudes within the natural attitude. Sensitivity to this fact is required in order to avoid either assimilating phenomenological awakening to the pattern of mundane awakenings or else overlooking that it is an awakening at all.

To live in the natural attitude means to understand life as transpiring in the world. Living in this way, one takes over and develops convictions about life in the world, about various types of life situation and about life itself. We speak of a "life attitude" when these convictions pre-reflectively organize broad fields of activity, making actionable certain ways of dealing with things and making salient just those things that require dealing with in these ways. It is possible to make such convictions explicit and to justify them. They then take the form of a system of judgments about what is important or good, how to get along, or simply "the way things are" for human beings under various circumstances. The life attitudes of others and other groups are naturally available through observation and communication. Typical attitudes toward life and life-spheres can thus become familiar features of a cultural world. As such, it is possible to understand them, even to appreciate their aesthetic or intellectual value, without their becoming effective. However, the original function of these attitudes is to govern one's own life in the world. The detached appreciation or understanding of a life attitude contemplates what it would be like to live under it.

A judgment that expresses an effective life attitude is not merely a claim on truth. It is a claim on behalf of an established style of dealing with the world or one of its domains. Its being true is thus a matter of great personal interest. The very personality of the person who lives from the attitude is involved. This is the case even with life attitudes that have cultural standing as "philosophies." Because effective life attitudes determine what and how things matter, they tend to perpetuate themselves. But they are not permanent. The worldly person is grounded in her attitudes while simultaneously anticipating their enrichment or cancellation in the course of further experience. She even approaches foreign attitudes as possible guides to her own life. One can experiment with these attitudes to see if they "catch on" by resonating with implicit opinions and reorganizing life activities in a satisfying way. Alternatively, one might find that one's ways of dealing with typical situations have imperceptively shifted such that a propositionally explicated life attitude has lost its previous efficacy.

This brief sketch is sufficient to illuminate how the devaluation of life attitudes within the natural attitude differs essentially from the devaluation of the natural attitude itself. A devalued life attitude ceases to frame involvement in the domain to which it pertains. If I now entertain that attitude, things in its domain can still be made to fit into the intellectual perspective it affords (this is what makes the attitude conceivable for me as actual), but this act of entertaining precisely interrupts my involvement with what is important. The explication of an effective attitude captures the things themselves as they are in my various spheres of involvement. A devalued attitude, on the other hand, is like an abnormal light source that gives things interesting appearances, thereby drawing attention to itself. If I am someone who is no longer a "Nietzschean" or a "Marxist," these attitudes have not necessarily become less fascinating or logically consistent. The crucial point is that they no longer guide me in my involvements.

When the phenomenological awakening devalues the natural attitude as naïve, it does not displace its universal guiding function for life in the world. Even when suspended, the natural attitude remains effective in the sense that it captures things as they are in my involvement with them. The world is there for the natural attitude. The phenomenological awakening uncovers what was presupposed in this being there. It has before it accomplishments of world-constitution and the constituted world *as they are framed in* the natural attitude's interest in discovering, articulating, and transforming reality. The awakened ego no longer pursues this interest in reality, but it is interested in the whole life shaped by this interest. Although the phenomenologically awakened person cannot return completely to her previous naïveté, her natural-attitude life continues to show her the real world, not its image or representation. This holds also for those particular life attitudes effective for the person in natural life. From the phenomenological perspective, they are naïve with respect to their presupposing complexes of constitution unnoticeable in the natural attitude, not because they fail to be "neutral" or "objective."

Because the phenomenological attitude does not deal directly with things and situations in the world, it is not tied to the formation of a particular personality type. The case is similar to the paradox of the "moral personality" presented by Kant in his *Anthropology* (1978, 204). Because the person of genuine character wants to bind herself to principles given by reason, she will likely appear as an eccentric from the standpoint of convention. However, because her only motivating principles are those that would be valid for everyone, she is never an eccentric, never "a character" in that sense. Analogously, the habitual adoption of the phenomenological attitude may lead to a new relativization of life attitudes, but this relativization never provides justification for another life attitude discoverable within the framework of natural-attitude life. The devaluation of transcendentally naïve life poses no threat to my personality as it is shaped by attitudinal commitments about living in the world.

Despite these differences, the phenomenological awakening remains a devaluation of natural-attitude life as naïve. Transcendental life and natural-attitude life do not coexist as complementary perspectives within an ego. The former contains the latter within itself. Diurnally awakened, sleeping and dreaming are there to be understood as activities of a real ego unaware of its reality. Phenomenologically awakened, world-directed life is there to be understood as an activity of a transcendental ego unaware of its transcendentality. As Husserl puts it, the natural attitude becomes "a particular transcendental attitude" (1970, 205/209).

12. Phenomenological Awakening and Jeopardy

The phenomenological awakening poses special problems regarding the demand for appropriation as well as the kind of appropriation that fulfills it. Our general analysis outlined how an experience of jeopardy prompts the awakening ego to appropriate its naïve life (A § 8). A genuine awakening jeopardizes me because it threatens to undermine a project I was interested in accomplishing and which is important because I have, to some degree, understood myself as its accomplisher. This faces me with a predicament in which I stand because of my lapse of basic integrity. What escaped notice should have been noticed in order to reach some live objective. The wakeful appropriation of naïve life proceeds in light of this objective. By bringing what was unnoticeable into play, and diagnosing the effect of consuming interests, the appropriating ego converts its naïve history of accomplishment into a history wakefully understood. On this basis, a decision becomes possible about whether and how to resume pursuit of the objective.

Failing this experience of jeopardy and the predicament to which it corresponds, the ego is not urged to transform any of its projects from naïve into wakeful accomplishments. We called such experiences pseudo-awakenings because they are concerned with precisely what need not be taken into account for the important matters in which I am involved. We opposed the mood of urgency characteristic of genuine awakenings to the contemplative mood of pseudo-awakenings. However, we also became sensitive to how everydayness restricts the sphere of what warrants attention. Perhaps there are no pseudo-awakenings, only provincial egos. Bearing these reflections in mind, we now ask: Is the phenomenological awakening merely contemplative?

Initially, it seems that it is. The phenomenological awakening presents the ego with a new activity over which it has never exercised responsibility: transcendental constitution. But this activity, because it is unreal and without real conditions, shares no context with any activity pursued on the ground of the world. Accordingly, in discovering its previous negligence and exercising its newfound responsibility, the awakened ego no longer pursues anything in the naïve ego's sphere of interest. World-constituting life is not a factor that should have been taken into account in order for the naïve ego to have reached some live objective.

Wakeful appropriation cannot take over something of consequence already underway in naïve life. This apparent discontinuity of interest undermines the critical import of the awakening.

Within the natural attitude such discontinuity can be overcome by reframing reflections. Where a presupposition appears irrelevant, a reinterpretation of the ground within a broader field of interest can make it matter that I presupposed. For example, the world occluding tendency of everyday life can be such that a structurally sound house is not a relevant circumstance for the goal of entertaining dinner guests. This tendency can be counteracted by critical reflections that expose the provinciality that enables the impassivity of the contemplatively awakened ego. By localizing its context within a broader horizon, the ego may realize unavailable convictions that inform its routine accomplishments. However, the unearthed conviction can only jeopardize because of an unbroken world-interest exercised in taking account of the local context from a more comprehensive perspective. Because it discontinues this interest, the awakening to transcendental life cannot inform any mundane accomplishment, regardless of how open one is.

A sign of this is that transforming the world into a ground relative to the presupposition of transcendental constitution does not call into question any particular convictions about the world that have formed in the natural attitude. Because the phenomenological awakening is not directed toward the world, it can neither confirm, nor deny, nor reassess any position of importance to naïve life. The realized relativity only introduces a new mode of egoic accomplishment and a new mode of correlative validity into which the naïve life of natural subjectivity must be integrated. Husserl often emphasizes that the phenomenological attitude neither interprets nor changes the world, but clarifies it just as it is. This posture of neutral clarification not only distinguishes the epoché from a skeptical stance toward reality as a whole. It also entails letting alone the particular truths about the world already acquired during the course of natural life: "Through the 'inhibiting' of the epoché, I have lost nothing from this life that was mine … Neither have I lost the world and mundane judgments, theories, etc.. All my knowledge remains available to me, even if everything has altered its mode of validity in a certain way" (2002, 83). For example, to attend to a perceived thing in its dependence upon a vast network of constitutive accomplishments leaves the material, value, and practical determinations of the thing just as I had naively taken them to be.

The perfect aloofness with which phenomenological wakefulness leaves mundane being alone is unrivaled by any posture of acceptance possible within the natural attitude. Within my world-directed life, I can resolve to rest content with reality simply as it is, to reconcile myself to negativities of all kinds exactly as they are. But this resolution depends upon a judgment directed *at reality*—it is worthy of acceptance. Universal acceptance is a life attitude. By contrast, the phenomenological attitude is interested in the world-constitution through which all mundane being first of all occurs. It offers no judgment or interpretation about mundane beings. Here, the leaving alone of what naïve life took to be reality is not the opposite of rejecting it. It is the opposite of having it as a theme at all. We look in vain, then, for any "stoic" significance in phenomenological awakening.

In arguing for the harmlessness of his academic skepticism, Hume claims that it "strikes in with no disorderly passion of the human mind, nor can mingle itself with any natural affection or propensity" (1993, 26). He means that, unlike "easy" moral philosophy, his investigation of human nature refrains from promoting any specific life attitude, all of which can interact with particular personalities to yield bad results. But precisely because Hume's orientation remains psychological, his attention to the contribution of the human mind to the coherence of its world counts against that coherence, even if one cannot help but affirm it. The principle of custom, for instance, thanks to which humans are sure of anything beyond what is directly seen or recalled, belongs to the makeup of a particular creature. Common sense is thus a kind of fatality, which prudent, modest thinking identifies as such. This modesty and prudence, however, are themselves components of a life attitude. When reason acknowledges that nature prevails over reason, it humbles itself and consents to inhabit an opaque world. Because phenomenology does not relativize the appearance of mundane being to a particular creature, it leaves reality alone without a hint of psychologistic modesty and its prideful renunciation of imprudent attempts at superhuman knowing.

In its leaving alone of mundane being, phenomenological awakening also differs from the Socratic awakening to eidetic being. Naïve thought is devoted to sensuous beauties and goods without being "able to follow" the implication that points to the beauty and goodness they manifest (*Republic* 476c).[25] Having opinions in this mode is thus like dreaming, which is unaware of its nocturnal status. For itself, it is the enjoyment of power and vision. The Socratic practice follows the maxim of wakefulness. Awareness of naïveté is preferable to the functionality that comes from having established opinions, even when the extrinsic value of this awareness is nil, that is, when it incapacitates and benumbs (*Meno* 80a-b). However, Socratic conversation promises a *better* functionality to those who pass through this bewilderment. This is because the eidetic realm includes the realm of real particulars as that to which it affords standards. The spatiotemporal world continues to occupy the philosopher as the sphere of application for philosophical insights. Socratic awakening uproots opinions relevant to established practical interests and aims at a reform of those interests in light of the true standards afforded by knowledge. The relativizing of worldly reality to eidetic being thus enjoys a critical power totally absent in the relativizing of worldly reality to transcendental life. Eidetic judgments carried out within the phenomenological attitude no longer include reality as a basis, even in the mode of arbitrary instantiation. Their basis is rather the arbitrarily instantiating pure experience.[26]

Phenomenological awakening thus seems entirely contemplative because the naïveté it discovers has not jeopardized the ego as the accomplisher of something important for its articulated world-interest. The awakening leaves untouched not only the established facts relied upon in one's definite accomplishments but also every life attitude that guides these accomplishments. Although the scope of the phenomenologically determined presupposition is universal, its centrality seems fixed at zero. But perhaps we can discover how the ego is jeopardized by natural naïveté by broadening our focus. The realization of transcendental life seemed unable to jeopardize because it did not take place in the world or depend upon any mundane conditions. However, let us now attend to this very fact: the ego has realized that its life is not contained in the world. The phenomenological attitude does not merely discover the transcendental depth of what was naively given. It discovers new truths about what my life and the world fundamentally are. Do not these truths uproot projects that require wakeful appropriation?

In discovering as mine a life that is not in the world, I seem to revise my established self-conception. In the natural attitude, I understood my life as "first-personal." Phenomenologically awake, my life is seen to transcend what is first-personal. This transcendence becomes prominent at the limits that define first-personal life. After outlining the phenomenon of first-personal life, we will consider a few aspects of this transcendence and then ask whether their realization jeopardizes the ego in any of its worldly undertakings.

Living in the natural attitude, I understand my life as limited by a broader world that contains it. There are things in this world that are my concern, for which I am responsible, that figure in my activities, and there are things that are not my concern, but perhaps yours, theirs, the concern of past or future people, or perhaps nobody's concern at all. This is not just a matter of temperance. When

I make the distinction in manifold ways between what does and does not "have to do with me," I call attention to the boundaries that define my personal life. In general, I, like each person, only have limited and partial access to the reality in which I live. I am responsible for knowing, evaluating, and acting with respect to those matters in my sphere. But there is a wide world of things beyond my concern. This "beyond my concern" is a basic determination of my life as first-personal, as centered on one person among many in the world.

As a phenomenologically awake ego, my life is the transcendental life in which the world is constituted with just the meaning that it has. It is clear that this life cannot be placed somewhere in relation to a beyond. This is clearest precisely in those experiences in which the beyond is constituted. Consider the experience of the spatial beyond. Living in the natural attitude, there are zones of spatial reality that are indeed out there, but that are not where I am. As I look out at the ocean from the Atlantic coast, I reflect that the African continent lies somewhere far off in that direction. But my perception is not there. My perception takes place in this and not that particular sector of a broader spatial reality. Now, phenomenologically awake, I am responsible for *having* these forms of absence through the modes of constitution that present them "emptily" as targets for possible fulfilling experiences.[27] As we outlined earlier, these constitutive accomplishments result in the perception having the meaning "taking place in this particular location," but they themselves cannot be found in a particular location. The phenomenological investigation of natural-attitude life shows that my taking the world as my limit is not itself limited by the world. Transcendentally, the beyond is my concern as much as the here. Mundane attention reaches into the remote (A § 7), which, for transcendental attention, is already "here" as meant along with the near.

Consider a related kind of transcendence of personal by egoic life. In the reality that contains my natural-attitude perspective, there are also entities with their own inwardnesses, their own perspectives on reality. In the natural attitude, the world is there for my perspective, but this is only one perspective belonging to an organism in a particular spatiotemporal location. The others are elsewhere and have their own perspectives. These perspectives are reflected in the natural use of personal pronouns. The first-person perspective shows me second and third persons, each of whom is also a first person with her own perspectives. These other perspectives may include me as a second or a third person, but they are not mine. The experience that is mine is a perspective determined by its place in this intersubjectivity, with which I am always in communication, as I especially notice in attending to foreign, abnormal, animal, or departed others.

By contrast, the phenomenologically awake ego has this whole system of personally attributed experiences before it *as mine*. The perspective of the second or third person, the foreigner, the child, and the animal, as well as the first-person perspective limited by and in communication with them, are all in need of appropriation in terms of *my own* world-constitution. Husserl's great achievement here is to show how my own apperception of the other ego, as a domain of subjectivity to which I can never win direct access, is the only way to understand the evident experience I have of the perfect independence of the other. "My own," in this context, does not assign experiences to one human animal as opposed to others. The very having of experiences as articulated into mine, ours, yours, and theirs is a complex accomplishment, the subject of which I recognize as myself, not as one person in the world, but as I now am, a unique ego responsible for (whose "thinking" matters for) any and all mundane being. The life now appropriable as mine incorporates the perspectival system that characterizes involvement in the world, but only to understand it as genuinely perspectival. I am responsible for the being there of the others precisely as absolutely transcendent with respect to my subjectivity. The ways of communication are appropriable in an egoic solitude unknowable in first-personal life. In the natural attitude, one may dispute whether meaning is public or private. In the phenomenological attitude, the public and the private are thematic as meant.[28]

There are still other ways that the phenomenologically awakened ego is the subject of a life in which the defining limits of personal experience occur, but which is not itself limited by them. "I was born, will die and am an organism of a certain species" is a complex natural-attitude truth that the appropriating reflection leaves alone as true while clarifying its sources in transcendental subjectivity. But this truth, because it pertains to the life of a psychophysical being in the world, does not establish anything about the nature of transcendental subjectivity itself. Of course, one should not for this reason apply to transcendental subjectivity the conceptions the natural attitude opposes to birth, death, and biology. It is better to employ privative language: transcendental subjectivity is birthless, deathless, and unbiological. This leaves birth, death, and species membership as life-limiting facts for the human being. It is simply that they no longer count as conditioning the most encompassing dimension of my life.

Does this strange transcendence of the limits of mundane life force the wakeful conversion of any project that was underway for the naïve ego? Having experienced and judged in the phenomenological attitude, I can never return entirely to my natural naïveté. The latter is now backlit by a transcendental apperception. With respect to my sense of self, it includes the awareness that my egoic being is not exhausted by my psychophysical existence. I now know that I am also the subject of a life of constitution in which every mundane being, including myself as a human being, has acquired whatever being and sense it has for me: "My human life has transcendentally 'behind it' my transcendental egological life, the life constitutively functioning, the life of consciousness" (2014a, 80). The question is what effect this knowledge has on my world-directed life. Is there some project underway that stands in need of critical reflections that will enable me to accomplish wakefully what I was naively?

It might seem that life in the natural attitude entails taking my first-personality seriously in a way no longer possible in light of the transcendental apperception. Prior to phenomenological awakening, I privileged as mine those spheres of concern bound to my location in the broader world as one person among others. Because I can now inhabit a reflective attitude for which all mundane being is equally my concern, my first-personal commitments are no longer as binding as they were before. This would follow if the phenomenological perspective, in and of itself, included any judgment about the importance of projects underway in natural-attitude life. The transcendental apperception involves awareness of an ability to temporarily suspend my interest in the world. This interest is no longer consuming. But relativizing this interest does not involve any new stance about its importance. Stances about the life-significance of specific life projects or of life as a whole arise in the natural attitude through evaluations aimed directly at the world. Rather than diminishing the seriousness of first-personal life, the transcendental apperception indicates a new first-personal possibility, habitual phenomenological reflection, the life-significance of which is an existential problem. In the second part of this study (IIB § 13), we will see that Husserl understands this problem precisely in terms of how to take oneself seriously as a philosopher.

People may discover all kinds of transformative significance in phenomenological awakening. But these discoveries are idiosyncratic. In Kantian language, these personal transformations make discretionary use of the transcendental apperception. There is no inherent inconsistency in having relativized natural life to its transcendental presupposition and standing committed to any life attitude or project. For instance, the discovery of my transcendental life has, in and of itself, nothing to say against the very "worldly" attitudes of acquisitiveness or ambition. From the transcendental perspective, these are not more worldly than their ascetic opposites. It is possible, of course, that one's life attitudes are provincial or otherwise unjustifiable. But here,

Sokolowski's insight is again pertinent. It is broader world-directed experience that will uncover and correct this, not transcendental reflection. What likely happens in attempts to invest the latter with a specific transformational meaning is that the need for transformation has already been substantiated within the natural attitude, which then motivates a discretionary use of transcendental apperception. This leads to the unsurprising illusion that the phenomenological attitude is the natural ally of prevailing life attitudes in the people who exercise it.

The awakening to transcendental life flows into natural-attitude life in myriad ways. To this point, however, we have been unable to discover how it introduces an imperative to transform any tradition in which I was naively involved. Perhaps there is no non-discretional use of the transcendental apperception. Perhaps phenomenological awakening does not force me to reconsider how to pursue those interests that shape me as a person in the world. Perhaps it does not matter for life in the world that this life has been transcendentally naïve. Perhaps the most fundamental exercise of integrity does not enable the wakeful fulfillment of any possibility to which natural-attitude life has dedicated itself and is without "historical meaning" in this sense. This is possible, even if it should prove practically intolerable.

13. The Idea of an Enlightenment Project

The foregoing reflections have emphasized the radical disconnection between the natural and phenomenological attitudes. This disconnection made it seem that transcendental naïveté was perfectly irrelevant to every established interest of natural-attitude life. But the case may have been overstated. We now consider the possibility of a historical project of such a kind that transcendental naïveté would jeopardize anyone who stood committed to it. We may indicate the nature of such a project by recalling the maxim of integrity: If I am naïve, I want to find out that I have been, no matter the consequences. Whereas we previously considered this maxim in light of the capacities belonging to an ego as such, we now consider the possibility of its animating a movement within actual human history. This project, although discernable in human thoughts and deeds, would exhibit a commitment to wakefulness as an absolute value, regardless of its relevance to whatever interests might otherwise orient human life. The pursuit of this project would not only advance the infinite tasks of self-responsibility in the natural attitude but also require overcoming that attitude in order to clarify and fulfill its animating vision of a maximally wakeful humanity.

It seems that only such a preexisting project, dedicated to wakefulness as such, could be uprooted by the discovery of transcendental naïveté.

Were such a project to be in effect, the natural attitude would undergo a new form of devaluation as inadequate to the realization of the live objectives of the project. Correlatively, phenomenological wakefulness would also attain an historical importance commensurate with that of the project. The existence of such a project would also introduce a broader set of concerns in terms of which the phenomenological awakening matters. The centrality and scope of the phenomenological awakening would thereby acquire a variable dimension. Just what this project is, how and when it was established, for whom it is "in effect," in what ways it jeopardizes this dedicated community, and just how all of this could be ascertained are problems for the assertion that there is such a project. We have merely outlined how the project would affect the parameters of phenomenological awakening.

However, there are problems even for the idea of a project related to phenomenological awakening in this way. On the one hand, the project itself cannot have brought about the discovery of transcendental naïveté. The epistemic authority of wakefulness dictates that the true explanation for the transition from naïveté into wakefulness adopt the wakeful, not the naïve, perspective. While attention to the historical occasion for phenomenological awakening helps ward off the illusion of recollection, the occasion itself cannot be responsible for the awakening. In this context, Fink's critique of "ways" into phenomenology is pertinent: "If we take ways into phenomenology to mean a *continuity of motivation* that begins in the natural attitude and by inferential force leads into the transcendental attitude, then *there are no such ways*" (1995, 32–3). No project established in the natural attitude can lead, via its own developmental logic, into the phenomenological attitude. Descartes already alluded to this in the opening to his first meditation. There is no suitable time for the destruction of mundane wakefulness. How could circumstances arise within the purview of that wakefulness that would urge this destruction upon us?

On the other hand, the phenomenological attitude cannot itself determine the existence and nature of this project. As a matter of principle, this attitude cannot substantiate claims about the facts of human history. Further, in order for the phenomenological awakening to jeopardize me in this project, I must have already been committed to it. This means that the devaluation of the natural attitude as inadequate to the goals of the project is based upon their prior establishment and pursuit in the natural attitude itself. The goals cannot be imposed from this side of the awakening. While the necessity of phenomenological wakefulness to the fulfillment of the project only becomes apparent after the suspension of the natural attitude, this necessity must also become apparent *in* the course of the natural-attitude pursuit of the project. The phenomenological attitude must be the condition for the transformation and fulfillment of that project, not its retroactive invention.

Because it is provided neither by the course of the project, nor by the mere attainment of phenomenological wakefulness, evidence for this transformation must be forged in an historical interpretation. The interpretation is contestable for several reasons. First, the phenomenological attitude is essentially subsequent to the natural attitude, which will have shaped the project throughout its historical development. The established understanding of the goals, methods, and interests that define the project is inevitably transcendentally naïve. There is thus a resistance to appropriation internal to the project. The purported phenomenological transformation seems to abandon the interest that determines the project's meaning. Second, because it runs against established understanding, the interpretation can only find motives for phenomenological transformation *in* the history of the project by appealing to latent intentions that lack unambiguous expression. Third, the interpretation cannot claim impartiality in its attitude toward historical evidence. While the imperative to appropriate the preexisting project must arise out of the history of that project, there is also an imperative to find some such imperative. The alternative is to consign life in the world to naïveté as a natural condition from which it needs no liberation. This is a practically impossible option given commitment to the project.

14. The Presupposition of an Enlightenment Project

We can anticipate the focus of the second part of this study by noting that Husserl undertakes his entire work as a participant in such a project. Naming this project after the Enlightenment is not always Husserl's practice, but it finds some traction in his texts. In the *Kaizo* articles, for instance, he uses the term "Period of Enlightenment" (*Aufklärungsperiode*) to describe the historical epoch during which the ideal of a philosophical culture determines "the fundamental character of modernity" (1989, 84). This epoch lasts so long as the ideal animates actually existing culture to achievable goals in a "free ascendant development" (ibid.). In the *Crisis*, Husserl characterizes the "Age of Enlightenment" (*Zeitalter der Aufklärung*) in terms of its "inspiring belief" in the ideal of a universal philosophy that could guide a rational reform of human culture (1970, 10/8). Dedication to the Enlightenment project in this sense is the historical worldview to which Husserl is unconditionally committed. The general intention of the Age of Enlightenment, he writes, "must never die out in us" (1970, 197/200). This is the case even though Husserl's assessment of the Enlightenment conception of rationality is that it was thoroughly mistaken and naïve (1970, 197/200, 290/337, 292/339). The critique of Enlightenment is immanent to Enlightenment. This is the name for the project that is wakefully transformed and brought to the fulfillment of *its own* objectives through the overcoming of its transcendental naïveté.

To assert that the phenomenological tradition initially presupposes the Enlightenment project means that this project is the operative historical orientation in terms of which the transformative claims of phenomenological awakening can first of all arise. At the center of this project is *Wissenschaft*. The transformational meaning of phenomenological awakening thus lies, first of all, in the predicament it creates for science. But the predicament is highly ramified. It embraces an array of accomplishments that require critique and conversion from the wakeful perspective. Most narrowly, it is psychology, the natural-attitude study of subjectivity, that cannot achieve its goals without overcoming its transcendental naïveté: "Psychology had to fail because it could fulfill its task … only through a radical, completely unprejudiced reflection, which would then necessarily open up the transcendental-subjective dimension" (1970, 211/215). More generally, *any* science that would participate in the unconditional pursuit of truth is uprooted because of its consuming world-interest: "Once the goal of absolute truth has been established … the sciences of this [world] positivity are consequently deemed imperfect [*unvollkommene*]" (2002, 66). This applies even to the science of objective nature. The transcendental clarification of natural-scientific theorizing "is not a mere appendage to natural science, but belongs to it itself as its correlative, subjective side. Only through this phenomenological, natural-scientific work does it become fully substantiating science [*vollbegründenden Wissenschaft*]" (1993, 135). More generally still, philosophy, the universal theoretical enterprise encompassing all science, can only emerge from its "centuries-old failure" (1970, 11/9) by overcoming "its own unnoticed naïvetés" (14/12) through a phenomenological transformation: "all the philosophy of the past, though unbeknown to itself, was inwardly oriented toward this new sense of philosophy" (18/17). Finally, the predicament of philosophy jeopardizes the historical community that had seen it as the key to the possibility of a wakeful life. Participation in this community is the broadest form of "involvement" in science or philosophy. The precarious state of philosophy implies "at first a latent, then a more and more prominent crisis of European humanity itself in respect to the total meaningfulness of its cultural life, its total '*Existenz*'" (1970, 12/10).

The connection between the phenomenological attitude and science is the result of a particular historical development. To emphasize this, we will reserve the term "phenomenological attitude" for the simple orientation toward transcendental life. In principle, this attitude need not serve theoretical or scientific ends. A seeing and judging about transcendental life shorn of all scientific aspiration is a privative concept in the tradition initiated by Descartes, for whom scientific interests already motivated the upending of mundane wakefulness. However, not only is such a minimal logos of phenomena conceivable, its conception also highlights the fact that phenomenological theory involves complex spiritual conditions beyond the capacities of attention belonging to an experiencing ego. We will use the term 'phenomenological-theoretical attitude' to refer to the modification of the phenomenological attitude by which it is oriented toward the advancement of scientific goals.

Husserl's systematic introductory works are dominated by the phenomenological-theoretical attitude. They take over and pursue goals of the theoretical tradition. In taking over these goals, phenomenological attention is already fastened on what is relevant to their achievement. Primarily relevant are those characteristics of world-constituting life that allow it to serve as a foundation for theory in general. Preoccupation with the foundational aspects of world-constituting life is a consequence of the awakened ego's involvement in science. Live objectives of the theoretical project, taken over in the new attitude, motivate a task that is first with respect to those objectives: demonstrating that world-constituting life is a domain for systematic inquiry that includes, grounds, and certifies all others. World-constituting life thus takes on a structural function within the construction of theory.

Among the highest scientific objectives taken over in the phenomenological-theoretical attitude are (1) attaining insight into the whole of what is, within which every discoverable entity will have its place; (2) supplying ultimate explanations; and (3) gaining access to a realm of indubitable evidence. The phenomenological-theoretical attitude has before it the task of establishing the viability of these objectives and, negatively, their unviability within the natural attitude. The true universe is consciousness, not world. Final explanations are constitutive, not mundane. Certainty attends immanent, not transcendent perception. The definition of phenomenologically reduced consciousness as a universal, grounding, and certifying domain lays the foundation for the secure pursuit of theoretical goals in the phenomenological attitude. The whole of naïve life in its cognitive, evaluative, and volitional aspects, in its scientific and prescientific forms, falls within its purview, as do the methods of phenomenology itself. Of course, traditional forms of scientific discipline guide this entire enterprise. The theoretical project is taken over, not discovered, in the phenomenological attitude. However, the concepts employed in this traditional discipline require their own justification, which is furnished only by phenomenological investigation. We here see in outline the bold idea of phenomenology as universal, rigorous science. The classical methodological and substantive concepts of phenomenology develop in its light.

In Husserl's later work, and particularly in his final attempted treatise, the phenomenological-theoretical attitude is folded into the purview of a new attitude. The theme of this attitude is precisely phenomenological work, but now considered as a developing practice in the midst of the human world. Reflections in this new attitude contend with the realization of a presupposition operative in the phenomenological-theoretical attitude. The belief that phenomenological wakefulness is the necessary condition for the fulfillment of scientific aims has as a necessary condition for *its* truth a contentious historical interpretation that the phenomenological-theoretical attitude itself cannot apprehend, but upon which phenomenological-theoretical thinking is based. The presupposition is that human history is such that a transformative appropriation of science in the phenomenological attitude is possible.

Thinking in the phenomenological-theoretical attitude stands committed to the *historical* view that transcendental naïveté has inhibited the realization of the goals that have actually animated the scientific tradition. While established within the consuming interest of the natural attitude, the theoretical project points beyond the natural attitude in such a way that it can only reach maturity in the phenomenological attitude. This view depends upon an interpretation of science that weds it to a particular conception of an Enlightenment project. The point of science, as a sphere of human activity, has always been to overcome naïveté, rather than, for instance, to predict the course of objective reality. This vision of science must be discernable as the driving force of the historical development in which the phenomenologist stands. But the phenomenological-theoretical attitude is in no position to carry out the historical interpretation of which it makes use, let alone confront the difficulties, outlined above, that it involves.

The historical existence of theory and its epistemic ideals is an obvious background condition for phenomenological-theoretical work, and phenomenological reflection may explicitly allude to it in positing itself as philosophy. What remains unavailable in the projection of phenomenological theory is that this very projection implies an interpretation of scientific history, broadly and narrowly construed. The theorizing phenomenologist is the naïve representative of a historical worldview. We will call "ultimate presuppositions" those convictions that constitute this worldview. As we will see, they are realized when the very goal of philosophy becomes questionable in terms of its meaning for human life.

The appropriation of such presuppositions reconsiders phenomenology as a theoretical project in light of the historical interpretation implied by this self-understanding. The appropriating attitude is thus non-phenomenological in that it is directly concerned with the historical world; but it also depends upon the prior attainment of the phenomenological attitude and its concomitant devaluation of the natural attitude as naïve. If the integrity of phenomenological theory demands the appropriation of the ultimate presuppositions, then it demands a return to the history of natural-attitude life, not as neutralized or transcendentally apperceived but as the domain in which to win clarity of purpose about the life-significance of philosophy or universal science itself. We call "critical-historical" the attitude responsive to this task.

15. Critical-Historical Appropriation

The straightforward pursuit of phenomenology presupposes an interpretation of philosophical history in which the latter realizes *its* objectives by overcoming the naïveté of the natural attitude. Awakening to this presupposition is a meta-awakening. It realizes a naïve interpretation of natural-attitude naïveté. This awakening jeopardizes me as someone making sense of and participating in historical traditions, particularly those connected with "philosophy." The appropriative tasks called for here thus direct the ego back toward realities in the world of human culture and its unique historical present, in which first-personal responsibilities are at stake.

To confirm that philosophical history spans the natural and phenomenological attitudes, it is necessary to employ the form of appropriative reflection we earlier called teleological reconstruction (A § 10). The appropriative reflection on philosophy, however, belongs to a class of reflections to which we did not devote special attention. These are critical reflections that concern interpersonal and intergenerational accomplishments in which the reflecting ego is a participant. In such cases, the teleological reconstruction involves additional forms of interpretation.

The conviction that I cooperate with others always depends upon an interpretation of their actions and expressions. Such an interpretation is inherently fallible because deception, reticence, contextual differences, and sheer accident can lead to misunderstandings. When the others are only indirectly present through their works, there is the additional complication that I cannot refine the interpretation through direct dialogue. Ordinarily, established narratives mask the fragility of this situation. They allow for participation in historical tasks without a recovery of the past willful intentions that are embodied in documents and other works. However, it is also possible to execute actively the interpretations upon which such narratives are built. I can empathetically revitalize the goals of my predecessors on the basis of their works and orient myself toward these goals in the awareness that our shared tradition inevitably makes of me a carrier or miscarrier of their wills. The resulting criticism and appropriation of my predecessors does not arise from a comparison of my purposes with theirs, but from an emerging clarity about how my purposes *are* the continuance and transformation of theirs. This active communication of wills in the present can then motivate the construction of an optimally grounded teleological history, whether this coincides with or reforms established narratives.

This form of historical interpretation mediates the recognition of consuming interests that concealed what should have been noticed for the realization of the live, intergenerational objective. From the perspective of "historical objectivity," this leads to bad history. My historical appropriation will not understand predecessors as they understood themselves. Rather, I will criticize predecessors for not having seen what I myself claim they could not (in fact) have seen, but which they should have seen in order to reach the objective I have in view. This is unfair. However, our previous analysis has shown that I am equally unfair to myself in appropriating my own naïve life-phases. When I look into the naïve life-phase, I do not recount what I then experienced. I understand things from the enhanced scope of responsibility claimed in my awakening. The reconstruction is unfaithful to the past in order to be true to it. Furthermore, it will tend to construe my past naïveté as both inevitable and inexcusable. The explanation by way of consuming interests shows why what should have been noticed was in fact unnoticeable. When this kind of reconstruction involves a historical tradition, worries arise about understanding others in terms of oneself, the past in terms of the present. But this kind of understanding is just what the wakeful appropriation of naïveté requires.

Although it holds predecessors responsible for the presuppositions implied in their works, the critical-historical appropriation is ultimately concerned with reestablishing the integrity of the appropriating ego as a participant in an intersubjective project. It holds others responsible for their naïveté only in order to take responsibility for my own. The awakening has jeopardized me in my orientation toward an historically established goal. It is thus *my* historical interpretation that requires appropriation. The construction of a teleology in which the goals of philosophical history are fulfilled in the prospects of phenomenology aims primarily to rectify the naïveté of the practicing phenomenologist. The narrative and evaluative features of the appropriation are those proper to self-critique, not the attribution of unrealized presuppositions to others (A § 3). This is because, as the subject of the reflection, I understand the others in a "we" of which I am a responsible member.

The critical-historical appropriation is susceptible to its own illusions that we will consider in the second part of this study (IIA §§ 8–9). We can anticipate them in light of the general appropriative illusions outlined earlier (A § 11). The illusion of recollection here takes the form of irresponsible teleology. An irresponsibly teleological reconstruction attributes to naïve history of the power to wake itself up. The awakened subject that comprehends the development as oriented toward the fulfillment of the wakefully posited objective says: history requires this fulfillment. And this is true. The reconstructed tradition appears animated by a driving force that struggles to express itself through predecessors' works, and that only becomes a clear object of the will in the present resumption of the uprooted accomplishment. However, this dynamic appearance is founded upon the present need for a wakeful resumption of the uprooted accomplishment: to carry out this task with clarity of purpose, I require this historical self-understanding. The course of history was not the self-alienation of the wakeful subject's accomplishment. Rather, the wakeful subject has to recapitulate the history to which he belongs to gather himself in his commitment to an aim. Any "historical necessity" manifest in the reconstruction is a consequence of the wakeful annexation of naïveté, which always has available in the present what had to remain hidden in the past.

In critical-historical appropriation, the illusion of recollection coincides with the epistemic illusion. Every awakening jeopardizes me as the subject of an accomplishment that has importance or centrality in my life. Minimally,

I was handling a routine task at the periphery of my self-conception. Maximally, I was dedicating myself to a vocation I cannot let go while remaining who I am. An increased centrality of the uprooted accomplishment corresponds to an increased necessity that it be wakefully resumed. This is a "personal" necessity of remaining oriented toward ends that actualize certain values. The awakened ego is personally invested in the viability of the uprooted accomplishment. This investment already orients the ego in its reconstruction. Whereas historical necessity characterizes the successful reconstruction, personal necessity is the source of the imperative that it be successful. Where this imperative becomes categorical, as in the case of vocationally dedicated subjectivity, it is tempting to seek a guarantee by treating historical necessity as the object of disinterested contemplation. Rather than cultivate historical roots that support a freely affirmed personal necessity, irresponsible teleology avoids the existential trial and takes shelter in fatalism.

The pragmatic illusion here takes the form of wishful thinking. The teleological reconstruction is an exercise of epistemic authority by the awakened ego over a history dominated by presuppositions. Because of its access to consuming interests, it understands predecessors better than they understood themselves. Yet, the works through which it understands predecessors also indicate historical facts that in turn imply historical possibilities and necessities (e.g., what was written when and where by whom implies chronological and geographical limitations on possible influence). The authority of wakeful attention over naïve life lies in its ability to determine the truth of that life. It must adhere to and not evade the facts of "objective history." Facts are the material out of which a teleological reconstruction is formed. A disregard of this requirement undermines the integrity of the appropriation by divorcing success from wakeful accomplishment and indulging in mythmaking. Personal necessity is here a possible source of self-deception that would conceal wishful thinking from itself. The reconstruction must guard against wishful thinking and its tendency to become invisible. Its aim is to transform the sense of a living tradition. It fails if it is not guided by facts that contending interpretations can recognize as constituting the tradition itself.[29]

However, so long as the reconstruction has a foothold in facts, it is free to discover for itself which facts are important. For instance, the claim that the interest in reliable determinations of reality is an offshoot of a more fundamental objective at work in philosophical history—that of overcoming naïveté—need not maintain that this latter objective was pursued more often or with greater energy. Its minimal form is that the more fundamental objective was once discovered as more fundamental, and that subsequent history has the meaning of a superficialization or deviation. The decisive moments in the reconstruction would then be the original discovery and the first deviation. A preponderance of evidence that the superficial interpretation has in fact carried the day would not speak against the reconstruction of a more profound history one is called to carry forward. Selectivity is dangerous only when the activity of selection and the interests driving it are concealed. This concealment, some motives for which we have already addressed, especially plagues reconstructions that coincide with established narratives. There is no such thing as an "objectively important" historical fact. The semblance of such facts indicates a failure to appropriate established narratives.

Finally, it is an illusion of false modesty to regard the results of the critical-historical appropriation as of merely local significance just because they too are "in history." According to this view, as soon as a history is meaningful as ours, it inevitably has its full meaning outside of itself in the broader development to which it belongs, but which it cannot comprehend. This applies also to the significance of the objectives the critical-historical appropriation promotes. The objectives matter only for participants in a particular cultural tradition. To think otherwise is a symptom of provincialism. There are, of course, many historical reflections for which this is a fitting description. The illusion that one knows that it describes all historical reflections obscures the very possibility of an Enlightenment project, as well as the special problems that arise precisely because such a project, if it exists, is also of local significance.

16. The History of Philosophy and Philosophical History

The historical appropriation of the Enlightenment project concerns two histories. The first is the history of philosophy as expressed in works. In these works, the appropriation aims to reconstruct a frustrated aspiration toward the phenomenological conversion of philosophy. Each work decisive in this history opens up possibilities for future thinking that point toward a phenomenological culmination, but fails to realize this culmination itself because of consuming interests that shaped the intellectual situation. While it is from the outset clear that these consuming interests are rooted in the fundamental interest of the natural attitude, the reconstruction is concerned with the concrete ways that this interest has shaped the attempt to think philosophically. It wants to understand those particular restrictions that explain why a given author was unable to advert freely to everything relevant to his theoretical work as seen from the present, wakeful perspective. Through historical influence, the accomplishments of one author become the starting point or object of criticism for another. Each predecessor thus earns a place in history because of what he was and was not able to do for philosophy.

The appropriative reflection regards philosophy as a kind of work undertaken in the midst of the human world, and the phenomenological attitude as a "vocational attitude" correlated to this work. When Husserl uses this term, he means to emphasize that the attitude fits into one's broader personal life as a habitually exercised focus that provides continual access to a particular field of activity. In this limited respect, the phenomenological attitude is perfectly analogous to the attitude of the architect or the police officer. Every such practice has a distinct significance for the life of the community in which it persists as an intergenerational cultural form. If phenomenological awakening heralds a transformation of the philosophical-scientific tradition, it concerns the whole cultural life in which this tradition persists. The focus on the history of philosophy is an abstraction from philosophical history.

At this level, the appropriative reflection aims to develop a historical sense of who "we" are who stand committed to an Enlightenment project centered on science and philosophy. A community that answers to this description will have emerged through remarkable transformations that introduced new forms of life into human history, forms oriented by concepts of truth and being initially unavailable in world-directed life. The appropriation has to reconstruct these transformations in a way that shows not only that they are historically possible but also that they actually occurred to a definite people or peoples under definite circumstances and that their effects reach into the present. By way of a plausible narrative, it offers an invitation to identify with this community and the tasks that define it. In identifying with this community, "we" become responsible for the Enlightenment project. We become heirs of a history that has endangered this project by discovering and pursuing it in transcendental naïveté. But we also become the subjects of its possible vindication through a wakeful transformation of its sense.[30]

17. Crisis and Hope

"Crisis" is Husserl's name for what these reflections on philosophical history are about. The second part of this study will examine the crisis closely. We can already offer a tentative definition in light of our general reflections. A crisis is a predicament characterized by two features. First, the uprooted project is a calling to which one has dedicated oneself, that is, it is so central that it cannot be abandoned without betraying oneself. Second, despite the obscurities caused by a history of naïveté, the project is accomplishable if transformed from a wakeful perspective. The disclosure of crisis is the *goal* of the appropriation of philosophical history. It is worth recalling that Husserl begins the *Crisis* by acknowledging that for an audience assembled in a place "dedicated [*gewidmeten*] to the sciences" the claim that the sciences are in crisis risks seeming ridiculous (1970, 3/1; also 1993, 103). This is because many of the sciences have become quite effective at realizing epistemic and cultural goals within the constraints of the natural attitude. Whatever the degree of success enjoyed by the sciences, it belongs to phenomenology's basic historical situation that "the point" of science will have been traditionally understood in transcendental naïveté.

To show that there is a crisis, the reflections will have to unseat established narratives that construe the progress of science and scientific culture with respect to transcendentally naïve ideals. The kind of progress envisioned here (overcoming superstition, predicting and controlling the course of nature, distinguishing between subjective seeming and real being, etc.) is really progress. The reflections will have to show that "our" pursuit of such progress springs from a deeper commitment to an Enlightenment project that such progress alone cannot bring to fruition. To think along with the reflections is to transform one's sense of what is at stake in the history to which one belongs. Being "dedicated" to scientific culture will now require confronting a situation in which its loftiest goals are put at risk.

At a minimum, a crisis is a situation that is not entirely hopeless. If there is a crisis, revealing it is thus an effective bulwark against despair. According to Husserl's formula, the teleological reconstruction is what "we" who need to believe in "our" vocational commitment must do in order to be able to believe. Equally, a crisis is a situation in which the viability of "our" commitments is threatened. If there is a crisis, revealing it is thus an effective bulwark against complacency. The success of science and scientific culture is dangerous because it conceals the aspirations with respect to which it is a failure. Being able to believe also means not being satisfied with false consolations. A responsible teleology aims at clarity of purpose. History does nothing for us; it only charges us with responsibilities.

This way of sustaining commitment to an endangered Enlightenment project is a non-discretional use of the transcendental apperception through which the phenomenologically awakened subject understands natural-attitude life. The continued pursuit of this project, if it is indeed in effect, is impossible under natural-attitude constraints and becomes possible again only through a wakeful appropriation of its naïve history. The discovery of this transformative significance of phenomenological awakening is in no way idiosyncratic. However, it does not lack personal significance for the phenomenologist. In fact, the life situation toward which the phenomenologist is obliged to have an effective life attitude is the crisis, considered in all of its ramifications (A § 11). Within human history, there is a philosophical history, the decisive events of which shape the world in which she comes to understand "the point" of her theoretical work. As with all life attitudes, the judgments that articulate the situation to which it pertains are rooted in the personal commitments of the judger, and so stand open to the appropriative ideals of worldliness and authenticity.

18. Phenomenological and Critical-Historical Appropriation

The relationship between phenomenological-theoretical work and critical-historical appropriation invites skepticism about philosophy itself as a systematic inquiry oriented toward maximal wakefulness. The phenomenological-theoretical attitude is historically naïve. However, the appropriation of this naïveté requires taking transcendentally naïve positions, which themselves require phenomenological appropriation. The second part of this study will turn to Husserl's crisis writings to show that this reciprocal relationship between attitudes is not only harmless but also gives a systematic finish to philosophy. For now, we can dispose of certain misunderstandings that would obstruct our investigation.

First, the historical naïveté of the phenomenological-theoretical attitude does not prevent it from securing and exploring its own, proper theme. The history of philosophy is simply not something that the phenomenologist needs to know in order to reflect on transcendental life. However else historical understanding may aid the phenomenologist, it cannot function as a source of phenomenological evidence. Neither does following a historical narrative first open the phenomenological domain by force of its internal coherence. Historical understanding becomes *necessary* to phenomenology only when it seeks to overcome naïveté about the *Lebensbedeutsamkeit* of an already available method for discovering theoretical truths. Recognizing the necessity of critical-historical appropriation does not entail any compromise with historicism.

Second, the critical-historical appropriation does not respond to an exigency that confronts phenomenology from the outside. The idea of a phenomenological philosophy is problematic because of the way natural-attitude interests have shaped philosophical history. This situation is inherent to the historical emergence of phenomenology and need not result from particularly exacerbating circumstances. The assumption that the crisis is an especially bad state of historical affairs that elicits engagement from an otherwise aloof philosophy implies one of two things. Either there is a ready application of phenomenological-theoretical findings to social emergencies or else phenomenology utilizes social emergencies to harness the pathos of urgency for its own purposes. The first notion is patently absurd given the nature of phenomenological subject matter. The second notion is belied by Husserl's statements about the methodological importance of the critical-historical reflections. We will develop the view that phenomenology is driven to its crisis interpretation by philosophical motives. As external exigency, "crisis" can only be the occasion for the realization of the historical viewpoint presupposed in the phenomenological-theoretical attitude. The appropriation of this viewpoint will reveal that the crisis arises *within* the Enlightenment project in which phenomenology itself participates. Not only is crisis interpretation carried out in pursuit of philosophical motives but the crisis itself, if it exists, is a moment of a history that is philosophical.

Finally, it is true that the critical-historical reflections are ultimately world-directed, not transcendental. There are two reasons this mundane focus does not undermine the project of phenomenological philosophy. Once transcendental life has been discovered as a theme for ongoing reflections, it counts as "the only absolute concretion" (1973b, 84/117). The human world is understandable as what it is in transcendental reflections, whereas the transcendental domain is not understandable as what it is in world-directed reflections. This is a matter of principle independent of psychological facts about attention. As a subjective rule of method, the phenomenological epoché is already "complete" when it prevents my using natural theses as theoretical premises. It does not require a totalization of phenomenological attention.[31] Even though the historical understanding won through appropriation enters into a background awareness failing which the phenomenologist's theoretical work would be naïve, it does not undermine the absolute nature of the field engaged by that work.

Phenomenological reflection can also convert into constitutive themes everything involved in the conviction that phenomenology is important for philosophical history. However, this kind of reflection cannot provide the sort of clarity required in the face of the ultimate presuppositions. This has implications for the presentation of critical-historical appropriation in a philosophical system. A phenomenological reflection on the very possibility of critical-historical appropriation would not actually appropriate the presuppositions operative in the phenomenological-theoretical attitude. It would achieve theoretical clarity without clarifying the historical sense of purpose naively invoked by interpreting phenomenology as philosophy. Therefore, a systematic presentation of philosophy should actually perform the critical-historical appropriation against the historical background available to the phenomenologist. This means that it will project the theoretical tasks of phenomenology in light of a crisis.

Part Two

The Crisis Problematic

In the first part of this study, we outlined a framework for understanding presuppositions as they become evident in the natural, phenomenological, and critical-historical attitudes. We concluded by considering what is involved in appropriating the "ultimate presuppositions" that place phenomenology in a philosophical history. In the second part, we will examine how Husserl understood and tried to appropriate these ultimate presuppositions. We will present Husserl's crisis writings as an exemplary engagement with this sphere of problems, which we will term the "crisis problematic." Because the crisis problematic requires the phenomenologist to attempt an historical interpretation of his own contingent situation, it can seem to be of primarily biographical significance. In the case of Husserl, perhaps, it would offer a glimpse of a recognizable man at work behind a relentlessly rigorous procedure of reflection. The humanist may even find here a confession that, all told, it is finally the familiar world of politics, economy, and culture ("Germany between the wars") that concerns the philosopher, despite his abstractions. We make a distinction, though, between a philosopher's interpreting his situation and his attempt to claim for that interpretation a systematic importance. Indulging biographical and historical curiosity can obscure that systematic importance. As the domain of ultimate presuppositions, the crisis problematic is of abiding interest for phenomenological philosophy. By viewing Husserl's crisis writings in terms of a problematic in which they claim a position, we can highlight their properly philosophical significance while making room for competing positions.

Division A

Husserl and the Ultimate Presuppositions

1. The Idea of an Independent Introduction

In his final attempted treatise,[1] Husserl incorporates the appropriation of the ultimate presuppositions into a systematic presentation of phenomenology. The *Crisis* discovers the phenomenological-theoretical field in the context of sweeping teleological-historical reflections. These reflections aim to establish that a phenomenological reorientation of philosophy is a practical necessity. They operate in the two dimensions of appropriation outlined in part one of this study (IB § 16). First, a reconstruction of modern thought since Galileo aims to show that the project of universal science has faltered because of paradoxes in the understanding of subjectivity that only phenomenology can resolve. Second, a reconstruction of European history aims to show that the phenomenological conversion of philosophy will revitalize a civilization that has become unable to believe in its defining mission.

From a perspective concerned solely with theoretical certainty, the historical reflections are unnecessary and unhelpful.[2] They burden a phenomenological-theoretical method with contestable claims that have no bearing on that method's proper subject matter. However, this perspective restricts the maxim of wakefulness to one privileged form of evidence. To neglect the wakeful appropriation of what one is doing because it involves one in uncertainties is to fall prey to the epistemic illusion (IA § 11). It does not appear that Husserl made this mistake. His express view was that the historical-teleological approach of the *Crisis* addresses a form of naïveté impervious to the methods that discover consciousness as the domain suitable for universal, grounding science. This naïveté consists in presupposing that it makes sense to understand phenomenology as an appropriation of the goals that define philosophy as a sphere of human endeavor. It is because the *Crisis* would thematize and critically assess this understanding that it could stand on its own as an introduction to phenomenological philosophy.[3] Husserl preferred the *Crisis* to his other introductory works precisely because it wrestles with the ultimate presuppositions.

This is made clear in *Teleologie in der Philosophiegeschichte*, a 1937 essay in which Husserl explicitly discusses the ultimate presuppositions. Let us briefly outline the import of this discussion. The ultimate presuppositions (*die letzte Voraussetzungen*), Husserl says, will dominate philosophical work as long as one has not radically questioned philosophy itself as an operative working goal: "das Ziel 'Philosophie selbst' ... radikal in Frage zu Stellen" (1993, 383–4). This questioning does not wonder whether phenomenological knowledge is possible. It is rather like the reflection a worker might pursue when, sure that his tools, methods, and skills can get the job done, he wonders about the true purpose of his work, about "the point of it" in terms of personal and interpersonal interests. Accordingly, Husserl's statement that, failing the resolution such questioning might provide, phenomenological methods may prove futile (387) does not concern their epistemic soundness. It concerns the relevance of phenomenological work to a live objective: philosophy. These reflections consider philosophy as a vocation integrated into a network of human interests.[4] The question of phenomenology's futility is thus historical in nature. Does the realization and appropriation of transcendental naïveté jeopardize and transform the "philosophical" objectives of humanity or does it rather abandon the ground upon which knowledge serves human interests? The responsible phenomenologist is obliged to appropriate the presupposition of those historical conditions that make former alternative possible. This appropriation requires that we intervene in our history in order to transform it into a teleology: "wir müssen in unsere Geschichte eingreifen um sie zu eine Teleologie zu machen" (397).

These reflections are meant to justify the historical-teleological approach to phenomenology as presented in the already published parts of the *Crisis*. Husserl claims that this approach is more principled and systematic than those taken in his earlier introductions to phenomenology, particularly *Ideas I* (1993, 426). However, if confronting the ultimate presuppositions means reflecting on phenomenology's relationship to philosophy as a working goal, this hardly warrants privileging the *Crisis*. Throughout his lifework, Husserl developed many strategies for negotiating phenomenology's relationship to the task of philosophy, or universal, grounding science. Why are these strategies naïve from the standpoint of the awakening to the ultimate presuppositions?

2. From Philosophical Epoché to Historical Intervention

We can address this question by comparing Husserl's final approach to philosophy as a working goal to others he had previously taken. Without claiming to be exhaustive, we will consider four kinds of approach. The first shows that a prohibition against using or rejecting theoretical results won in the natural attitude is required in order to discover the phenomenological domain, in which theory is *also* possible. The second argues that this prohibition and shift in attitude are *demanded* by the goal of theory itself. The third proposes to *derive* this demand from a reflection on the nature of scientific activity. The fourth accomplishes this derivation through an *intervention* in philosophical history that transforms it into a teleology.

The first kind of approach appears throughout the career of Husserl's transcendental phenomenology. Here is a synopsis: If I am to leave alone all mundane beings and the system of reality in which they are arranged, I must also abstain from passing judgment on all extant theoretical assertions about them. This is simply because phenomenology is not concerned with the reality that world-directed science opposes to subjectivity. An epoché of world-directed science is thus a prudent step toward establishing and fixing the phenomenological attitude. At this point, Husserl anticipates the objection that there is nothing to study in the phenomenological attitude. If the entire world is off-limits to judgment, is there anything to accomplish scientifically besides repeating the single proposition "*cogito*"? Husserl answers by demonstrating that pure consciousness also admits of scientific treatment of a recognizable kind. In the phenomenological domain too, there are diverse species and hierarchies of species, essential laws, wholes analyzable into parts, and so on. To discover these, and to express them systematically, is an ongoing theoretical task.

This is an argument that a familiar form of theoretical discipline is possible once the domain traditionally engaged by theoretical interest has been placed off-limits. It is necessary to place it off-limits because of what the phenomenological attitude demands. In the second kind of approach, the relationship of necessitation is reversed. A familiar form of theoretical discipline now requires the practicing phenomenologist to abide by certain principles that ensure phenomenology's independence from existing theory.

The paradigmatic case of this second approach is *Ideas I*. Husserl here explicitly understands the suspension of the natural attitude as a means to discovering a new scientific domain. In fact, he presents the method of suspension as linking up with an essential moment in Descartes' procedure of universal doubt in the service of first philosophy (§ 31). The question raised by this approach is whether it introduces an element of historical dependence into basic phenomenological methods. Does the possibility of phenomenological suspension depend upon previous advances in the history of philosophy? Husserl guards against such dependence by adhering to two rules: the philosophical epoché and the principle of all principles. The former simply states that the phenomenologist shall take no interest in evaluating the content of past philosophy (§ 18). Above all, he will not appeal to any finding of past philosophy as a premise in any argument (§ 30). The principle of all principles is the positive complement to the philosophical epoché. It asserts that the only legitimate source of justification for knowledge claims, especially those concerning scientific principles, is what is originally present to the investigator. When a claim is grounded in this fashion, it counts as an absolute beginning (§ 24). These two rules allow for an independent engagement with philosophical history. For instance, Husserl treats Cartesian doubt as the instantiation of an essential kind of experience. Facts about what Descartes actually did are irrelevant to the development of the method of phenomenological suspension. All that matters is that I can attempt to doubt and can reflect on what this attempt entails.

It is noteworthy that Husserl develops this methodological policy as a response to the requirements of "genuine science" as characterized by the absence of bias (§ 19). This means that while the philosophical epoché enforces independence from previous philosophical doctrine, certain ideals animating the project of philosophy remain in effect; even the absolute beginnings afforded by the principle of principles, as well as the principle itself, respond to them. Husserl is aware of this obvious fact and draws attention to it repeatedly. This second kind of approach to philosophy as an operative working goal simply does not find in this obvious fact any problems requiring examination.

The third approach draws a distinction between relying on existing doctrine and taking up the aim of genuine science and then explicitly confronts the problem of how to appropriate this aim. This approach is epitomized in the line of thought expressed in the *Cartesian Meditations*. Husserl's solution to the appropriative problem utilizes a method that was not needed in the first and second approaches. Roughly: I adhere to the philosophical epoché and take no interest in the truth of any scientific theory of which I am aware. But I am free to think myself into the kind of intellectual effort indicated by these theories and to clarify the special kind of convictions at which it aims by virtue of being scientific, rather than journalistic, legal, political, or everyday-pragmatic. This will present me with the "final idea" that animates scientific practice, of which I can articulate the essential moments (§ 4). Husserl now derives the principle of all principles from a reflection on this final idea (§ 5). This derivation depends upon the premise that actually existing science is basically "Cartesian" in its aspirations: that it is guided by the ideals of absolutely grounded judgments and perfect evidence. Husserl makes use of a generally agreed upon concept of genuine science to which the assessment of actual sciences appeals.

What is the status of this assertion about the character of genuine science? Husserl has science in view here as a cultural practice. What such practices are really all about is a matter of contestation within the tradition of the practice. In light of ongoing experience, members of the community for whom the practice is meaningful engage in critical reflections that revise its governing norms. For instance, a dispute about whether pitch clocks accord with the essence of baseball is only resolvable by looking to the history of baseball as embodying and shaping norms. There is no access to what "genuine baseball" might be outside of this history. At certain decisive moments in the development of a practice, one deliberates over its history in order to discern what it is really all about and brings some developmental tendencies to fulfillment at the expense of others. When ideals lose purchase on actual praxis, their persistence as ideas does not alter the fact that the practice has turned away from them. The game, one says, has changed. So too, it would seem possible that science is "genuine" insofar as it provides reliable, useful predictions. However, the historical contestability of genuine science does not interest the third approach.[5]

The fourth approach directly engages in the historical contest over genuine science. It presents science as a tradition, the genuine sense of which is exposed to betrayal in the present. In taking over philosophy as a working goal, phenomenology wants to aid in the resolution of a crisis. This approach is already foreshadowed in *Philosophy as Rigorous Science*, employed in *Formal and Transcendental Logic*, foregrounded in the writings leading up to and including the *Crisis* and justified in *Teleologie in der Philosophiegeschichte*. It considers science, not only as a kind of activity, but primarily as the concrete development through which this kind of activity has been practiced. Figures in the scientific tradition do not instantiate pure possibilities for thinking as they do in the second approach. They rather author historically determined projects aimed at definite ends, which open up and close off definite possibilities for their successors.

This fourth approach is an exercise of historical responsibility. It seeks to show not only that the research program of phenomenology instantiates a kind of ideal-oriented activity but also that it fulfills the will of those particular predecessors who have struggled to achieve genuine philosophy in the past. To show this, it delves into the development of the tradition, explicating its implicit intentions and critiquing them in view of phenomenological principles. Pernicious and promising trajectories are discerned and traced into the present. The result is not a comparison of phenomenology with other positions in the history of philosophy, but the awareness that phenomenology is a transformation of the tradition that rescues it from betrayal. The reflection effectively makes philosophical history into a teleology that culminates in phenomenology.

How should we compare these various approaches to philosophy as a working goal? Our proposal is that all four are compatible, but that we would overlook the peculiarity of the fourth approach by assuming that it does better the very same thing that the others aim to do. The first three approaches demonstrate that the appropriation of the natural attitude is a scientific task. Because phenomenology frames its subject matter quite differently than natural-attitude life and science, it is not obvious that there is a phenomenological field of inquiry; this field has to be illuminated. Further, the scientific rigor of this inquiry is not immediately apparent because it cannot assimilate methods or concepts of natural-attitude science; it has to be demonstrated by appeal to general epistemic ideals that animate science as such. Among these ideals is the resolve to assert only what one sees for oneself, rather than what tradition prescribes. The first three approaches address these matters. However, only the fourth aims to appropriate the ultimate presuppositions. Only the fourth approach responds to the realization that the sense of phenomenological-theoretical work depends upon one's participation in a certain sort of history. The teleological reconstruction justifies the belief that one does.

3. Philosophical Epoché versus Historical Intervention

We will now develop the thesis that the teleological intervention in history has a different aim than the other approaches to philosophy as a working goal. In several interpretations of the *Crisis*, Carr has advanced the view that the primary aim of the teleological-historical reflections is to accomplish the philosophical epoché more rigorously than was previously possible. Our thesis can be refined by way of contrast with Carr's view.[6]

In *Ideas I* § 18, Husserl announces the philosophical epoché as a policy already in effect. Carr understands the historical reflections of the *Crisis* as the method for arriving at this policy as a legitimate result. In his *Translator's Introduction* to the *Crisis*, he proposes that "Husserl's entire treatment of the *facts* of Western philosophy could be seen as an attempt to accomplish what he *thought*, in the *Ideen*, had been done in one sentence" (1970, xxxviii). Because philosophical interests develop within the orientation provided by a historical tradition, it is facile to claim independence from that tradition simply by suspending interest in what it teaches. Instead, one must pursue an independent relation to the history of philosophy precisely by making explicit that history's orienting power. In *Phenomenology and the Problem of History*, Carr argues that such thoughts lead Husserl to a hermeneutical approach that would "overcome the historical prejudices of consciousness, which, no less than the natural ones, prevent the philosopher from grasping the *Sachen selbst*" (1974, 186–7). This method, which Carr calls the "historical reduction," overcomes the weight of history, not through a willful disinterest, but through a "reliving of our philosophical prejudices, a repetition of the philosophical *Selbstverständlichkeiten* under which we turn to philosophy in the first place" (117). For Carr, this new reduction is the methodological core of Husserl's final treatise: "the *Crisis* is essentially the construction of a history which reflects the philosopher's own philosophical prejudices for purposes of overcoming those very prejudices" (1987, 90).

It is important to emphasize that the historical reduction targets the context that shapes the theoretical concerns of the individual philosopher. The method, writes Carr, "aims precisely at the particular configuration of historical-cultural prejudices peculiar to the philosopher and his own age" (1974, 264). These are the prejudices that, failing a critical appropriation, render philosophical work provincial. They make it obvious which problems, concepts, methods, and results are controversial or settled, interesting or uninteresting, promising or exhausted. Participating in this obviousness, the philosopher is released from having to make these determinations himself. Whatever he accomplishes in this way, however brilliant, is theoretically irresponsible. The question is whether the historical approach of the *Crisis* is best understood as enabling the phenomenologist to overcome such prejudices.

Husserl is clearly interested in how his philosophical predecessors were blinded by historical prejudices. In the historical sections of the *Crisis*, he considers how canonical thinkers inherited convictions they could not (in fact) think about because they were preoccupied with what these convictions made relevant. Although such presuppositions had to remain hidden at the time, in attending to them we understand the limits that define each philosopher's true place in the historical development (1970, 53/54, 75/77). It would seem that reflecting on how these presuppositions have shaped the history of philosophy could also reveal how the practicing phenomenologist is captive to the prejudices of his own context. The problems, concepts, methods, and results with which he works belong to the very history upon which he reflects.[7]

However, Husserl only undertakes his critique of past philosophers because he does not think he belongs to history in the same way they did. Husserl regards himself as having accomplished the final establishment (*Endstiftung*) of philosophy. The practicing philosopher no longer has to wait upon future historians of ideas to clarify what he really understood. He has this clarity for himself in the form of an "apodictic method which, in every step of achievement, is a constant avenue to new steps having the character of absolute success, i.e. the character of apodictic steps. At this point philosophy, as an infinite task, would have arrived at its apodictic beginning" (1970, 72/73–4). It is precisely because Husserl thinks his phenomenological-theoretical lifework has developed this method that he invests his historical reflections with a special epistemic authority. When Husserl asserts that the final establishment allows us "to understand past thinkers in a way they never could have understood themselves" (73/74), he is not relying upon the retrospective advantage that any present has over its past. He is relying upon the apodicticity of phenomenological wakefulness. We see, then, that Husserl does not regard the historical reflections as enabling the discovery of an unbiased philosophical method for grasping the *Sachen selbst*. Instead, the possession of that method calls for a definitive account of the philosophical past.[8]

The purpose of Husserl's historical reflections becomes apparent when we distinguish between two sorts of presuppositions in philosophical practice. On the one hand, there are those particular ideas the philosopher unthinkingly inherits from his tradition. On the other hand, there are those "ultimate presuppositions" operative in the belief that philosophy is a coherent task at all. Husserl describes these latter presuppositions in *Teleologie in der Philosophiegeschichte* by noting that the rational will to pursue philosophy depends upon having discerned the "original sense-giving motives" that determine the point of philosophy for human life, and that confer upon it a purposive unity underlying conflicting philosophical systems (1993, 374). If the unity of the philosophical task has not been discerned, every problem, concept, method and truth that counts as "philosophical" is futile, no matter how rooted in original evidence.[9] The historical reflections of the *Crisis* aim to appropriate the phenomenologist's own naïve pursuit of philosophy as a goal. The critique of traditional prejudices in past philosophy is not animated by the worry that these prejudices might cloud phenomenological vision. It is animated by the need for a history that supports commitments the awakened subject can affirm as his own.

History is relevant to the appropriative reflection at the ultimate level, not primarily as a source of unsubstantiated convictions that threaten to disburden theoretical insight, but rather as a source of purposive clarity about philosophy as a vocation. This does not settle the matter, however, of whether and how a method like Carr's historical reduction counteracts historical prejudices that prevent one from grasping the subject matter of phenomenological-theoretical work. This is an important and difficult issue for phenomenology. We here offer only a few indications.

Working through a history of the philosophical present cannot enable a "grasp of the *Sachen selbst*" if this means facilitating the original attainment of the phenomenological attitude. In the natural attitude, working through history can illuminate the locality of one's orientation in the world. This also applies to the history of those specialized worlds that orient particular practices. But such historical reflections derive their critical power from the fundamental world-directedness of the natural attitude. They overcome provinciality by locating world-contexts within the wider world they occlude in accommodating routines. The vista that opens to the worldly person does so through the transcendental naïveté in which world and world-context are first of all there. The ideal of worldliness actually bars access to the phenomenological attitude if it underwrites the dogmatic view that the interplay between world and world-context is the source of all awakening.

However, if "grasping" the *Sachen selbst* means describing what is given in phenomenological reflection, then historical prejudices can pose problems. Phenomenological-theoretical work inevitably takes over a natural language or languages and the conceptuality of an established theoretical tradition. By no means does this inheritance stand between phenomenological cognition and its object like a screen. Instead, the phenomenological conversion of natural language and conceptuality exploits their expressive power. All the same, there are multiple true descriptions of a given structure of transcendental life. By interacting with natural languages and conceptualities in singular ways, each sets into relief different aspects of reduced phenomena. The routinization of particular concepts and descriptions impoverishes what can be seen phenomenologically. Phenomena are presumed to "fall under" descriptions readily available in established terminology. A historical reduction that targets this routinization shows that descriptions first articulate what seems to fall under them and that they are always articulable otherwise.[10] This effectively restores the expressive endeavors underlying norms of usage (IB § 3).

Exploring the history of theoretical problems may also alert the phenomenologist to how certain conceptual frameworks are bound to the limitations of the natural attitude. For example, the empiricist approach to consciousness explains memory by means of a present datum that gets interpreted as past. If I study this approach critically, I can see that this present datum is required by the general natural-attitude conviction that experience is a mundane event. When I investigate memory from a phenomenological standpoint, I can now guard against the expectation that I should find a present image-datum, an expectation fueled by everyday descriptions of memory as well as the authority of empiricist theories. Although the historical reduction serves this precautionary function and may help explain mistakes retrospectively, it does not settle any philosophical issue. The question of how memory represents the past is answered strictly on the basis of what is given to phenomenological reflection.

Finally, though, we may even acknowledge that what is given to phenomenological reflection is itself obscure failing a historical critique. Aldea (2016) makes an interesting proposal along these lines. She draws attention to the "modal potency" of types, their ability to project "entire systems of conceivable possibilities" (32). This potency is not undone by moving from the natural to the phenomenological attitude and is indeed relied upon in the methods of variation that aim to discern transcendental eidetic structures. The arbitrariness of the example that supports an eidetic insight must be established across typical epistemic styles (37). This, in turn, requires historical reflections that expose "covert epistemic and normative transfers" (29).

Husserl preferred to contrast the directness of phenomenological seeing with historical research rather than extol the benefits of a method like the historical reduction. He was right to worry that a focus on history can create the illusion that its authority eclipses that of intuition. However, confined to its supporting role, historical reduction only enhances the rigor of the philosophical epoché. According to the above classification, it fits into the second approach to philosophy as a working goal and its concern with securing the independence of phenomenological judgment.[11] There may be many ways to employ historical reflections for this purpose. The fact remains that the historical reflections of the *Crisis* have an entirely different aim. Husserl expresses this aim plainly in the foreword to the published sections: to ground the necessity of a phenomenological reorientation of philosophy. Insight into this necessity is based in the clear awareness of crisis.

4. The Inevitability of Crisis

The crisis interpretation aims to show (1) that ramified projects in philosophical history have been uprooted by their transcendental naïveté and (2) that these projects are nevertheless accomplishable through phenomenological transformations. Whether this situation exists is a historical question. It requires an experience of jeopardy in a dedicated community and a devaluation of the natural attitude as inhibiting the attainment of objectives first established in that attitude. The appropriative reflections can demonstrate that these conditions hold only by interpreting the historical background available in the present. Even if the crisis exists, whether it continues to exist is also a historical question. There are two ways for the crisis to end. Either the project is wakefully appropriated or else appropriation becomes practically impossible because the objectives that would require the phenomenological transformation of the project have ceased to animate it in practice. When reflecting on the crisis at its most encompassing level, Husserl recognizes these two possibilities: "there are only two escapes from the crisis" (1970, 299/347). However, the multivalent nature of the term "crisis" in the *Crisis* has encouraged the view that the crisis is inevitable, permanent, or otherwise irresolvable.

We can address this interpretive difficulty by fixing a concept of crisis that distinguishes it from two other kinds of scientific deficiency that concern Husserl throughout the *Crisis*. These latter forms of deficiency cause science to fall short of theoretical ideals that characterize genuine science on Husserl's understanding. They are thus forms of "unscientificity" (*Unwissenschaftlichkeit*). Following Husserl's general usage, we term them "meaning-emptying" (*Sinnentleerung*) and "objectivism" (*Objektivismus*). The first from of unscientificity is inevitable for any actually existing science. The second form of unscientificity results from transcendental naïveté and motivates the crisis. However, we do best not to identify either form of unscientificity with the crisis of science itself.[12] These distinctions will allow for a definition of crisis that highlights the function and content of Husserl's appropriative concepts.

The unavoidable features of unscientificity arise because science is a historical tradition. In various places, Husserl reflects on how progress in scientific thinking depends upon practices that allow and even require this thinking to lose touch with itself. For instance, no thought is available to an endlessly open scientific community without its being documented. But documented thoughts can be referred to and relied upon without being thought through again. Addressing a complex problem requires making use of methods as mere techniques, that is, without clarifying why the method is legitimate. In general, the traditionality of science means that it necessarily operates at a distance from the intuitive sources that justify its procedures and results. Scientific integrity only demands clarifying the closing of this distance as possible in principle. In explaining why this clarification has itself become impossible (in fact), Husserl has recourse to objectivism, a form of naïveté rooted in the consuming interest of the natural attitude.

Objectivism arises from the attempt to understand and pursue the highest aims of science in light of the problematic conception of subjectivity that governs mundane life (IB § 1). It is inevitable only in the sense that appropriative reflections can explain why it had to result from consuming interests functioning within a tradition. Objectivism places true reality, the universe of what is, beyond the seeming to be that characterizes subjective perspectives. Theoretical reason invents and executes ways to transcend these perspectives and reach the world that is identical for everyone. Within this theoretical framework, the subjective life in and through which domains of reality are constituted is inaccessible and presupposed. With this presupposition at its disposal, Husserl's teleological reconstruction treats objectivism as a fateful prejudice from which phenomenology finally liberates the philosophical tradition. Freed from the objectivism that concealed objectivity as an accomplishment, theoretical rationality can assume responsibility for the thoughtlessness that facilitates its functionality and clarify the intuitive sources of its field-defining concepts.

Husserl begins *Crisis* § 1 by equating the crisis of science with a lapse in scientificity. However, he quickly effects a "change in the whole direction of inquiry" so that the topic of scientific crisis encompasses *the motives* "for subjecting the scientific character [*Wissenschaftlichkeit*] of all sciences to a serious and quite necessary critique" (1970, 5/3). Why should the scientific character of the sciences be a matter of such gravity? The motives for thinking it so concern the "role ascribed to the sciences" in "our culture" (ibid.). In particular, they concern a wavering of faith that science can fulfill this role. Objectivism and the consequent concealment and exacerbation of *Sinnentleerung* are developments internal to science that explain the emergence of this crisis. But the crisis itself is the distress of no longer being able to believe that science has a certain significance or importance for human life. According to Husserl's heading for *Crisis* § 2, the crisis of science is the loss of this *Lebensbedeutsamkeit*.[13]

On this definition, the crisis is resolved if the phenomenological transformation of *Wissenschaftlichkeit* restores the belief that science might fulfill its "ascribed role" and thereby enable a certain type of culture. Husserl envisions this role as facilitating a praxis of "universal critique," the aim of which is to "transform [humanity] from the bottom up into a new humanity capable of absolute self-responsibility on the basis of absolute theoretical insights" (1970, 283). Universal critique is no more reducible to philosophy than the human body is to the brain.

As we will see in upcoming sections (IIB §§ 7–9), it encompasses the whole cooperative effort to build and sustain a culture that promotes the exercise of basic integrity in all its dimensions. Philosophy, as universal science, would vindicate such a culture through the ongoing demonstration that humanity *is* capable of absolute self-responsibility, that humanity is wakeful, responsible for what is, not just what seems to be. In a text from 1930, Husserl describes the cultural work of a phenomenology that "clarifies, substantiates, [and] absolutely secures absolute autonomy" (2014a, 440).

The *Lebensbedeutsamkeit* of science derives from this projected function in a culture of universal critique. It is because objectivistic science cannot satisfy this function that it provokes a crisis—a wavering of faith in this meaning. The crisis concept thus includes reference to a historical vision of science as integral to an Enlightenment project, a vision still in effect for a community dedicated to it. For every uprooted project, Husserl's crisis interpretation invokes a "we" who cannot let it go. This imperative to continue the project is irreducible to the imperative to find an imperative to continue the project. The appropriative reflections must actually discern a historical development in which "our" culture requires this service of science: "theoria (universal science), arising within a closed unity and under the epoché of all praxis, is called (and in theoretical insight itself exhibits its calling) to serve mankind in a new way ... This occurs in the form of a new sort of praxis, that of the universal critique of all life and all life-goals" (1970, 283/329). Husserl seems to think that it is practically impossible to give up on one's dedication to philosophy and philosophical culture (1993, 400, 410; 1989, 243). This is consonant with Kant's claim in the *Anthropology* that the first introduction of a universal principle into an individual life marks the "beginning of a new epoch" and that the radical transformation it demands is, for that life, "unforgettable" (1978, 206).

At the historical level, however, the mediating function of cultural expression makes it questionable whether the dedication ever really occurred and, if it did occur, whether it is still in effect. This questionability remains even though, as Husserl emphasizes in the *Kaizo* articles, the most general coherence of tradition ensures that "no lost culture-idea is really lost" (1989, 90). The first use of "lost" signifies that the idea is no longer a guide for purposeful activity in common life (*Zweckidee*). Cultures can turn away from ideas such that they become totally disempowered, even if this turning away implies the possibility of a turning back. When an idea has become dormant in this way, merely talking about it, however persistently, or merely remembering it, however fondly, cannot reactivate it. Even granting the Kantian thesis about the irrevocability of principled commitments, we would do well to heed Williams's warning against mistaking the "intellectual irreversibility of Enlightenment" for an historical irreversibility (2002, 254). The possibility of crisis depends upon the contingent circumstance of "our" belonging to a community still dedicated to the project of self-responsibility that requires *Wissenschaft* as its "functioning brain" (1970, 290/338).

5. Crisis as a Medical Concept

We earlier offered a tentative definition of crisis as a situation one faces (IB § 19). More fundamentally, crisis refers to the facing of that situation, to being, oneself, in crisis. Crisis is primarily a concept of jeopardy, secondarily a concept of uprootedness. It is personalities who are in crisis because a project to which they are dedicated has been uprooted. Crisis is the subjective condition of having lost touch with an undertaking that can and must be resumed because it is central to one's self-conception. The critical-historical reflections aim to induce this condition. Crisis consciousness, not crisis resolution, is the measure of minimal success for the appropriation of the ultimate presuppositions. This heightened awareness of everything endangered and redeemable in the present predicament is the goal of an intervention in historical understanding that Husserl presents as a form of spiritual medicine.

When Husserl describes the crisis in medical terms, he is not using metaphors.[14] Rather, medicine itself is a discipline with two sides, only one of which has been thoroughly developed. In its familiar form, medicine looks after the health of psychosomatic individuals, considering their mental and physical life either in abstraction or in reciprocal relation. The other side of medicine looks after life in its spiritual form. Roughly speaking, this is human life as studied by the humanities. Here, human life is not in view as a psychosomatic occurrence, but as the agent and patient of culture (1970, 270/315). As such, it stands in relation to an orienting world that matters. For it, even the nature that causes belongs in the orienting world that matters. According to Husserl, this life can also get sick and requires its own kind of medicine.

Husserl's idea of spiritual medicine depends upon conceptions of health and sickness alluded to in several texts, including *Philosophy as Rigorous Science*, the *Kaizo* articles, the *Vienna Lecture*, and *Crisis I*. Husserl equates spiritual health with powerful thriving (*kraftvolles Gedeihen*). This condition describes the person or the higher-order personality (group, organization, institution, etc.) in its orientation toward values requiring actualization through action. The subject of thriving life enjoys the full exercise of power in dedicated activities. On Husserl's view, this vital energy derives from and is sustained by a faith that the actualization of genuine values through activity is possible. Faith amounts to believing that one can pursue successfully what one must pursue in order to remain true to oneself (1970, 291/338). This belief is self-fulfilling insofar as it summons the resolve necessary to attend to the task. Husserl characterizes faith as energizing (*Schwunggebender*) (10/8) or as sustaining of momentum (*Schwung haltender*) (1981, 326). However, if it is to serve this vital function, it cannot be blind. Faith requires a clear understanding of the situation of action as supporting the actualization of values, familiarity with methods of actualization, and the experience of at least partial actualization. Faith, clarity, and success reinforce one another in thriving life.

Spiritual sickness, on the other hand, is a kind of atrophy (*Verkümmern*). This condition again refers to the person or higher-order personality in orientation toward values requiring actualization through action. We can thus distinguish between spiritual sickness and spiritual death, in which this orientation has been given up. The distinction is important because spiritual medicine works through renewal, revitalization, or rebirth. It does not raise the spiritually dead. In the final division of this study, we will argue that the crisis problematic requires a warm body, a "subject of crisis," and that this subject can cease to be viable. In *Crisis I*, Husserl makes a fundamental distinction between "humanity which has already collapsed" and "humanity which still has roots but is struggling to keep them or find new ones" (1970, 15/13). It is this struggling humanity to which spiritual medicine attends.

Sickness is a weariness of the will, a condition in which it has become difficult to summon the power and resolve to act. Husserl traces the source of this weariness to a practical skepticism that is the opposite of faith. The world does not seem conducive to the actualization of the values to which the subject stands committed. Just as belief, clarity, and success reinforce one another in thriving life, so do skepticism, obscurity, and failure in atrophied life. Unclear ideals are easy targets for skepticism; failure provokes suspicion that action is senseless. The defining feature of sickness, though, is a wavering of faith in oneself as an agent of value actualization.

Given these general concepts of sickness and health, we can understand crisis interpretation as a form of spiritual medicine with diagnostic, curative, and preventative dimensions. In spiritual medicine, diagnosis and cure are inseparable. Acknowledging sickness and understanding its etiology is already a form of recovery. In psychophysical medicine this is not necessarily the case. Knowledge about the human organism obviously does not, of itself, relieve a headache, nor does it enhance the efficacy of aspirin. For this reason, the tasks of diagnosis and treatment can fall to someone who is not the patient, whereas in spiritual medicine self-diagnosis and self-treatment are essential. Discovering spiritual sickness is a task in its own right because such sickness is often concealed by what Husserl calls "consolations" (*Crisis* §§ 2, 4, 23).[15] These are actualizable surrogates for the values that seem unactualizable. By affording the experience of success, they tend to cover over the resignation through which they came to orient the will. Understanding this success as a symptom of an underlying failure, exposing consolations as such, and recovering orientation toward the actualization of values that seem unactualizable is the first step in crisis interpretation. This is why the historical reflections already succeed by discovering the crisis. Recognition that one is sick, mere consciousness of crisis, is already to improve one's health.

The wavering of faith in the orienting values has its motives. These point to the etiology of the disease. Diagnosis investigates the motivational history of the patient, identifying sources of obscurity in aims and methods, and the failures to which they have led. The curative moment demonstrates that the experience of frustration does not justify abandoning the task to which one stands committed, and thereby aims to restore the faith that gives energy to purposeful life. This occurs through a critique of methods and projected goals. At a minimum, it shows that the obscurities and failures of the past are surmountable through reforms that keep the orienting values in view. It projects a plausible success story of which failure will have been only a moment. Finally, even in the midst of thriving life, such a critique can function preventatively by confirming the sense of methods and goals and guarding against skepticism and consolation.

Once it has dispensed with false consolations, crisis interpretation is guided by a methodological optimism that sustains belief. In a manuscript of 1923, Husserl presents this optimism in the form of an ethical imperative: "If I grasp the slightest real possibility that the world might 'accommodate' humane purposes, then I must treat this supposition as a certainty and act accordingly" (1997, 235n; see also 225–6). The difficulty with this position is that it seems at cross purposes with philosophical culture itself. It seems that in order to avoid the conclusion that the idea of philosophical culture "is merely a factual, historical delusion" one sets about deluding oneself (1970, 15/13). This is because the imperative allows the demands of practical reason to exert such pressure on theoretical reason that the latter is in danger of succumbing to the unreason of wishful thinking or self-deception.[16] In his *Kaizo* article of the same year, Husserl acknowledges that in *our* culture ... this faith can "move mountains," not merely in fantasy, but in reality, only if it is transformed into prudent, rationally insightful ideas, only if it is in them that it brings to complete determination and clarity the essence and possibility of its goal and the method by which it is to be attained ... only such clarity of thought can summon joyful work and give the will, the resoluteness, and the all-pervasive power to carry out acts of liberation. (1981, 327)

We can defend the role Husserl accords to optimism in spiritual health by distinguishing between two kinds of practical intelligence. The first, deliberative, assesses a situation in light of the opportunities it affords various courses of action. The second, orientational, concerns which features of the situation should be borne in mind once deliberation has established commitment to a certain course of action. If applied to deliberation, the imperative to treat the "slightest real possibility" as a "certainty" is clearly indefensible. It would determine courses of action under the assumption that variables in the practical situation will conform to the wishes of the agent. A charitable interpretation of the imperative has it govern the orientation of a committed agent. Such an agent has ideally decided upon a course of action in a deliberation free from the distortions of wishful thinking. Indeed, the imperative applies only given a real possibility that the world is responsive to one's purposes. On this basis, it requires that the committed agent adopt a certain stance about the practical relevance of this possibility compared with the alternatives. Following it, I do not confuse my desires with probabilities; it counsels confidence in action, not optimistic prediction. Returning to a deliberative attitude, I can confirm objective probability assessments that describe the unlikelihood as such. The imperative requires me to treat the scenario in which the improbable obtains as the only relevant scenario for committed action. It does not tell me what to see, but where to look: "Look to that which makes you strong!" (1997, 226).[17]

The alternative to a recovery of philosophical culture, which Husserl calls "barbarism," is a real, perhaps likely, possibility. But from the perspective of participation in the Enlightenment project, it is practically irrelevant. The crisis interpretation furnishes the justification for hope and protects the will to philosophical culture from the threats of futility and consolation. At the beginning of the *Crisis*, Husserl asks: What must we, who believe in the goal "philosophy," do, in order to be able to believe (1970, 17/15–16)? The teleological reflections that follow are the answer. They are the self-administered medicine. They transform our historical moment so that it is charged with an unfulfilled but viable project in pursuit of which "we" can be true to ourselves.

6. Husserl's Appropriative Concepts

The appropriation of the ultimate presuppositions depends upon the discovery of a crisis of science. The crisis of science, in turn, depends upon there being a subject capable of undergoing such a crisis: ultimately, a historical community dedicated to the Enlightenment project. This subject is at the center of any crisis interpretation. The crisis is ultimately *its* crisis. For reasons considered in part one of this study (IB § 13), this subject must be discovered through the appropriative reflection itself. The project that requires the phenomenological transformation of philosophy is appropriable as mine neither in the natural (pre-phenomenological) nor in the phenomenological-theoretical attitude. The appropriative reflection has to discern *in* the particular history to which one already feels responsible a self-conception defined by dedication to ends uprooted by transcendental naïveté.

The concepts that describe the subject of crisis are ambiguous for a number of reasons. The same term may refer to the bearer of crisis, that is, to the responsible jeopardized subject, to the uprooted project to which this subject stands committed, and to the ideal that orients this uprooted project. Further, the appropriative reflections refer to the subject precisely and only as the bearer of a historical movement that the subject has never adequately grasped. Finally, although the subject is only at stake as a subject of crisis, the reflection can only reshape an already effective history, which means that the subject has a self-understanding extrinsic to the crisis perspective. This guarantees a tension between the conventional use of the concept and its use in the crisis interpretation. Husserl's concept for the subject of crisis at the concrete level of philosophical history is "European humanity." At the abstract level of the history of philosophy, he tends to name the movement, "the transcendental motif," but also speaks of "we modern philosophers."

These concepts are indeed concepts, not ideas "in the Kantian sense." They refer to communities animated by ideas and only secondarily to the ideas that animate them. In the appropriative reflection, the concepts must function in judgments that discern a developing unity of spiritual life in which the realization of the relevant ideas is evidently at stake. *The subject-concepts are thus historical.* The historical formations to which these concepts refer must include the author of the crisis interpretation as a participant. The historical reflection is simultaneously an exercise in self-clarification. The appropriations must reconstruct the history that has made "us" who "we" are, not a history available to indifferent spectators "from outside." Husserl's comment that a history of the latter sort "might as well be Chinese" serves not only to fix attention on historical materials that we can recognize as ours but also to fix an attitude for which it matters that they are ours, rather than regarding them such that they "might as well" belong to a foreign or even fictive community (1970, 71/72). *The subject-concepts are thus personal.* The appropriation promotes the spiritual health of the subject of crisis. We have seen that spiritual health consists in purposive clarity about the realization of objectives to which one stands committed. The interest in history reflected in the use of the subject-concepts is not primarily theoretical. It does not address the question of what I can know, but rather the question of what I am entitled to hope so that I may act with resolve. *The subject-concepts are thus practical.*

We will examine the content of Husserl's concepts in the final division of this study. The meaning of "Europe" and the "transcendental motif" will give a specific, contestable character to Husserl's appropriation of the ultimate presuppositions. In the remainder of this division, we will examine the novel use to which these concepts are put, a topic that contains its own difficulties. Our aim is to identify a general methodological function that any ultimate appropriation in the Husserlian spirit will fulfill. A series of brief comparisons with similar methods from the history of philosophy should serve to highlight the specificity of Husserl's "crisis approach" to the systematic presentation of philosophy.

7. The Practical Extension of Phenomenological Reason

The appropriation of the ultimate presuppositions carries phenomenology beyond its sphere of theoretical competence. It is true that as Husserl developed the scope of phenomenological investigation, he increasingly emphasized the temporality of consciousness and the constitutive problems related to intersubjectivity, culture, and history. However, the *use* of history that characterizes Husserl's engagement of the crisis problematic is not phenomenological in the strict sense. The phenomenological attitude takes an interest in mundane being only as a clue to its transcendental constitution. The crisis interpretation, on the other hand, turns to events in human history precisely in order to attain clarity about what one is trying to accomplish in the world. It does not want to know how a unitary tradition is evident, but to regain a sense of participation in a unitary tradition. To employ a distinction from the *Crisis*, this mode of attention moves on the ground of the pregiven lifeworld; it does not inquire into how it is so given.[18]

It is also true that Husserl repeatedly denies that the historical reflections of the *Crisis* are history in the "ordinary" or "usual" sense. This claim, though, requires examination. The conception of ordinary history Husserl invokes as a foil would treat temporal development "from the outside" as a domain of "facts" regarded with objective indifference and ordered into "an external causal series" (1970, 71/72). Husserl thereby emphasizes the "inner" and "teleological" nature of his historical reflections, which seek to clarify the task our own history assigns to us. This distinction may differentiate Husserl's history from certain forms of historical scholarship, but not from the most ordinary histories of everyday life. When someone is unsure about what he is doing in his marriage, his career, or his country, he often has recourse to historical reflections that are simultaneously "self-reflections on what he is *truly seeking*" (ibid.). Inner, teleological histories are the stuff of storytelling practices that provide orientation for life in the natural attitude. There is nothing inherently phenomenological about them.

In engaging the crisis problematic, the phenomenologist has to take a stance on non-phenomenological matters. In this sense, the crisis problematic requires an extension of phenomenological reason. The extension is also accomplished for "practical purposes." In both *Crisis I* and the 1937 essay on teleology, Husserl characterizes the appropriative reflections as the response to an existential contradiction that confronts the philosopher. He stands committed to ends of reason that he "cannot give up," but neither can he "hold onto his will" or "believe his belief" because of their apparent incongruity with conditions in the surrounding world. The extension of phenomenological reason seeks to overcome this apparent incongruity. It succeeds if it enables one to believe what one must (1970, 17/15–16). The comprehension of crisis is the product of judgment guided by an unconditional commitment.

Despite important differences, this approach warrants comparison with the Kantian practical extension of reason in which "my interest, because I *must* not remit anything of it, unavoidably determines my judgment" (2002, 181). Kantian postulation differs from positive thinking that caters to psychological needs because theoretical reason asserts what practical reason requires only if the latter is pure. This purity refers to the determination of the will by an aim that is a priori necessary, independent of every discretionary purpose. In Husserl's extension, we can detect a parallel conception of aims that directly determine the will. The Enlightenment project and the philosophical program it requires appeal to my basic integrity and are thus mine in a preeminent sense. In the 1937 essay on teleological history, Husserl argues that the goal of philosophy (let us construe it broadly as philosophical culture) is a lifegoal of such a nature that, once I have discovered it as mine, I know that it would have still been mine even if I had never come to formulate it as a lifegoal. The imperative to hold onto the goal is "categorical" because no one, *not even I myself*, can impose it upon me "from the outside" (1993, 410–11).[19] Its appropriateness to me is not contingent upon my changing life attitudes and personality. It is a goal imposed upon me by my very being a self. And yet, sustaining commitment to the goal requires that it be commensurate with some sense of who I am as a person in the historical world of human culture.

For the phenomenological extension, both the apparent futility and the actual attainability of the necessary end are products of historical understanding. The contradictions between diverse philosophical systems, the positivistic reduction of the scientific idea, the dominance of theoretical and commonsense dualism, a widespread view that limits the promise of scientific culture to the satisfaction of natural needs—these are facts. The crisis interpretation attempts to integrate them into a more profound history for which they count as divergences or failures. It discerns the philosophical goals animating "our" historical development and traces the effects of transcendental naïveté in thwarting their attainment. The result is an awareness of the "inward orientation" of past philosophical history toward its phenomenological conversion (1970, 18/17). This historical approach marks an obvious departure from the Kantian extension, in which the necessary end is apparently futile in the sensible world, but thinkable as possible in the intelligible world.

In phenomenology's historically oriented extension, the problem of the degree to which interest may determine judgment is particularly difficult. For Kant, theoretical reason freely asserts the postulates with just the content required for their practical function. Because they do not belong to the realm of possible cognition, theoretical reason does not have to "yield" any of its claims. Its primary job is to protect the orientation of the rationally determined will by guarding against the speculative pretense to cognize the existence or nonexistence of the postulates (2002, 172). The phenomenological extension also involves the use of practically determined concepts, most crucially "crisis" and its subject-concepts. However, this use incurs upon an established domain of historical cognition. Concepts organizing a competing crisis interpretation or concepts organizing an interpretation that undermines the "crisis" altogether may better fit the historical facts. Husserl emphasizes that his subject-concepts do not apply to everything conventionally included in their extension (1970, 98/101, 276/322). However, they must find some historical traction. To succeed, the appropriative reflection must show that there were transcendental philosophers and European institutions in the conventional sense whose work embodied the will definitive of "Europe" and the "transcendental motif" in the sense defined by the practical extension. Husserl never specifies the threshold of historical evidence required for the crisis interpretation. But there must be circumstances under which one is no longer *able* to believe, for instance, in "Europe as the historical teleology of the infinite goals of reason" (299/347). Otherwise, the appropriative reflections would not be necessary to secure the ability to believe.

The phenomenological extension thus confronts despair in a way the Kantian extension does not. This is true even if we assume a view like that of Despland, who interprets Kant such that the objects of rational faith only become effective for a human life when an historically instituted faith translates them into the concrete world (1973, 206). The crucial point is that these objects themselves are not historically acquired. For Kant, because the postulates have their source in a requirement of pure reason, I claim them in an assertion of my rational personality, even if only through the unschooled conviction that they are true concepts (2002, 170). Any fortification of the postulates through teleological reconstruction in the world of sense is a supplemental effort, the failure of which would leave intact fixed and unchangeable coordinates for willing the necessary end (177, 184). For Husserl, on the other hand, the basis of hope is itself historically acquired and therefore historically fragile. Human history may "collapse" so that even crisis consciousness is no longer possible. The phenomenological extension first enables the assertion of its practically determined concepts through a trial of sincere belief. Husserl indicates as much in the 1923 manuscript cited above. The ethical requirement to assert that failing which a practically necessary task would be futile is conditional upon the discernment of its real possibility, not merely the thought of its logical possibility.

If the phenomenological extension risks despair, it also wagers less than the Kantian extension. Precisely because the connection between phenomenological wakefulness and the Enlightenment project is historical, the former is not falsified if pursuit of the latter should prove fantastic. Kant, who posits an a priori connection where Husserl discovers an historical one, seems to hold that the futility of promoting the necessary end would falsify the fact of reason itself.[20] For Husserl, the "truth" of the phenomenological attitude and its attainability for human beings are not mere ideas unless linked to an additional object of the will. The phenomenological attitude is an inviolable contemplative stance independent of any connection to philosophy and its historical ramifications. It is only under certain contingent conditions that this connection is evident.

Husserl emphasizes this contingency in the *Vienna Lecture*, where he presents as one of three historical possibilities the situation in which philosophy "is called" to facilitate the praxis of universal critique. The first possibility is that no objective synthesis between the philosophical and practical attitudes is available. This is the scenario in which the contemplative significance of phenomenology does not uproot any live objectives for naturally interested life. The second possibility is that the practical interests of natural life subordinate philosophical inquiry by restricting its scope and function in light of what these interests require. Husserl calls such "finitization" (*Verendlichung*) the "obvious" mode of synthesis between theory and practice, probably because it has increasingly governed the modern understanding of science (1970, 283/329). But to the extent that it governs, finitization supplies surrogate forms of success to scientific culture and thereby conceals its own operation. The triumph of finitization would put an end to the crisis by ushering in an age of barbarism. The third possibility is the historical development in which "we" happen to stand. Philosophy has a practical vocation because it has been called "to serve mankind in a new way" (ibid.), an assignment neither inherent to, nor appropriable in, the phenomenological-theoretical attitude. This responsive character of the crisis interpretation distinguishes it, in Husserl's eyes, from a speculative imposition that confronts history with a priori demands (275–6/321). At the term of the reflection, we understand ourselves as responsible to reconstituted traditions, not to principles.[21]

An extension of reason for practical purposes is motivated by the pursuit of a necessary end. For Kant, the source of this necessity is that the end is required by a principle of pure practical reason (or at least this principle as it applies to human beings) and thus compels my dedication regardless of circumstance. On Husserl's understanding, the ramified goals of philosophy are necessary through an imperative that determines the will directly. At the same time, the crisis interpretation presents this end as originating in a historical development such that the pursuit of the end is a response to and a fulfillment of that development. This is a situation impossible for the conventional Kantian: an end "derived from reason" is also "derived from history." This feature of the phenomenological extension suggests a second point of comparison—the Hegelian philosophy of history.

8. Historical Teleology: Contemplative and Interventionist

Hegel can understand an end derived from reason as simultaneously derived from history because he regards history as the self-realization of reason. The purposive activities of human beings are the vehicle for fulfilling this absolute purpose. This higher aim is initially unconscious, but must eventually become conscious because it consists in intelligence contemplating its actuality (1956, 25). Understanding our history is thus the same as understanding the ends of reason because historical phenomena are how reason comes to itself in the temporal dimension.

Despite Husserl's explicit anti-Hegelianism, his appropriation of the ultimate presuppositions results in a historical teleology that has several Hegelian features. Further, these features seem to follow from the attempt to grasp a historical development the fulfillment of which requires the overcoming of transcendental naïveté. We have seen why this requirement is unintelligible for an interpretation that simply tracks the development from its own naïve perspective. If the development is indeed historical, the alternative seems to be to appeal, with Hegel, to a destiny of reason in the world (1956, 16). The phenomenological standpoint, grasped concretely, would be the result of spirit's historical path to self-consciousness. The *Crisis* contains several formulations that make this characteristically Hegelian appeal. Indeed, in *Crisis I*, Husserl defines philosophy as "the historical movement through which universal reason, 'inborn' in humanity as such, is revealed" (1970, 16/13–14). Another Hegelian feature of Husserl's appropriation is that it proceeds from an authoritative present (the *Endstiftung* of philosophy) that assigns to each phase of the historical process its true significance, as opposed to the apparent significance it had in the past. Finally, this authoritative perspective construes the conscious aims of historical figures as ways of promoting an aim of which they lack clear awareness. Husserl, like Hegel, invokes a historical level of instinctive movement correlated to the *dynamis* of reason (Hegel 1956, 30, 57; Husserl 1970, 18/17).

While Husserl's history has these Hegelian features, its function in the crisis problematic gives it a very different epistemological status and practical import. Most importantly, it is not a scientific description of any subject matter, and thus not phenomenology in the Hegelian sense (1977, 31–6, 56). For Husserl, the reconstruction of philosophical history is the only way to understand ourselves as philosophers of the present. However, the method suited to understanding ourselves as philosophers of the present is not the same as that method of self-understanding that is philosophy qua strict science. Claims about the relations of influence between philosophical schools, or about the mood of a particular generation of Germans, for instance, cannot meet standards of phenomenological rigor. Phenomenology turns to world history as a final domain of appropriation in which it purchases clarity of purpose by forfeiting the fullness of theoretical insight.

To this point we have emphasized that the inner and teleological nature of Husserl's history does not distinguish it from the ordinary storytelling practices of the natural attitude. However, the telos at which this history aims does distinguish it from ordinary storytelling. It discerns a development that can only realize its animating objective through a phenomenological transformation. So while the history is phenomenologically naïve, its appropriative concepts express a unitary development in which that naïveté is overcome. For Husserl, history is at issue precisely as the dimension in which reason, in the form of infinite tasks, is manifest. He thus shares the Hegelian perspective that history is a "spiritual" rather than merely anthropological or biological phenomenon. The appropriative concepts refer to communities insufficiently characterized by the universal categories of historicity (such as the home/alien relation) because they are dedicated to tasks that transcend empirical traditions and express what is essential to humanity as such (1970, 15/13, 275/320). Although their defining work can never be complete, these communities pursue a project that is unsurpassable. In Hegelian fashion, Husserl too claims that these spiritual shapes represent an end to history insofar as they are explicitly oriented by a final telos that is not itself an episode in a larger drama (14/12; 1989, 73).

However, Husserl's historical method, unlike Hegel's, does not describe an absolute that has proven its rank by coming to itself in historical time. It is true that Husserl defines history in *Crisis I* as a movement through which the universal reason inborn in humanity is revealed and philosophy as the form in which this reason is fully conscious of itself. These statements, though, are in the subjunctive mood. One *could* claim reason's historical sovereignty if the crisis *were* resolved (1970, 15–16/13–14). The historical development is not a complete object for contemplation, but a synopsis of what is at stake in the present. While Hegel's teleological account of spirit is itself the theoretical demonstration that reason is sovereign in history, Husserl's presents a crisis motivated by the practical intolerability of a history in which it isn't. The audience addressed through the subject-concepts of the crisis interpretation consists of we who cannot console ourselves with a merely anthropological history (7/4).

One might object that this "crisis" is a mere dramatization because its reconstruction assumes a perspective from which it has already been resolved. The epistemic authority of the appropriation depends, as we have seen, upon the conviction that phenomenology is the *Endstiftung* of philosophy. The description of the so-called crisis, despite its urgent tone, would then exhibit a problem that has already been solved. If the crisis of science referred to its entrapment in objectivism, this objection would carry some weight.[22] Objectivism is a theoretical problem for which phenomenology is a theoretical solution. But objectivism is only the motive for the crisis. The crisis of science refers to our wavering commitment to its *Lebensbedeutsamkeit*. This practical problem is resolved only when "our" civilization energetically pursues its mission of Enlightenment. Phenomenology as such merely makes this pursuit conceivable by removing the motive for its apparent futility. The historical reconstruction transforms our sense of what is possible in order to call us to action. For the phenomenologist, the required action includes a return to one's philosophical work (1970, 72/73). However, the tasks associated with building a culture of critique are manifold and endless. The goal projected in the crisis interpretation is not the phenomenological philosophy of the present, but a "great and distant future" in which humanity enjoys the true fruits of Enlightenment: "life-inwardness" and "spiritualization" (299). The accusation that Husserl articulates the crisis from the standpoint of its accomplished resolution is thus incorrect. The historical reflections first clarify the crisis as resolvable.

Husserl's interest in establishing the possibility of an end makes his engagement with history in the *Crisis* decidedly un-Hegelian. Husserl's history is the product of an intervention aimed at restoring the vitality of a dedicated will. It offers we who recognize ourselves in its subject-concepts a sense of historical identity that we may embrace by pursuing the tasks with which we are charged. The truth of statements about who we are, as subjects of the crisis, depends upon our dedication to these tasks. Further, by making explicit the "existential contradiction" from which it begins, the crisis interpretation refuses to support this dedication with anything beyond the historical roots it cultivates for itself. One may, as Steinbock has, sum up the difference between Hegel and Husserl by stating that whereas the former sees history as a consummated teleology of reason, the latter sees it as an open and contested teleology of reason (1998, 186, 195). The primary role of historical reflection in the crisis problematic, of course, is not to present the view that history is a contested teleology; it is to engage in the contest. Crisis history is teleology for a practical purpose, ultimately springing from and reinforcing an original commitment to what is most important.

This practical orientation determines two complementary abuses of the subject-concepts that we can describe in Kantian terms. Each abuse presents as theoretical knowledge a historical reconstruction that has its truth only in supporting dedication to a project. The abuses are difficult to avoid because the subject-concepts serve their function only when they organize a course of actual events in our historical background. These concepts are indeed concepts, though they refer to communities oriented by ideas. The abuses undermine our participation in these communities by defining them otherwise than through the tasks by which these orienting ideas are effective. A critique of these abuses in thus integral to understanding ourselves as subjects of the crisis.

The first abuse is anthropomorphism. It would have the subject-concepts refer to communities as defined by special anthropological features. Since these features would qualify a given community to bear an Enlightenment project, it is appropriate to describe fixation upon them, echoing Kant, as "superstitious." In the arena of philosophical history, anthropomorphic superstition would define us, who are dedicated to a philosophical culture, by certain religious, political, economic, or ethnological forms. It would even apply to the fixation upon generally "human" attributes insofar as they describe facts about organisms. In the arena of the history of philosophy, the superstition would define us, members of the philosophical movement redeemed in phenomenology, with reference to particular philosophical personae and *their* schools or doctrines rather than to the movement itself. The subject-concepts organize a history in which certain cultural forms and intellectual tendencies in our historical background play decisive roles. However, they are decisive precisely insofar as they trace the development of a humanity that becomes responsible to ideals that relativize allegiance to every cultural tradition.

The second, opposite abuse is fanaticism. It would have the subject-concepts organize a history that actualizes an absolute will and intellect, itself known through the historical reconstruction. Since this position is only possible through direct acquaintance with the absolute perspective, it is appropriate to describe it, with Kant, as "theosophical."[23] In both arenas organized by the subject-concepts, fanaticism would interpret history such that every phenomenal manifestation is from and of the absolute. This approach avoids anthropomorphic superstition. However, it leaves the terrain of the crisis problematic altogether. The reflection on crisis seeks in history not theoretical knowledge of an absolute intellect and will but rather a merely human understanding of everything pending for a fragile will. By understanding myself as a subject of crisis, I develop an orientation from which it is possible to *believe* that something absolute is at stake in human history, that humanity is in imperfect possession of logos, not of a mere "anthropo-logos," but of logos itself, and is also cognizant of this possession and its perfectibility, that is, that human history is a philosophical history.

The distinction between the Hegelian philosophy of history and the use of history in the crisis problematic does not primarily concern what has or has not yet been accomplished in history. The decisive question is whether history becomes systematically relevant for a contemplative or practical interest. The subject of the Husserlian reflection is a dedicated subject who turns to history seeking clarity of purpose about a goal she cannot let go. The resolution of Husserl's crisis consists in an experience of purposive self-possession, not the attainment of absolute knowing. Reason is sovereign in history insofar as this sovereignty is effectively willed.[24] The teleological intervention in history aims at a self-understanding that supports this will. The quiet, self-restraining contemplation of history is the goal neither of the method nor of history itself.

9. Mythmaking and the Will to Believe

Husserl stresses that his historical reflections do not aim to generate theoretical knowledge. They are, as he says, relative to our situation and attempted for "existential reasons" (1970, 59/60). These existential reasons arise from the "painful existential contradiction" of being dedicated to a necessary end without being able to believe in the possibility of its realization (17/15). If the crisis interpretation alleviates this contradiction by enabling belief in the goal, and if belief is needed for its "energizing" function in pursuit of the goal, then is it not pragmatically justified regardless of its truth? It is perhaps easiest to find clarity of purpose in a true historical narrative. However, when the purpose at stake is central to one's self-conception, isn't one permitted to find confidence in mere myths if the truth is not available or compliant?

There are instances of mythical discourse in ancient Greek philosophy, most notably Plato, that do not seem to be remnants of pre-philosophical thought, but rather the products of a philosophical method that fosters confidence in the strange, novel goals that define *theoria*. Socrates characteristically warns that he cannot fully vouch for the truth of these myths, but that they are good to believe because they make us courageous lovers of wisdom. While the nature of the contents involved limits what can happen in a believable myth, Socrates here appeals to a dimension in which one is generally free to believe what one needs to. Further, these myths are not mere stepladders to be dispensed with upon initiation into the philosophical vocation. The myths are integral to this vocation because they tell stories about the human condition that help us understand who we must be if we are indeed responsible for the truth.

The case of *Meno* is especially relevant to our comparison because it clarifies the philosophical task by understanding the past. Socrates counteracts the apparent futility of philosophical ends by deriving the human capacity for philosophy from an account of where the soul has been and what it has seen (81a–e). The account itself is an object of trust rather than knowledge. However, Socrates espouses it because doing so makes us brave and industrious truth-seekers (86b–c).[25]

This form of mythmaking is explicitly oriented by ends of reason, which it connects to the human will through narration. It thus survives Kant's critique of postulating for discretionary purposes (2002, 154). However, if Husserl employs such a method, he is involved in a contradiction. The historical community capable of undergoing Husserl's crisis is defined precisely by its refusal to rely on mythical understanding for ultimate orientation (1970, 285/331). If this community can only strive for the goals associated with rational culture through a mythical self-understanding, then we must draw one of two consequences. Either myth invariably provides ultimate orientation for rational culture, in which case rational culture on Husserl's understanding is impossible, or else Husserl's historical reconstruction is compromised by its reliance on myth. Crisis interpretation fails as spiritual medicine if it depends upon beliefs that are merely salutary rather than salutary and true. Husserl requires of his teleological reconstruction that it be true, albeit in a "peculiar" way (73/74).

The most obvious difference between Socrates' story in *Meno* and Husserl's reconstruction is that the latter remains within the recorded history of human events while the former makes use of a dimension of existence anterior to human life itself. There is a corresponding difference, then, in the standard of plausibility. The plausibility of the Socratic myth depends upon a combination of religious authority and conformity to the essential nature of things. Within these restrictions, the possibly true narrative is affirmed if it is pragmatically justified in light of philosophical practice. The Husserlian reconstruction, while free from religious authority, is additionally bound by historical knowledge about the course of human events. However, there is also significant variability possible here regarding the narrative qualities of events. Again, a possibly true history will be affirmed if it is pragmatically justified in light of philosophical practice.

The fact that the crisis interpretation stays within the bounds of available human history has an important consequence for the affirmation of a narrative that "might be true." In a history that is retrievable for participants in a unified tradition, claims about the narrative qualities of past events can be *made* true or false through the action of those participants. The reconstructions of the past that "might be true" because they conform to essential possibilities and historical knowledge also "might become true" because they will be consistent with the outcomes of unresolved controversies in the tradition. As participants engaged in these controversies, we are also agents of historical truth. Husserl's 1923 imperative has this feature as well. It is not just that one ought to treat as certain an empirical possibility, the fulfillment of which would support the actualization of values. Insofar as action in the present shapes what the historical situation is, it can eventually confirm the truth of the interpretation that supports it. The truth conditions for the interpretation are analogous to those of present-tense "mission statements" about the defining purpose of an institution or community. One says, for instance, that the United States is a "country of immigrants," by which one means that a certain internationalism and openness is built into its very identity. However, not only does this assertion depend upon the narrative construal of particular historical events as foundational or deviant, the very plausibility of that construal also depends upon the present and future stances the nation takes toward immigration policy, and so on.

The Socratic myth might be true and should be treated as such because it enables the pursuit of philosophical ends. Husserl's appropriative history might be true in the sense that it can be made true through the pursuit of philosophical ends that it enables. Affirmation of the history thus falls under the general Jamesian category of lawfully willed beliefs about "personal relations." These are permissible not only because they pertain to dilemmas that are theoretically undecidable but also because believing what I want to believe can motivate action that creates a situation in which the desired belief becomes true (1956, 23–4).

Defining the truth of the reconstruction in terms of conformity to historical facts and their construal according to narrative qualities that stand or fall with future actions does not yet distinguish it from a mythical conception, even according to Husserl's own standard. For Husserl, mythical understanding is defined by its practical-universality and locality. It is practical-universal because it orients human beings with respect to the whole cosmos in which their endeavors take place (1970, 283/329–30). It is local because its orientating power is always relative to the particular community whose welfare is at stake. Confronted with alternative accounts of the whole, relative to other communities, their traditions, and practices, mythical understanding may incorporate or reject foreign elements, but it cannot contribute to an account of the whole that would hold regardless of tradition. A myth is "true" in the context of a particular historical community.

In light of this general definition, it seems sensible to suspect that Husserl supports the aims of rational culture with a mythical understanding of history. The subject-concepts appeal to a group membership already efficacious in the historical background. When applied in the reconstruction, they organize circumstances, persona, and events that we recognize as part of our familiar heritage. If this were not the case, the resulting history would be impersonal and, as Husserl says, "might as well be Chinese." The purposive clarity won through the reconstruction is thus itself relative to a particular traditional community. The problem of how to negotiate encounters with foreign traditions of Enlightenment seems to loom large. To the extent that this problem is not addressed, the locality of the crisis interpretation seems to render it provincial.

In the next division, we will see how Husserl's most concrete subject-concept allows him to circumvent these problems; we will ask whether he thereby invites problems even more difficult. It is already clear, though, that to overcome mythical understanding, the subject-concept must draw upon the historical background in a paradoxical manner that unsettles self-conceptions based in geographical, religious, political, or other cultural affiliations. This requirement accords with the avoidance of anthropomorphic superstition, which would undermine the end the reconstruction is supposed to support.

10. Relation between the Two Dimensions of Appropriation

Husserl's appropriative reflection operates in two dimensions: philosophical history and the history of philosophy. The former refers to the historical development in which philosophy is charged with spearheading a transformation of human culture. The latter refers to the philosophical movement that attempts to fulfill that charge. In the first part of this study (IB § 16) we anticipated a certain priority of philosophical history for the appropriative reflection. We now take up this issue explicitly.

The critical-historical attitude considers phenomenology as a praxis in the midst of the human world. Let us stipulate that the understanding of a praxis is concrete to the extent that it grasps the social whole of which its activity and ends are a part. It is abstract to the extent that the activity and ends simply refer to each other in an isolated field of work. We propose to interpret Husserl's perhaps too bureaucratic sounding discussions of philosophers as "functionaries" in light of this distinction.[26] To be aware of oneself as a functionary is to have an optimally concrete consciousness of philosophical praxis. This will help clarify the priority of philosophical history as a dimension of appropriation.

Let us reflect briefly on being a functionary in general. If I am conscious of myself as a functionary, I understand my will to accomplish some task as a moment of the will of a community of which I myself am a member. We might further distinguish between the genuine functionary, whose activity has been assigned by the community, the benefactor, whose activity serves the community, but was not so assigned, and finally the subordinate, whose activity serves the community, but who did not herself participate in the assignment. Functionary consciousness is awareness of my action as fulfilling an assigned task that I myself assign in my capacity as a member of the community. It is as a member of the assigning community that I achieve concrete understanding of my praxis.

Thus far, the description applies to both dimensions of the historical reflection, where having a task as assigned involves an identification of wills such that my will to accomplish the task *is also* the will of those spiritually united with me (1970, 71/73). However, functionary consciousness in the narrow sense requires that this assignment is specifically a "delegation." The assignment is directed toward the practitioner or community of practitioners from a larger community that includes them. Appropriation of the history of philosophy connects phenomenology to live objectives in an abstractly isolated vocational field. Appropriation of philosophical history clarifies the centrality of these objectives to the community that charges philosophy with their realization. It is as a member of this broader community, addressing himself to other members, that Husserl attempts the appropriative reflections in both dimensions. And it is as a member of this community that he is first of all "called" to undertake these reflections at all. Even if the philosopher is a benefactor to humanity as such, it is the community dedicated to universal critique that assigns his task. Husserl is imprecise when he addresses his audience as "*functionaries of mankind*" (17/15), more precise when he does so as "functionaries of modern philosophical humanity" (71/72) or "good Europeans" (299/348). The most fundamental level of appropriation is the historical reconstruction of this community. Only from its perspective is the teleological history of philosophy, in which the transcendental movement overcomes objectivism, decisive to the resolution of the crisis.[27]

This entire discussion seems fantastic so long as "assignment" and "delegation" are restricted to the social or even bureaucratic meaning they have in everyday life. One useful framework for social and bureaucratic delegation is Reinach's account of social acts. Such acts are not only other-directed but also fulfilled only if their content is actually taken in by the other; they are "in need of being heard" (2012, 19). They are thus necessarily linguistic. To assign or delegate here means to direct a certain utterance toward the other so as to instantiate the resulting obligation. Because an assignment is not a command, its accomplishment is dependent upon at least an implicit acceptance or co-assignment in the recipient. It also requires an underlying "inner act" of intending that the delegated task be accomplished—otherwise the social act of delegation is not genuine and questions arise about whether it is binding (22). Similar questions arise if the content of the assigned task proves to be nonsensical or impossible to realize. Husserl's talk of philosophical functionaries obviously does not invoke this kind of delegating social act, such as might have been voiced during the drafting of some Platonic constitution. However, delegatory assignment and all its vicissitudes emerge in modified form at the level of historical consciousness, where its vehicle is not simply linguistic utterance, but a matrix of narratives that shape the sense of one's provenance and prospects, and find confirmation in the possibilities available in the surrounding world. Dodd's study of the *Crisis* stands out in its recognition that history is there thematic as a dimension in which to clarify how one is "possessed," "claimed," or "necessitated" by a task (2004, 54, 64, 208). The very possibility of the crisis problematic, we might say with Dodd, depends upon "the human capacity to engage tasks and claims on the plane of historical existence" (210).

In his reflections on philosophy as a vocation among vocations, Husserl emphasizes that every vocational praxis renders a service (*Dienst*) that responds to a requirement or need (*Bedürfnis*) that originates from outside its own field of work (1993, 363, 378, 387). The vocation is required because it makes possible a certain form of life. A clarification and critique of various vocations along these lines is easy to imagine. One simply investigates the interests served by the vocation and why their fulfillment matters for the community. However, in the case of philosophy, the relevant *Bedürfnis* is not an expression of natural interests. The history in which philosophy has been assigned its task is one in which a community dedicates itself unconditionally to a form of life in which knowledge serves the interests of wakefulness. The appropriation of this history will have to reconstruct the emergence of the need for such knowledge through a realization of naïveté at the level of collective life, a realization that expands the purview of human responsibility into an infinite dimension (IIB § 7). From here, Husserl will trace "the developmental beginning of a new human epoch—the epoch of mankind which seeks to live, and only can live, in the free shaping of its existence, its historical life, through ideas of reason, through infinite tasks" (1970, 274/319).

This need for philosophy is connected to reformations and upheavals in cultural forms beyond philosophy itself, especially in those institutions that shape life attitudes. Clarity of purpose about what one is truly seeking as a member of the community defined by this need involves not only protecting the original knowledge *Bedürfnis* against the consolations of *Verendlichung* but also sustaining a critical posture vis-à-vis an entire mode of historical existence it is possible to relativize, but never leave behind.

11. Relation between the Practical Extension and Phenomenology Proper

We are now in a position to return to the question we raised in concluding the first part of this study (IB § 18). The phenomenological-theoretical and critical-historical reflections may be systematically ordered in two ways. If we divorce the critical-historical reflections from the practical extension of reason in which they function, then they appear as a first step in a layered reflection that moves from the available products of philosophical history, to the historical developments in the cultural world through which they were first made available, and finally to the transcendental life in which this world is first evident at all. Each stage of the reflection is transcendental in the broad sense that it traces results of subjective activity back to the activities from which they result. On this ordering, the phenomenological-theoretical reflections complete the series by arriving at a final dimension for the appropriation of naïveté.[28] Alternatively, if we restore the practical extension, the historical reflections that frame the phenomenological-theoretical program are ultimate because they appropriate for the latter a historical viewpoint to which it stands naively committed.

On our view, this second interpretation is more concrete. The first ordering is no doubt true from the phenomenological-theoretical perspective. However, that very perspective is unable to appropriate the historical standpoint to which it is naively committed. We are advancing this as a claim about the crisis problematic. As a claim about the *Crisis*, which never came to fruition, it is difficult to establish. However, we find valuable hints in those passages that effect the transition from the historical reflections to the transcendental reflections on the lifeworld. Husserl does not generally treat this transition as the "deepening" of a form of reflection already established in the historical sections. Instead, he describes two separate methods, characterizing the historical-teleological as existential and perspectival, the phenomenological as apodictic. In transitioning to phenomenological-theoretical considerations, Husserl "leaves behind" the historical orientation in order to fulfill the task with which it has charged us (1970, 120/123, 147/150). "Self-reflection," he writes in § 15, "serves in arriving at a decision; and here this naturally means immediately carrying on with the task which is most truly ours and which has now been clarified and understood through this historical self-reflection, the task set for us all in the present" (72/73). The phenomenological-theoretical reflections do not follow the historical reflections as a second, more radical stage in a progressive constitutive investigation. They follow a vocational reflection meant to clarify the significance of one's work by getting down to work in light of that significance. Husserl even suggests a musical analogy, comparing historical reflection to an overture and phenomenological reflection to the opera itself, "the actual work ... which [historical reflection] has created the vital readiness to understand" (102/435).

Although the historical reflections function as an ultimate appropriation, they remain subordinate to phenomenological-theoretical reflections as a means to an end. One engages in vocational reflection for the sake of working with clarity of purpose. One does not work in order to be able to engage in vocational reflection. The crisis problematic belongs to the system of phenomenology precisely as a propaedeutic to phenomenological theory. This propaedeutic exercise, however, is never finally dispensed with. The crisis is a developing and inherently unstable historical situation. Not only does it have variable factors (the state of historical knowledge, prevailing scientific practices, prevailing public attitudes toward science, the viability of the subject-concepts), but even the very existence of the crisis is a contingent product of historical understanding. Husserl's particular reconstruction remains true so long as it can compel recognition of the practical necessity of a phenomenological conversion of philosophy. However, the general task of appropriating the ultimate presuppositions is an abiding responsibility for phenomenological philosophy.

The reduction of the critical-historical reflections to the phenomenological-theoretical perspective is misleading, but legitimate within limits. The reduction of the phenomenological-theoretical reflections to the critical-historical perspective, however, is simply illegitimate. On this view, the historical reflections would be a paradigmatic case of phenomenological reflection, so that phenomenology would consist in the universal application of this method. The method consists, briefly, in "clarifying history by inquiring back into the primal establishment of the goals which bind together the chain of future generations, insofar as these goals live on in sedimented forms yet can be reawakened again and again and, in their new vitality, be criticized" (1970, 71/72). This form of hermeneutics exposes the historicity underlying the seemingly "private and nonhistorical" work in which one is immersed (71/73). If this historical sensitivity is equated with philosophical reason itself, a number of consequences follow that amount to the dissolution of the crisis problematic.

This view dramatically alters the very object of historical appropriation. It is no longer a project of *Wissenschaft* oriented by the ideals of perfectly grounded judgment, final explanation, and infinite inquiry into a defined sphere of absolute being. That dream would have to be abandoned.[29] Instead, it is a project oriented toward the telos of worldliness as described in part one of this study. This change in the historical project of science has a corresponding effect on its phenomenological fulfillment. Consciousness, previously a universe of true being, a domain of superior evidence, and final explanation, would become an abstract moment of a historical-cultural whole in which it is contained. Finally, the subject of crisis would forfeit its paradoxical striving to achieve cultural forms no longer bound by anthropological tradition. This "new sort of humanity, one which, living in finitude, lives towards poles of infinity" and its "new sort of historicity which distinguishes itself ... from historicity in general" (1970, 277/323) would attain proper self-understanding precisely as local formations within historicity in general. To employ Husserl's image, this humanity and its orienting telos would slip back into the spiritual sea "in which men and peoples are the fleetingly formed, changing and then disappearing waves" (274/319). These alterations describe the collapse of the crisis problematic itself. Reckoning with the possibility of that collapse is part of the ultimate appropriation, but the appropriation does not make history thematic in a way that guarantees that collapse.

Rather than asserting the encompassment of "historicity in general," the historical reflections bind us to a historical movement that aims to overcome history. We cite Dodd here at length:

> It is this *defeat of history* that we are called on to perform; that is what is required by the idea or telos that defines our historical being as such. To fix our historical relation to the task of science through inner critique is to clarify historical life of all naïveté, and in this sense to free life form a certain kind of historical experience. And it is *this* task, assigned by a *Stiftung* made in full awareness of the obscurity of history and acting against it, that gives birth to what Husserl calls "modern philosophical humanity." (2004, 71–2)

We now turn to the final topic of this study, an examination of the concepts that articulate Husserl's understanding of this "modern philosophical humanity."

Division B

Husserl and the Subject of Crisis

Our foregoing discussion has discovered constraints on any successful engagement with the crisis problematic. Actual engagement with the problematic, however, consists in an interpretation of the effective historical background. This requires taking a stance on which historical personalities and events are decisive for the Enlightenment project. The selection, ordering, and description of these materials amounts to an account of what has been uprooted by the crisis and what demands appropriation. Of particular importance are those subject-concepts that illuminate who we are in order to be responsible for the crisis at all. These decisions are all matters of historical judgment guided by a commitment to necessary ends. Because the commitment alone does not determine these judgments, the crisis interpretation, even when it conforms to what the problematic generally requires, remains an object of controversy.

The following sections will consider Husserl's attempt to carry out a crisis interpretation with particular attention to the concepts "transcendental motif" and "European humanity," which orient the teleological reconstruction in the respective dimensions of the history of philosophy and philosophical history. We will begin with the appropriation of the history of philosophy as organized by the transcendental motif. Husserl's subordination of objectivism to transcendentalism in the development of modern thought depends, we will show, upon his characterizing as a consolation a certain vision of science. The justification of this characterization, in turn, lies in his appeal to our participation in "European humanity," the essential features of which we will then examine. The legitimate use of "Europe" as the subject-concept of crisis depends, finally, upon avoiding the abuses of anthropological superstition, theosophy, and mythmaking, as well as meeting a vague standard of historical plausibility that we will discover by way of a discussion of hypocrisy.

The resulting philosophical history is meant to grip us, not in spite of our practical identities, our involvements in definite roles, relationships, and projects but through them. It connects our present to specific efforts in the past that might be redeemed in the future. We become custodians of a paradoxical tradition that opened up and struggled to sustain those new forms of self-responsibility that make naïve reliance on tradition intolerable. Sustaining this orientation is an ongoing struggle because of the tendency to place the paramount value of integrity in the service of natural interests.

1. Two Ideas of Science

Husserl's continuous intellectual history in the *Crisis* is restricted to the modern era. This era is defined by a conflict between two opposing interpretations of the Greek idea of episteme, a universal knowledge of all that is. On the one hand, objectivism takes the task of episteme to be the determination of what really is in the world, "what is unconditionally valid for every rational being, what is in itself" (1970, 68/70). On the other hand, transcendentalism takes the task of episteme to be the reflection on "the subjectivity which *ultimately* brings about all world-validity" (69/70). Modern philosophy is thus a "single struggle between two ideas of science" (207–8/212). This struggle concerns the overall orientation of scientific questioning, not a particular problem in epistemology or ontology unrelated to other fields of inquiry. Insofar as special fields belong to the broader project of science, the meaning of their subject matter and method is at stake. This is so even if the decisive battle between the objectivist and transcendentalist tendencies is waged in a single science, namely psychology.

The protagonists of Husserl's intellectual history are those philosophers who develop the transcendental motif such that a predicament emerges in which a decision to realize its potential becomes necessary. Their number can finally be reduced, for Husserl, to three: Descartes, Hume, and Kant (1970, 192/194). Together, their work accounts for the basic plot elements that make the formation of this predicament intelligible. Of course, this selection is made in the interest of appropriating the presupposition that phenomenology realizes the highest objectives of our theoretical tradition (IB § 14). This focus involves an overt tendency to simplify, draw broad equivalences, and ignore both entire dimensions of concern and an abundance of details. What is negligence for historical scholarship is necessity for teleological reconstruction. Husserl seeks insight into the unifying aspiration of our theoretical tradition. One will never find this by surveying academic islands of discourse where philosophers survive as distinct literary figures and philosophical "areas" enjoy separate and equal status.

Each of these names, "Descartes," "Hume," and "Kant," refers to a subject of crisis. They partake of those ambiguities we outlined with respect to such subjects in particular (IIA § 6) and critical-historically appropriated subjects in general (IB § 15). There is a discrepancy, not only between Husserl's use of these names and the conventional use but also between the understanding each thinker actually had of what he was doing and what he was actually doing. The freedom of interpretation enjoyed in such appropriative reflections, however, ought not be confused with the complete freedom from historical fact Husserl rightly invokes in a different context. Philosophical claims inspired by a historically false interpretation of another philosopher are not for that reason false. If Husserl was inspired by reading Plato to a phenomenologically clarified conception of the *eidos*, this conception stands or falls apart from considerations about Plato's authorship of certain dialogues, whether Socrates was being "ironic," the quality of translations, and so on (1993, 49; 1970, 394/512). The crisis interpretation, however, makes claims about a continuity of motivation detectable in extant works. If historical research were to show, for instance, that Hume did not have access to Descartes' actual ideas because he relied exclusively upon bad translations, this would threaten Husserl's position about the profound philosophical motives at work in Hume's reception of Cartesian thought.

Husserl treats his historical protagonists strictly in terms of what they do for the transcendental motif. The essential functions of Descartes, Hume, and Kant are, respectively, to introduce the transcendental motif, but objectivistically misconstrue it, to show the absurdity of this construal, but rest content with the resulting skepticism, and to initiate the task of a scientific transcendentalism, but fail to execute it concretely. Each thinker is hampered by his naïve conception of psychology, broadly understood as the science of subjectivity. Ultimately, the development of genuinely psychological concepts will serve as the occasion for the phenomenological discovery of the universe of world-constituting life.

We will briefly discuss the three central protagonists in this reconstruction, emphasizing their relationship to the transcendental motif and drawing attention to what is more latent than patent in Husserl's text. There is no need to repeat or explicate his well-known interpretation. In particular, we will resist the temptation to supplement Husserl's account with a more detailed or comprehensive picture of Cartesian, Humean, or Kantian philosophy. Husserl's abridged treatment of these thinkers was not intended as a first gesture toward a history that would do justice to the full scope of their thought. For an understanding of the crisis problematic, it is better to pick up on Husserl's reductive tendency rather than counteract it and bring into focus exactly how his "Descartes," "Hume," and "Kant" prepare an insight into the necessity of the phenomenological conversion of philosophy.

2. Descartes

To succeed, Husserl's reconstruction needs to show that our scientific tradition is oriented toward the goals of transcendentalism. Because of the essential historical priority of the natural attitude, objectivism functions as the default orientation for science. The relevant tradition must therefore begin as a struggle to *redefine* the scientific idea. The beginning is so rudimentary that the impulse to break with objectivism not only fails but also fails to raise this impulse to the level of a conscious attempt. At the same time, the beginning is so radical that the self-conscious overcoming of objectivism is possible only by working out what was really implied in it (1970, 75/77). Descartes, specifically the author of the first two meditations, initiates the transcendental motif.

In a sense, Descartes' realization of the cogito has already achieved everything essential to the program of transcendentalism. The cogito is the "absolutely apodictic presupposition" (1970, 78/80). It thus furnishes a final and universal domain for the appropriation of naïveté. Because this domain is my own egoic life, I am assured that my power to presuppose is equaled, in principle, by my power to appropriate. Everything that counts as being for me does so within this life of "thinking," to which I am now awake. "The new motif of returning to the ego," writes Husserl "introduced a new philosophical age and implanted within it a new *telos*" (80–1/82–3). Husserl's decision to restrict his appropriation to the modern philosophical age has deeper motives that we will identify in upcoming sections. At the level of the history of philosophy, it is justified by the originality of Descartes' beginning.

From the perspective of this beginning, objectivism is a relapse or a deviation. This is true even of Descartes' own objectivism, which determines his interpretation of the cogito *from the start* (1970, 78/80). Descartes' ability to methodically present such a profound discovery while overlooking its importance is explained by the influence of Galilean science. The Galileo sections of the *Crisis* are for this reason an indispensable prelude to the movement that begins with Descartes.

In Husserl's judgment, objectivism dominates the entire history of philosophy up to Descartes. With Galileo, however, a fundamentally new, embracing form of objectivism takes shape. It is precisely the novel features of Galilean objectivism that enable both Descartes' discovery and his misinterpretation. The effect of Galileo's infamous "surreptitious substitution" is to prohibit subjectivity from any direct contact with the world. Mathematically idealized nature is not experienceable in perception or imagination. Because this idealization applies, via indirect mathematization, to the entire sensuous display of the surrounding world, reality can only be indicated or represented by mere appearances. Experiential knowledge is accordingly compromised: "If the intuited world of our life is merely subjective, then all the truths of pre- and extrascientific life which have to do with its factual being are deprived of value. They have meaning only insofar as they, while themselves false, vaguely indicate an in-itself which lies behind this world of possible experience" (1970, 54/54). Husserl repeatedly asserts that previous philosophy had no reason to carry out the radical quasi-skeptical epoché that leads Descartes to the cogito. While premodern skepticism attacked the universal claims of episteme, it never ventured so far as to question the entire world of sense experience (76–7/78). It is Galileo's conception of a mathematical nature that provokes a novel procedure of doubt that, at least initially, suspends the being of the world itself. By forcing a return to a life of thinking that has no worldly existence, the mathematization of nature prepares a critique that will eventually undermine not only physicalistic but also perennial philosophical objectivism.

Descartes himself, however, introduces the transcendental motif with the paradoxical intention of grounding objectivism subjectively. Husserl points out that he can only do this by failing to take his own epoché seriously. The results of this mundanized epoché create the framework in which an ill-fated modern psychology will try to understand subjectivity. This framework makes it impossible to see that (1) the epoché shows all being to be meant exactly as it is in acts of thinking (as *cogitata*), (2) the realm of *cogitata* includes scientifically determined reality—and all reality established through acts explicitly oriented toward truth, as well as (3) the intersubjectivity implied in the natural use of personal pronouns. This blindness allows common sense to determine the ontological interpretation of the ego cogito cogitatum. Rather than treating it as the unique encompassing domain of apodictic being, Descartes treats it as the first-personal certitude of mental interiority, beginning from which it makes sense to infer a physical outside. The thinking thing thus takes its place as a finite substance constituting one side of a psycho-physical dualism.

Husserl emphasizes the objectivism in Galileo's project because it blinds Descartes to the true meaning of his discovery and prepares the way for modern psychology as a special science. However, he is also attuned to an inheritance of Galilean science that will ultimately aid the development of the transcendental motif. Descartes was not serious about the ego of the epoché. He was, however, serious about the ideal of a single, encompassing science that would methodically explain an infinite but self-enclosed field of being: "This new philosophy seeks nothing less than to encompass, in the unity of a theoretical system, all meaningful questions in a rigorous scientific manner, with an apodictically intelligible methodology, in an unending, but rationally ordered progress of inquiry" (1970, 8–9/6). This general sense of scientific rationality, shorn of its physicalistic interpretation, will make the skeptical rebuttal to Descartes, brought to maturity in Hume, intolerable for a thinker like Kant, who inherits the tradition of post-Cartesian rationalism (91/93–4). The empiricist critique of objectivism thus inspires the project of a *scientific* transcendentalism. In the end, phenomenology will claim to discover the single realm of being implied by the idea of a single, encompassing science. Transcendental subjectivity is a genuine universe of being: "completely closed off within itself" (112/114) and of "inviolable unity" (113/115).

3. Hume

Hume's basic service to the transcendental motif is to revive the insight, stillborn in Descartes, that all possible validity is accomplished in subjectivity. Husserl admires Hume for having let this insight provoke the recognition that all knowledge of the world is a problem for examination. Where Descartes presupposed a Galilean nature, Hume treats all access to objectivity as "an enormous enigma" (1970, 89/91). For Husserl, Hume makes possible "a *completely new way* of assessing the objectivity of the world and its whole ontic meaning" (90/92).

Hume's form of critique represents a twofold correction of the tradition. On the one hand, it undoes the objectivistic link between rational constructions in the cogito and a transcendent, univocal in-itself. On the other hand, it exposes the circularity of the psychology that tried to ground this in-itself while making use of it in its accounts of subjectivity. Hume effectively reveals the naïveté of both Leibnizean rationalistic metaphysics and Lockean materialistic epistemology.

Hume's inability to make a positive philosophical contribution is explained by his adherence to the data sensationalism bequeathed by the project of naturalistic psychology. Once Galilean mathematization had placed reality beyond direct intuition, immanent experience could not claim to disclose any qualities of things. The subjective residuum, what is "directly experienced," is sense data (1970, 30n/27-28n). This is the historical result of a consistent working out of Descartes' claim that he does not really see men, but hats and coats. For hats and coats are also unities constructed out of visual data. Cartesian objectivism could explain the presence of these data in consciousness via a causally effective reality that they do not resemble, but to which they correlate. Hume's insight that any such reality must first of all take shape in consciousness prohibits this explanation. Falling back on the data complexes themselves, which he too treats as primary, he concludes that nothing beyond them is ever truly present. Our propensity to believe in identical realities is the result of associative laws that express our subjective nature, not an objective world.

Husserl's basic critique of Hume is that although he recognized consciousness as a life of accomplishment, he did not recognize that it is an accomplishment of reason (or unreason). This critique operates at two levels. First, Hume continues to work with the psychologically adulterated version of Cartesian intentionality (1970, 83/85), according to which our confidence that we see things is the symptom of an unrestrained judgment that goes beyond the data. If we learn to reflect on the "really" given data and are aware that the objectivistic inference to an in-itself is unsupportable, everything beyond this "reality" becomes "fiction": "All categories of objectivity—the scientific ones through which an objective, extrapsychic world is thought in scientific life, and the prescientific ones through which it is thought in everyday life—are fictions" (87/89). The error here is to overlook that sense data are an abstract moment functioning in an overall accomplishment directed toward, and fulfilled in, things themselves. Hume divorces transcendentalism from a concern with true being.

At a deeper level, this critique concerns Hume's "philosophical ethos" (1970, 88/90). Husserl's complaint is not only the standard one that skepticism cannot account for its own claim to truth and thus "cancels itself out" (ibid.). He also charges that Hume rests content with this situation because of an intellectual frivolity that masquerades as sophistication. It is as if Hume does not take thinking seriously enough to worry about the universal fictionalism his critique of knowledge implies. The ultimate consequence of the *Treatise* is a paradoxical solipsism for which all identical things and egos (including even oneself) are illusions. And yet, philosophy is simply an intellectual entertainment; the world gets along fine without it. Husserl's diagnosis is that, for Hume, *reason itself* must be a fiction (87/90). The aim of Hume's transcendentalism is thus not really to attain "a coherent self-understanding and a genuine theory of knowledge" (88/90), but to point out the overreaching of those metaphysicians who claimed insight where they had none. Descartes' struggle to know God and the external world is actually anthropological through and through. The pretension to do metaphysics is itself an unfortunate human disposition. Hume thus "remains in the comfortable and very impressive role of academic skepticism" (88/90). Meanwhile, the everyday, natural-scientific and mathematical experience of truth remains incomprehensible. Hume's satisfaction with this situation is a sign that surrogate goals have occupied the philosophical tradition.

4. Kant

Husserl credits Kant with realizing that the school of rationalism to which he belonged was jeopardized by Hume's skeptical intervention. His primary service to the transcendental motif was to unite it, and its critique of objectivism, with the rationalistic spirit driving the development from Descartes through Spinoza, Leibniz, and Wolff. Husserl writes of the Kantian system that it "is the first attempt … at a truly universal transcendental philosophy meant to be a *rigorous science*" (1970, 99/102). Kant's limitation is that he cannot advance beyond Hume except by evading the enigma he discovered. This evasion is explained by his erroneous concession to empiricism that psychology is a science of "inner experience." Given that starting point, transcendentalism cannot advance through direct, progressive methods and relies upon regressively constructed concepts essentially unavailable to intuitive insight. The systems of German Idealism after Kant only exacerbate this problem, coupling a convincing critique of objectivism with a confounding notion of absolute subjectivity. The result is a positivistic reaction in the name of scientificity: "the great transcendental philosophies did not satisfy the scientific need for … self-evidence, and for this reason their ways of thinking were abandoned" (1970, 200–1/204).

We summarized Husserl's assessment of Hume by saying that the latter saw conscious experience as an accomplishment, but not an accomplishment of reason. Kant restores to experience its role as an accomplishment of reason, but this restoration is not evident because reason's work in experience is essentially concealed. Kant's starting point is the insight that mathematical natural science is incomprehensible as a priori knowledge of a mind-independent reality. He moves from the premise that the things of experience *must* be susceptible to a priori knowledge to the conclusion that they can only be so if they are already formed by a transcendentally functioning intellect (1970, 94/97). As transcendentalism, this approach treats the real world as a "result" of subjectivity. However, I can never appropriate as my own the work of constitution underlying my naïve acceptance of the real world. This is because my concrete life is already formed by transcendental faculties. Concrete life is the subject matter for an empirical science of subjectivity, the conditions of possibility for which philosophy deduces: "Because he understands inner perception in this empiricist, psychological sense and because, warned by Hume's skepticism, he fears every recourse to the psychological ... Kant gets involved in his mythical concept-formation" (115/117).

By referring to a life that is mine, but which I cannot own, these mythical concepts wed transcendentalism to an appeal to an unknowable mode of existence failing which knowledge itself becomes incomprehensible. The mythical, then, is leveraged by the needs of science: "It helps not at all to try to explain the incomprehensibility of the transcendental constructions by outlining, in the same spirit, a constructive theory of the necessity of such incomprehensible things" (1970, 200/203). According to Husserl, this constructivism is inevitable for Kant because, fearing psychologism, he refuses to approach life and its world directly. This is the meaning of his accusation that Kant took the lifeworld for granted. It would be equally wrong to accuse Kant of treating the phenomenal world as something apart from subjectivity as it would to accuse him of failing to see that knowledge of the world is an *explanandum*. Husserl's accusation is exactly that Kant explains the world by constructing subjectivity as its *explanans* rather than reflecting on how subjectivity actually discloses the world.

In relation to the transcendental tradition, this represents an abandonment of the most radical impulses in Descartes and Hume. The mundanization of the cogito by naturalistic psychology causes Kant to overlook that it is the ground and source of any rigorous transcendental knowledge. The kind of present-tense, egoic reflection introduced in Descartes' first two meditations no longer has the authority to make philosophical decisions. It gives way in Kant to deductions that make use of our commitment to the legitimacy of certain existing sciences. From Hume is lost the theme of questioning the obviousness of the pre-given world. Kant addresses the pre-given world in light of his concern to implicate in transcendental functions the nature hypothesized and constructed by modern physics. Here as there, scientific interest skips over the naïve forms of life we express in ordinary language. To the extent that transcendentalism needs to make use of this experience, it looks to psychological concepts that it prudently limits to what is as general and "obvious" as possible.

According to Husserl, Kant's scientific transcendentalism took the shape it did because the Lockean tradition had so alienated psychology from the essence of its own subject matter that any appeal to the psychological seemed to entail a naturalistic epistemology (1970, 116n/118n). This assessment emphasizes the importance of Brentano's intentional psychology as the forerunner to phenomenology. Brentano rediscovers intentionality as the being of consciousness and sets up an eidetic science of correlations between objects and their presentation. While he still conceives this as a regional project alongside the natural sciences, and thus overlooks its critical role with respect to all established world-knowledge, Brentano reopens a direct approach to subjectivity apart from the causal nexus and the inductive techniques that master it. When the systematic aims of a transcendental critique of reason emerge again, they will make use of this advance in psychology.

Though he does not say so, Husserl's self-conception is that he does for the transcendental motif what Kant might have done had he benefited from Brentanian psychology. Because the intimate relationship between intentional psychology and transcendental philosophy is now apparent, constructive methods are no longer necessary. Freed from the legacy of dualist misinterpretation, the ego cogito assumes its proper place in the transcendental system as the author and object of all philosophical knowledge. Intentionally included in this cogito are now all cogitata, scientific and non-scientific, having just that sense of transcendence and subject-relativity they do prior to reflection. Appropriating the mental accomplishments through which the world has its meaning and validity no longer entails a skeptical posture; it is a self-explication of reason. Furthermore, the critique of science is now just one facet of the general critique to which I am subject when I realize that my own life of transcendental accomplishment is the universal and apodictic presupposition for anything that counts as being for me. The tasks of self-examination traditionally restricted to the mundane domain of "behavior" or "action" now apply first of all to those constitutive accomplishments through which I have a surrounding world of nature and culture (1970, 246/250). The transcendental development of intentional analysis effectively synthesizes the Socratic ideal of integrity with the Cartesian ideal of science.

5. Decision between the Two Scientific Ideas

Husserl displays a teleological unity in our theoretical tradition from the standpoint that transcendentalism is its most fundamental tendency, driving through to realization in phenomenology. However, our theoretical tradition also clearly admits of a teleological reconstruction from an objectivist standpoint, according to which metaphysical constructions gradually give way to experimentally verifiable knowledge about the external world. In fact, one version of this history would describe how objectivism abandons the kind of physicalist realism targeted by Husserl's critique, instead understanding "reality in-itself" as a point of convergence for endless discovery and confirmation—an interpretation of mundane science with which Husserl agrees. Alternatively, a pragmatic reconstruction could focus on the increasingly obvious superfluity of the philosophically inflated idea of episteme, such that science, like other practices, eventually becomes content simply to serve the interests that emerge in natural life without justifying itself transcendentally or objectivistically. By every reasonable empirical measure, such as conformity to specialist consensus or to general educated opinion, Husserl's reconstruction loses out to these competitors. The mere fact of an established phenomenological research program does not resolve the issue in Husserl's favor either. The naïve historical standpoint that requires appropriation at the ultimate level is that this program is a transformative fulfillment that realizes what our scientific tradition has always been about.[1]

This stance that transcendentalism is what the modern scientific tradition is all about is not finally justified by theoretical considerations. Husserl rather appeals to "our" commitment to a vision of what science in general means for human life (1970, 5/3). At this level, the struggle over science has to do with the human interests that science advances. Here, transcendentalism is opposed to world-directed science as such, regardless of how the latter is justified. After exposing objectivism as a false interpretation of modern natural science, Husserl often poses the question of what the success of this science really means for human existence. His answers point to a group of related phenomena: "mastery" of the surrounding world (66/67), "prediction" and a "having in advance" of situations (51/51), "technical control of nature" (271/316), "power over ... fate" (66/67), "prosperity" (6/3), "happiness" (66/67). We can sum up this position by stating that the *Lebensbedeutsamkeit* of world-directed science is mastery (*Herrschaft*).

For Husserl, interest in mastery is not the symptom of an aggressive psychological disposition. It is built into the very structure of world-directed life; it is in this sense "natural." Normal perception is at once an inductive grasp of things and an experience of power and control centered on my own body: "through bodily 'holding sway' in the form of striking, lifting, resisting, and the like, I act as ego across distances, primarily on the corporeal aspects of objects in the world" (1970, 217/220–1). The act of moving my body in space is the localization of "my own originally experienced holding-sway" (217/221), that is, my having a grip on my environment as a realm for will-fulfilling action. While I cannot experience the holding-sway of others directly, it appears in their lived bodies. This is the condition for every form of cooperation and conflict between wills in the world. In acting for, with, or against others, inductive perception and judgment survey the realm over which humans hold sway, effectively measuring and traversing the "distances" across which egos act. Husserl projects a historical development whereby this induction becomes increasingly reflective and methodical, furnishes instruments for itself, and eventually leaps forward by subjecting the "corporeal aspects of objects" to idealization. This new way of measuring and calculating radically enhances the scope of human action and human control over outcomes. Husserl does not deride the happiness and prosperity that result from this revolution. Understood purely as a "theoretical-technical accomplishment" modern inductive natural science is a wonder of human culture, indeed a "miracle" (66/68).

Husserl interprets the success of modern science in this dimension as a consolation. The great danger, then, is not mastery, but that mastery might blind us to the fact that world-directed science fails to fulfill a deeper interest we have in science as such.[2] Husserl most often calls this interest "self-responsibility" or "autonomy" (1970, 338/272). In everyday life, it is pursued in acts of reflection that examine and attempt to bring to evidence what is "unquestioned and 'obvious'" (13/11). This taking responsibility proceeds in individual and collective life at a variety of levels. But it is a mere "prefiguration" of what philosophical or scientific reason aims to achieve (13/11). Just as everyday induction is "artless" compared to natural-scientific technique (51/51), so is everyday self-responsibility inadequate in light of the idea of autonomy formulated in scientific reason (338/273). The latter promises to make one "capable of an absolute self-responsibility" (283/329), providing ways of appropriating naïveté that will not themselves prove naïve. In light of the interest of self-responsibility, science thus appears as the "highest function of mankind" by "making possible mankind's development into a personal autonomy and into an all-encompassing autonomy for mankind" (338/273). In the *Crisis*, Husserl addresses "us" as bearers of this interest that world-directed science cannot satisfy, and in pursuit of which world-directed science itself requires appropriation. The failure of world-directed science is relative to an interest in science that bestows upon it the *Lebensbedeutsamkeit* of enabling absolute self-responsibility.

At a crucial point in the *Crisis*, Husserl presents as a failure of the modern scientific tradition its inattention to the subject-relative lifeworld in its very subject-relativity. Understanding this failure as a failure is the transition from the historical reflections to the phenomenological-theoretical reflections that take up the unsolved problem of the tradition. But in light of what interpretation of science's *Lebensbedeutsamkeit* is this a failure? If the point of science is to facilitate human mastery over the surrounding world, then such a study is senseless. Science, like every other human practice, has as its background the world of life and action. The presupposition that this world exists merely refers to the obvious setting condition for accomplishing anything that matters. The fact that science invariably "presupposes" the lifeworld that it aims to determine objectively only indicates that the presupposition of reality in general holds no cognitive or practical interest (IB § 4). Husserl can only demonstrate the need for a science of the lifeworld by appealing to an absolute interest in presuppositionlessness, an interest not exhausted by the cognitive-practical orientation of natural-attitude life. Tellingly, the appeal is in the form of a question: "Does philosophy fulfill the sense of its primal establishment as the universal and grounding science if it leaves this realm to its 'anonymity'? Can it do this, can any science do this which seeks to be a branch of philosophy, i.e. which would tolerate no presuppositions?" (1970, 112/114–15).

Husserl here questions his readers not as generic human beings but as inheritors of a particular historical movement that has explicitly posited presuppositionlessness as an absolute value that "consciously directs human becoming" (1970, 15/13). The *Lebensbedeutsamkeit* at stake is a "significance that was historically entrusted to philosophy, given to it as a task" (197/200). The subject of this meaning bestowal is "European humanity, which sought … to create the universal science as the instrument for giving itself new rootedness" (ibid.). The failure of world-directed science is then finally relative to the *Lebensbedeutsamkeit* invested in science by European humanity. The crisis itself, understood as the loss of this *Lebensbedeutsamkeit* (5/3), points back to this investment. So long as its aims had not yet been restricted by the paradoxes inherent in objectivism, "science could claim significance—indeed as we know, the major role [*führende Bedeutung*]—in the completely new shaping of European humanity which began with the Renaissance" (7/5). Husserl's history of philosophy aims to explain why science lost this leadership (*Führung*) and why it is salvageable (ibid.). In the *Crisis*, the history of philosophy thus belongs to the history of European humanity. The very title of the work makes this clear.

Husserl summarizes his *Vienna Lecture* by spelling out the fundamental role of Europe in historical reflections that diagnose the crisis: "In order to be able to comprehend the disarray of the present 'crisis,' we had to work out the *concept of Europe as the historical teleology of the infinite goals of reason* ... The 'crisis' could then become distinguishable as the *apparent failure of rationalism* ... of a rational culture" (1970, 299/347). It is from the perspective of the European teleology that this failure is legible as a failure at all, and then as merely apparent, that is, as surmountable. The failure is due precisely to the form of naïveté that dominated the whole modern period: "the most general title for this naïveté is *objectivism*" (292/339). But it is because of what European humanity sought in science that this naïveté eventually jeopardizes the whole "Modern Age," transforming its pride into a "growing dissatisfaction" and "distress" (294/342). In the *Prague Lecture*, Husserl writes that the collapse of universal science signifies an "existential catastrophe of European humanity. Just as science no longer lived up to its ultimate meaning as science, so too European man his ultimate meaning as European man" (1993, 108). However, this failure is merely apparent insofar as "we" can still understand and overcome objectivistic naïveté by bringing the transcendental movement to fruition. It is as "good Europeans" that Husserl's readers can recognize the fundamental importance of transcendentalism and take responsibility for the crisis of science (1970, 299/348).

Because Husserl's work on the crisis attempts to appropriate the ultimate presuppositions, it makes peculiar use of the authorial "we." In phenomenological-theoretical works, the authorial "we" is an invitation to participate empathetically in shaping and executing an investigation such that each of "us" reflects "for himself" on his own transcendental life. Occasionally, this "we" may coincide with the object of the investigation in its consideration of the ego in various attitudes and acts. In the crisis interpretation, philosophizing subjectivity acquires a historical specificity. This is most obvious in texts like *Crisis I* and *Vienna Lecture*, which make hortatory appeals to an audience in earshot. The novel use of the first-person plural, however, is required by any work that engages the crisis problematic and operates there implicitly if not explicitly. "We" who carry out the appropriative reflections are members of a historical community dedicated to scientific culture and struggling for the true meaning of that culture as a culture of autonomy and self-responsibility rather than of mere mastery and prosperity. Any actual engagement with the crisis problematic has to specify the historical provenance, limits, and prospects of this "we." At the same time, because this historical community is at issue precisely as the bearer of an Enlightenment project, its historical specificity must be reconciled with an anthropological indeterminacy that allows for participation irrespective of traditional inheritance. Husserl seems to have been well aware of this challenge in working out his concept of "Europe."

6. The Definition of Europe

Husserl's "Europe" names a historical community that seeks to overcome merely anthropological history. This entails that Europe has all the properties essential to any historical community without being defined by them. From an external perspective, this poses the definitional problem of how to apply historical categories to Europe. From an internal perspective, it poses the historical problem of how Europe defines itself over against history.

Husserl directly confronts these problems in *Crisis I* and the *Vienna Lecture*. A people or nation counts as European primarily because of its dedication to self-transformation in light of philosophical ideals. European humanity "seeks to live, and only can live" in the free reshaping of existence promised by philosophy (1970, 274/319). At the same time, however, "Europe" refers to this form of life as actually embodied in communities at various levels. This requires a degree of cultural coherence such that it is possible, even on Husserl's strict definition, to distinguish between Europe and non-Europe similarly to how one distinguishes between any two cultural worlds. The difference between home and alien, familiarity and strangeness, writes Husserl, is a "fundamental category of all historicity" (275/320). It thus functions in judgments about what does and does not belong to Europe and situates the European world in relation to an outside from which it can realize its locality. However, because Europe is not *merely* an empirical anthropological type (15–16/13–14), the application of this category "cannot suffice" to determine what is European about Europe (275/320). As we will see, European humanity is not itself a "people," defined by customary norms and a common heritage, but an open network of peoples committed to a common form of responsibility and freely claiming a common historical origin.

In the *Vienna Lecture*, Husserl asserts that he does not refer to Europe "as on a map." He thereby intends to distinguish his "Europe" from a purely geographical concept that would pick out the occupants of a certain area bound by coordinates on the globe. This is an odd contrast, however, because the understanding of world maps is typically cultural and historical in nature. Their boundaries refer to socially real demarcations in the landscape between those spheres of communal life Husserl himself calls "territories."[3] Mapped boundaries define not geometrical shapes that contain inhabitants but the sometimes-shifting places where complex unities of cultural life primarily develop, where certain ways of communicating and living are normal, where certain traditions are maintained and contested, and so on. If such are the territories one sees symbolized on maps, then Husserl does mean Europe as on a map, though not exclusively the territory conventionally called Europe on maps. He thus includes in Europe *other territories* such as the United States (1970, 273/318). By emphasizing that Husserl's Europe is earthbound and thereby mappable, we ensure that the critique of geographical reductionism does not justify the idealization of Europe, and thereby the evasion of the difficulties that attend its earthliness.[4] If we divorce the ideal from the real, then it is right to say, as Husserl does in the *Prague Letter*, that the meaning of European culture as a "spiritualization through scientific reason" is a "task consciously alive in empirical Europe" (1989, 241). Concretely, Europe is a historical community oriented by ideas.

Let us highlight some characteristics of historical communities in a way that clarifies the object of Husserl's reconstruction. European humanity does not refer to the whole of human history understood as a history of reason. Instead, it refers to a community *explicitly oriented* by the idea of autonomy, an outgrowth of the emergence of philosophy as a cultural practice (1970, 15/13, 276/321). European humanity is thus historical in the sense that it had a beginning motivated by definite circumstances. It is also a historical community in that it encompasses the whole continuous life of the societies that comprise it, within which discontinuous or goal-relative communities form. Europe is a "unity of spiritual life" that has *its* institutions, organizations, and so on (273–4/319). Philosophy is "the functioning brain" of European humanity, but it is one cultural form within the societal organism (290/338).[5] Philosophical history, determined as the history of European humanity, is irreducible to the history of philosophy. It includes the transformations philosophy brings about in the organization of the broader communal life. European humanity is also historical in that it is *a* historical community in the midst of others. Even if the entire Earth were to Europeanize, as was Husserl's hope (1993, 16), Europe would remain a territorially bound development exposed to possible communication with non-European rational animals. Finally, European humanity is a historical community in the inward sense that mature participation in the community involves cultivating a critical awareness of its historical definition: its beginning, its outside, and its organization.

In Husserl's reconstruction we can discern three features of European existence that define its paradoxical relation to human historicity in general:

1. Denationalization, which describes the development through which a pre-philosophical, but culturally developed nation breaks out of "political historicity" and charges philosophy with enabling a new kind of existence. This development is exhibited first in Greece as it is claimed by Europe's renaissance, but also in any process of Europeanization.
2. Renaissance, which describes the development through which Europe emerges by appropriating the Greek mode of existence across an intervening middle age. Presumably, a similar development also occurs for all subsequent Europeanization of non-European nations.
3. Europeanization, which describes the development of Europe into its non-European outside. This occurs through processes of denationalization and renaissance, and presumably also describes, in modified form, the historical maintenance of already constituted Europe.[6]

The exhibition of these features in "our" generally available history is meant to clarify our participation in an actually existing community dedicated to an Enlightenment project requiring maximally wakeful self-responsibility. This reconstructed understanding of Europe—not the conventional understanding—is the basis for any claims about which cultural forms promote or threaten its existence. Expanding upon hints in Husserl's crisis writings, the following sections piece together a Husserlian account of Europe and consider how it links European humanity to the engagement of specific societal problems that arise in the wake of philosophy.

7. The Nation and Political Historicity

In his crisis writings, Husserl consistently understands Europe in relation to the life of nations. It is in a specific nation that Europe has its "spiritual birthplace" (1970, 276/321). European spirit emerges in that nation through the realization of a peculiarly national naïveté (1993, 13, 286). The appropriation of this naïveté leads to an "upheaval of national culture" (1970, 288/335). Yet, Europe does not dissolve or subsume national communities. Europe itself is a "spreading synthesis of nations" in which each nation pursues its own historical possibilities (ibid.). In the *Prague Letter*, we encounter the following striking formulation: "Autonomy is not the concern of isolated individuals, but rather, *by way of their nation*, of humanity" (1989, 241; my emphasis). Husserl describes philosophical humanity as the result of developments in historical consciousness that transform and relativize, but do not negate, one's belonging to a national community.

The historical starting point for this development is "the ancient Greek nation in the seventh and sixth centuries B.C." (276). While this historical reference is essential to Husserl's reflections, his aim is not to recount the facts of Greek history, but to understand the new forms of life it unleashed. This goal is best served not by painting a vivid picture of the past but by thinking through structural modifications of our present, everyday life (1993, 380). The kind of collective "national" life out of which philosophical culture first emerged is still intuitively accessible in its relevant features, and indeed is still lived by the reflecting philosopher upon suspending the motivational power of certain ideas. The reflections attend to certain possibilities of historical existence in order to clarify a single course of events that has actualized them.

Why is the nation the staging ground for those transformations that initiate the history of European humanity? Historically, the antecedence of the natural attitude is experienced as the antecedence of a particular communal world into which one was born. Husserl's most general concept of nation means nothing more than this etymological sense derived from *natio* (1993, 9). As such, the national community and the national world is the inalienable orientation from which all discoveries of provincialism proceed (IB § 3), and in terms of which any existential individuation must occur (IB § 5). It is the inherently first ground for awakenings. More specifically, Husserl focuses on the nation at a particular phase of its development. It is not incidental that the ancient Greek nation stood "in contact with the great and already highly cultivated nations of its surrounding world" (1970, 285/332). Husserl calls "political historicity" (1993, 10) this form of life characterized by mutual awareness of home and foreign nations, each of which has evolved institutions that purport to provide for its subjects an encompassing framework for a satisfying life. Under certain circumstances, political historicity can realize its own provinciality such that a new form of life becomes practically necessary. The community into which one was born is not thereby abandoned, but relativized such that a new, infinite, community spiritually occupies it from within. While this new form of communalization introduces its own appropriative demands, it remains answerable to the ideals of worldliness and authenticity.

Let us begin by considering how the national community is uniquely encompassing. In any community (not a mere demographic class), I understand myself as a participant in a common undertaking. Correlative to this common undertaking is the common world in which and in terms of which it is undertaken. What "we" accomplish together may be a simple errand, a skillful activity, or a long-term program of action informed by certain values. In many cases, forms of communication specific to these communities illuminate their common worlds and facilitate their common endeavors. These brief indications suffice to highlight the encompassing nature of Husserl's "nation." Members of the national community do not, as such, pursue the accomplishment of any definite goal or type of goal. They instead pursue a common "life-praxis" through which the pursuits of a normal lifetime are pursuable (1993, 9). Correlatively, the national world is a common world into which I am born and which I *need never leave* in order to live a fulfilling life. The "leaving" at issue here is only geographical because it is spiritual. Even if I never exit my village or city, I am aware of sharing a language and other customary ways of behaving with a broader, indefinite community among whom I could live my whole life. Husserl thus refers to the nation as a "universal life-community" (1970, 281/327) and the national world as a "total-situation" (1993, 385) or a "complete [*totale*], practical surrounding world" (38).

In any communal activity and communal world, differences in understanding between people are, for the most part, readily understandable. This is already evident at the level of spatial perception. Apprehending myself and the other as examining the same thing from different perspectives involves the presumption that what the other sees differs from what I see because of her position. This is a position I could hypothetically inhabit. If I did, I would see roughly what the other now sees. A common natural world is thus the foundation for the communicability of perspectives, however these may be corrected or negotiated. At a more concrete level, differences in understanding are similarly understandable on the basis of a common cultural world. Cultural objects fit into recognizable contexts of action where they motivate people in familiar ways. Differences in how and to what ends people are motivated are understandable in terms not of a merely spatial position but of a social position within a framework of salient types of diversity (gender, age, vocation, region, etc.). The difference between my views and those of someone of a different type is itself a familiar feature of a common world and a common life that includes that difference, and therefore gives rise to no controversy. In everyday life, "other people" are not only there as subjects who understand a world of cultural objects. They are also there as cultural objects, immediately legible in their bearing. Cultural literacy about diverse types of people already guides the management of various life situations before any attempt to resolve the differences it considers as a matter of course.

Husserl emphasizes that when an interest does emerge in distinguishing true from false viewpoints, it makes use of the common national world as an ultimate hermeneutic frame for the giving of reasons. Again, there is an analogue here in simple perception. The true color of a perceived object is relative to a system of normal circumstances including, for instance, that the object is seen in daylight, from the right distance, and by perceivers whose bodies are healthy. The idea of an "irrelative true appearance" of the color, independent of all such circumstances, is nonsensical. Husserl's claim is that the idea of a truth about the world that would be irrelative to the life-praxis of the nation is equally nonsensical for political-historical humanity (1993, 9). Just as conflicts between sincere claims about true color are adjudicated with reference to normal perceptual circumstances, so are conflicts between sincere claims about practical affairs adjudicated with reference to normal cultural circumstances, themselves relative to the national community. Husserl writes: "The communal ground for all identifications, for all experiences and all validations of experience, for all propositions and propositional truths is the already valid traditional or historical world of the nation … Every dispute, every resolution of what is disputed, every perception and other experience presupposes this horizon, i.e. transpires in it as something valid *a priori*" (44–5). Husserl draws particular attention to the epistemic authority of "normal people" who have grown up in the traditions of the home nation, who understand the situations to which claims and justifications pertain and are therefore competent to decide when they are satisfying (8–9). The national world is composed of familiar practical situations "in which the practical interest belonging to them determines, through its normal fulfillment, what is true and what is false" (8). Truths describe the world in ways that reliably guide activity, always within the total-activity of national life itself. It is simply inconceivable (in fact) that there could be an effort to get at the truth apart from the life-praxis of the nation and its guiding light, the "reason of natural common sense" (386). The relativity of truth to the life of the nation is essential to its very meaning as truth.

In the "great nations" described in Husserl's reconstruction, the function of the national world as an ultimate horizon for human life is thematic in a special way. We can here follow up on a distinction Husserl occasionally draws between a mere nation (or *Volk*) and a "politically concentrated nation" (1993, 10–11, 387).[7] The latter, let us say, has evolved institutions that enshrine national life as a whole, concentrating power in leaders and functionaries who embody or attend to the national life-praxis as such (1970, 282/328, 284/330; 1993, 40). The nation, in all its diversity and as a whole, is itself present in the national world. For instance, the law, as code and practice, is a public display of binding norms that enable an orderly national life. The threat and spectacle of punishment makes explicit the actions that support or oppose this order. The military is a fighting force that acts on behalf of the nation. The war for which it readies exposes the contingency of the national life-praxis as such. The national religion combines a mythological understanding of the cosmos as a whole with an account of national history and its heroes. As a practice managed by a priesthood, religion interprets and appeases the mythical powers that determine the fate of the nation and its inhabitants. Husserl's descriptions of the national life proximate to the emergence of philosophical culture consistently mention such institutions. Not only members of the home nation but also curious foreigners can contemplate the picture they provide of a total national life-praxis.

In Husserl's reconstruction, the totalizing function of the nation is uprooted in an awareness of the national life-praxis and nationally grounded truth as *merely* national. This is achieved via a consideration of the home nation in light of foreign nations. However, foreign nations and their inhabitants are there for members of the home nation in a variety of ways, only one of which can motivate the realization that the national life-praxis is naïve. We can best track Husserl's account by outlining three modes of apprehension. First, foreign nations and their lifeways are themselves obvious and familiar features of the orienting world of the home nation (1993, 41n). Normal members of the home nation know about the differences that typically characterize foreign life-practices, as evidenced in foreign goods, customs, laws, myths, and so on. These differences, unlike intranational differences, are not readily bridged by cultural literacy, but they are registered by a general anthropological comprehension as abnormal variants of familiar phenomena (42). Second, the international difference is made salient in the attempt to understand the foreign life-praxis. Well-known facts about the foreigners indicate a foreign perspective for which the abnormal is normal. The attempt to take this perspective into account creates an ambiguous interpretive situation in which one's own homeworld can come into view as one homeworld among others, indeed as a foreign world for the foreign homeworld. Life in political historicity regularly requires this hermeneutic exercise. In commercial and military engagements, understanding the foreign perspective is obviously of great practical importance. Information about analogous vocational practices, perhaps discerned only in products of foreign work, may motivate practitioners in the home nation to consider aims and methods through the eyes of their foreign counterparts. Translation and even bilingual competence may become essential for these and similar reasons. Travel or emigration may lead to abiding interpersonal relationships with foreigners that disclose the foreign world through the rich medium of a person raised in its traditions. Husserl is thinking of such developments when he describes a nation in political historicity "entering into" the historicity of foreign nations (10) and encountering their "alien intelligence" (387).

Neither of these modes of foreign apprehension is the proximate motive for the emergence of European humanity in Greece. With reference to the second mode in particular, we note that the estranging localization of the home nation in international space does not devalue nationally relative truth as *merely* relative. Incompatible "true" descriptions of the world simply reflect the fact that there are conflicting encompassing life-praxes. The right way to do things in the foreign nation is really right, but for the foreigners. In political historicity, there is no method for resolving such incompatibility other than a contest between the life-praxes themselves—Husserl wonders how the truth of national world-interpretations fares once foreign armies have overrun the country (1993, 11n). Even in the case that an illuminating encounter with a foreign perspective provokes a correction of judgments at home, the correction still counts as true because it enhances the fulfillment of practical interests within the national life-praxis. Steinbock recognizes this explicitly in his account of home–alien encounters. When an alien encounter motivates a critique of home norms and traditions, its purpose "is precisely to realize more fully that very normality and tradition" (1995, 230); "Through liminal transgressive encounter with the alien, homecomrades realize their *own* possibilities" (1995, 245). The governing idea of traditional, anthropologically grounded truth survives the realization of provinciality in the face of the alien.

The third mode of apprehension depends upon the suspension of the practical interests of the national life-praxis. Encounters with foreign nations in light of diplomatic, military, commercial, or other social concerns lie within the "normal interest-driven life [*Interessenleben*]" of the home nation and leave no room for "general observations about relativities" (1993, 388). Especially in the *Vienna Lecture*, Husserl underlines that the decisive apprehension occurs in an attitude of curiosity, which he describes as a unique modification in life-interest, "an interest which has separated itself off from life-interests, has let them fall" (1970, 285/332).

> In this attitude, man views first of all the multiplicity of nations, his own and others, each with its own surrounding world which is valid for it, is taken for granted, with its traditions, its gods, its demons, its mythical powers, simply as the actual world. Through this astonishing contrast there appears the distinction between world-representation and actual world, and the new question of truth

arises: not tradition-bound, everyday truth, but an identical truth which is valid for all who are no longer blinded by tradition, a truth-in-itself. (1970, 285–6/332)

As a participant in political historicity, the international surveyor is sensitive to the depth of foreign nations as home worlds in their own right, but rather than entering into these worlds, he considers their outward appearance as interpretive wholes, especially as mythological pictures of the cosmos (1993, 388). Curious detachment from the home nation allows for its inclusion as one member in this multiplicity of surveyed worlds, and it becomes evident that *all* national life-praxes and the forms of reason they generate are identically naïve. This discovery of a universal human provinciality, which no syncretism of traditions could address, becomes the basis for new conception of reason oriented toward the one actual world that was always implied in national life, but went unnoticed. Philosophy can now emerge as the goal of a new vocational community.

The realization of human provinciality contains the impetus for both the transcendentalist and objectivist tendencies within the history of philosophy. Husserl recognizes that as a matter of fact the latter immediately becomes dominant. The new question of irrelative truth is first addressed, not to the actual world that appears only subjective-relatively but to a constructed, irrelative world that would underlie it (1993, 390–1). However, Husserl's origin story ties the emergence of philosophy to an absolute devaluation of naïveté as such. The totally novel "*Weltfrage*" that arises out of political historicity aims to "leave behind all naïve traditional commitment" (1993, 389). Because it is committed to the ultimate traditional datum, the pregiven world, the objectivist program cannot satisfy this interest. Ultimately, it is this same absolute devaluation of naïveté that accounts for the "universal and independent significance" of the transcendental investigation of the lifeworld (1970, 133/136). Beyond resolving those dilemmas raised by the history of objectivism within theory, the investigation answers to the basic need of philosophical humanity. Its purpose is to clarify not only science but also "all other acquisitions of human activity … [The lifeworld] must be considered in terms of the truly concrete universality whereby it embraces, both directly and in the manner of horizons, all the built-up levels of validity acquired by men for the world of their common life" (ibid.). This investigation applies the new question of truth to the naïvely given world itself, rather than abandoning it to "mere doxa." The rigorous appropriation of naïveté thus requires "a return to the naïveté of life—but in a reflection which rises above this naïveté" (59/60), a return to the life that "naïvely pregives the being of the world and then rationalizes or … objectifies it" (69/70).

8. Denationalization

Whatever the inner tendencies of philosophy, its appearance on the cultural scene as a new kind of vocation creates an unstable situation. Whoever has understood human provinciality cannot continue to live life according to the relative truths of the nation, the relativity of which now counts against their legitimacy. Simultaneous with the new idea of truth is its equally novel counteridea, seized upon by the Sophists, that there is no truth.[8] The negative assessment of traditional norms as mere conventions provokes a conservative reassertion of their dependability (1993, 389). It is in this precarious moment that a new cultural movement takes shape, rejecting both the sophistic and conservative responses to the destabilization of national life and posing afresh the question of what "our possibilities" might be. Husserl defines this movement by its projection of a life-praxis informed by universal critique, "the universal critique of all life and all life-goals, all cultural products and systems that have already arisen out of the life of man; and thus it also becomes a critique of mankind itself and of the values which guide it implicitly or explicitly" (1970, 283/329). It is only when philosophy, as a relatively closed vocational concern, prompts and sustains this movement that one can speak of a philosophical culture in Husserl's sense. Husserl's ideal of philosophical culture is neither that everyone should become a philosopher nor that philosophy should answer all of life's questions, but that the new idea of philosophical truth should inject a spirit of infinity into every exercise of reasoning about life in the world.

This "spirit of infinity" has a manifold sense that we can tease out from some elliptical passages in the *Vienna Lecture*. It consists in an explicit orientation toward (1) truths confirmable as identical now and later, for me and for you. The truth is infinite in the sense of being instantiated across space and time—it is an ideality; (2) truths that are unconditionally true, which implies that their justification is itself infinite, in the sense of unending. He who can give reasons for or against an assertion is "everyone," which now means, not any normally acculturated person but any rational person; (3) the endless building of truth upon truth by pursuing the implications of provisionally acquired truths. An infinite task on Husserl's view is a task that proceeds under this explicit threefold orientation (not any unbounded task that, like that of Sisyphus, admits of endless continuation). He can thus define philosophical culture as a "history of the cutting-off of finite mankind's development as it becomes mankind with infinite tasks" (1970, 279/325). This is tantamount, however, to the movement whereby "the general idea of truth-in-itself becomes the universal norm of all the relative truths that arise in human life" (287/334). Relative truths continue to count as true within their appropriate contexts, and praxis relies upon them as such. However, the epistemic situation includes new kinds of optima which may be invoked at any time.[9] Philosophical humanity "lives in finitude" but "toward poles of infinity" (277/322).

The spirit of infinity undermines the function of the nation as an ultimate life-horizon. Husserl distinguishes between "man in finitude," whose motivation "moves within his finitely surveyable surrounding world" and the new kind of man, motivated by infinite ideas (1970, 279/324), and aware of the "openly endless horizon in which he lives" (ibid.). In particular, the enshrining institutions of the nation are robbed of their ultimate authority. Truths about piety and justice, underwritten by the priesthood and other functionaries of state, are subject to the new critique, which is free to reject them or else transform them "in the spirit of philosophical ideality" (288/335). The new humanity is "irreligious," which does not mean secular, but critical of nationally bound religion (1993, 46). The critique also penetrates into the whole system of traditional norms that guide everyday life: "those of right, of beauty, of usefulness, dominant personal values, values connected with personal characteristics, etc." (1970, 287/334). The project of becoming a mature person is no longer relative to the paradigms of excellence that belong to the national world, its heros, its models of manhood and womanhood, for instance. Education now transcends inculcation in national traditions because it inculcates the habit of questioning these traditions as to their "true" value (ibid.). This amounts to a spiritual emigration from the national world. But the emigration does not move toward foreign traditions. Whatever the alien encounter discloses is itself a traditional datum that requires critical appropriation by "everyone" in the infinite sense. Gasché captures Husserl's intent when he claims that the foreign phenomenon that relativizes the Greek experience of the world is that of the universal itself (2009, 70).

Conversely, universal critique can only begin by working upon and through the matrix of traditions that constitute a particular national life-praxis. It is precisely the uprooted communal life in all its specificity that requires appropriation. The development of philosophical culture is thus engaged by particular contents and belongs, in an ambiguous sense, to national history. It is carried out in the Greek language, in relation to Greek religion, politics, art, and so on. The upheaval of national culture characteristic of European humanity "is accomplished at first within the spiritual space of a single nation, the Greek nation" (1970, 277/322). This space coincides with the territory of the nation as a political-historical reality. Husserl's practice of delimiting philosophical humanity with reference to units like "Greece," "the United States," or "the English Dominions" depends upon this (273/318). Paradoxically, then, the nation or group of nations transforming through critique reinstates the totalizing claim for its subjects, but now on nontraditional grounds. The new history that begins in Greece is "the epoch of mankind which seeks to live, *and only can live*, in the free shaping of its existence, its historical life, though ideas of reason, through infinite tasks" (274/319; my emphasis). In the same vein, Husserl asserts that there is no rational motive for a European to emigrate—spiritually—to a non-European world (275/320). We will examine this assertion in our section on Europeanization.

Greece is the paradigm for Husserl's European nation insofar as it undergoes the "immense cultural transformation which radiates out from philosophy" (1970, 286/333). We may summarize the features of such a national community as follows: (1) the normalization of a new personality type characterized by a critical "posture" that habitually subjects traditional norms and truths to the infinite framework of interrogation (287/334); (2) a "movement of education" that aims at cultivating this critical posture (286/333); (3) an ongoing struggle "in the sphere of political power" between this critical culture and the conservative defense of traditional authorities (288/335). We also mention the following problems implied by this transformation: (1) the tension between the upheaval of national culture and the nation's continued involvement in "commerce and power struggles" between political-historical territories (289/336); (2) the division of the national population into those who are and are not educated in the new sense (286/333); (3) the confusion of sophistry with critique, and critique—as compared with negativistic sophistry—with conservatism (1993, 389-90); (4) the temptation to finitization, that is, the reduction of scientific culture to the application of scientific results to natural interests (1970, 283/329); (5) the ambiguity between the new attitudes toward foreign cultures consequent upon the discovery of human provinciality and the familiar political-historical attitudes of chauvinism on the one hand and openness on the other (275/320).

Nowhere in the *Crisis* does Husserl expand upon this basic paradigm of European nationhood derived from the Greeks. His definition of Europe as a subject of crisis renders incidental many of those practices and institutions ordinarily invoked by champions of "the West." Husserl does not even privilege Athenian democracy.[10] He regards every rational reform of political, religious, legal, or socioeconomic life as a result of universal critique within the traditional matrix of a European nation or group of nations. But a nation is not European because it has carried out specific reforms. It is European just in virtue of the "spirit of free critique and norm giving aimed at infinite tasks" (1970, 289/336). The movement of rational critique within European humanity may even eventually reverse the process of political concentration out of which it arose. Europe is by definition a spreading synthesis of nations or peoples, not nation-states. Husserl's general concept of nationality contains wide variations, including the political unification of multiple peoples, the political division of a single people, and peoples lacking political unification under various conditions (1993, 10–11). At the limit, the projected development of Husserl's Europe includes the possibility of a stateless global (even interplanetary) community.[11]

9. Renaissance

Ancient Greece is the model of European nationhood. However, Europe has not already begun in Greece; it is a fundamentally modern development. Husserl defines European humanity such that it begins by modeling itself on ancient Greece. The historical reference for this moment of the Europe concept is the "well-known" phenomenon of Renaissance. Husserl does not specify which Renaissance he means. He points only to a general devaluation of the medieval "way of existing" in favor of the Greek or "philosophical form of existence" (1970, 8/5). This generality, coupled with Husserl's refusal, at least in the *Crisis*, to trace any special lineage that would bind particular contemporary peoples to the ancient Greeks, suggests a novel form of European historicity that guards the subject of crisis from anthropological superstition and suspends the guiding function of established self-conceptions. According to this view, the Renaissance is not a phase in a broader European history, defined ethnologically or geographically. Instead, any political-historical people of whatever ethno-geographic determination *becomes* European by leaping over its inheritance, its "middle age," in order to model itself on the universal criticism of tradition that broke through in Greece. Just as we heard the *natio* in nation, so should we hear it in Renaissance. It invests historical life with a new beginning for which each can make herself existentially responsible. This reconciliation of autonomy and historical rootedness becomes the basis for a spreading synthesis of nations in which none has a privileged claim to the Greek origin and each retains a distinct critical task through the reform of its own traditions.

The Renaissance in which Europe begins is independent of any allegiance to the contents of Greek culture. Husserl writes that "after some hesitation" Renaissance humanity determined that what was "essential" to the ancient

Greeks was "nothing less than the 'philosophical' form of existence: freely giving oneself, one's whole life, its rule through pure reason or through philosophy" (1970, 8/5). Husserl consistently restricts the object of Renaissance emulation to this form of life (*Daseinsart, Daseinsform, Daseinsweise*). The restriction even excludes the content of Greek philosophy. In fact, Husserl emphasizes that the modern philosophical project is based, from the beginning, on a decisive departure from Greek thought (21/18). The Renaissance is defined by its dedication to the reproduction of a form of life, not a particular style of scientific rationality, to say nothing of styles of architecture, art, or politics. It deviates from its proper sense the moment that it becomes mimicry or nostalgia. What it emulates in the Greeks is their pursuit of autonomy: "According to the guiding ideal of the Renaissance, ancient man forms himself with insight through free reason" (8/6).

The Renaissance must then be a free claiming of the Greek origin.[12] The historical link between modern philosophical humanity and Greece cannot depend upon lineage or inheritance. It is perhaps for this reason that the *Crisis* makes no attempt to reconstruct a continuous history that runs from ancient Greece up to modern Europe. There is no doubt that continuity exists and that such continuity is the historical condition for any renewal. However, it only enters into the account of European identity as the mere possibility of a reactivation through available artifacts. What is essential to the Greek humanity emulated in Renaissance is as effectively appropriated by a people totally isolated from any cultural continuum that might have "preserved" Greek culture as by a people solely responsible for this preservation. In Plato's *Republic*, Socrates' philosophical city cannot emerge historically because in order to begin, it must have already begun.[13] When Socrates is treated, in *Timeaus* (19b-26d), to the historical realization of his ideal, the paradox is resolved by the supposition that in archaic times Athens actually was a philosophical city, but that this Athens is completely inaccessible through historical backward references that would connect the present generation to its spiritual forbearers. Some natural catastrophe has obliterated every trace of its existence. A record of the city was preserved, so the story goes, by an Egyptian priest. Husserl's Renaissance enacts as a mode of historical self-understanding this Platonic insight that philosophical humanity relates to its origin, not as a familiar traditional inheritance but as a break with everything familiar in which it nonetheless recognizes itself.

We can clarify the notion of Renaissance historicity by reading the following passage from *Crisis II*:

We are what we are as functionaries of modern philosophical humanity; we are heirs and cobearers of the direction of the will that pervades this humanity; we have become this through a primal establishment [*Urstiftung*] which is at once a reestablishment [*Nachstiftung*] and modification [*Abwanderung*] of the Greek primal establishment. In this [*dieser*] lies the *teleological beginning*, the true birth of the European spirit as such. (1970, 71/72; translation modified)

We take the "*dieser*" in the final sentence to refer to the entire phrase "a primal establishment which is at once a reestablishment and modification of the Greek primal establishment." Europe has its teleological beginning in an *Urstiftung* that is also a *Nachstiftung* and modification of the ancient *Urstiftung*. It is a modification because the Greek origin is now appropriable as an origin across an intervening middle age for any people having attained "a certain level of prescientific culture" (1970, 288/335). In this respect, Europe "starts from Greece," but is a "supranationality of a completely new sort" (289/336).

The initiation of European history in Renaissance does not entail forsaking the traditions that orient a people in history. Each people becomes European by first of all subjecting its own life to critique. The cultural contents of its "middle age" are not and cannot be abandoned. By claiming the Greek origin as its own, a people prioritizes the commitment to the infinite framework of critique over traditional authority. It does not move away from its own traditions toward foreign, "European" traditions. Husserl assumes that each European nation will set about "pursuing its own ideal task in the spirit of infinity" (1970, 289/336). In the case of a people with a coherent tradition extending back before the Greek origin, the metaphor of "middle age" breaks down, but not the dual sense of beginning essential to Renaissance historicity. The whole traditional world of a people, back to its archaic empirical beginning, is rationally appropriable beginning from, that is, as a consequence of, the Greek origin. Modernity is a period in the development of a people that encompasses its entire development as the object of a novel critical comportment (14/12).[14]

Each European nation is alien to the others by virtue of its own historical coherence. They are united not only by their common pursuit of universal critique and their freely appropriated Greek origin but also by a new form of mutual influence that supplements those characteristic of political historicity. Husserl envisions a "giving and receiving" between European nations whereby "each nation, precisely by pursuing its own ideal task in the spirit of infinity, gives its best to the nations united with it" (1970, 289/336). The goods at stake here are "infinite ideals," by which Husserl seems to mean any normative conception produced through the new critical attitude. Critique in the spirit of infinity can yield results shaped by and suited to a local context. These results, however, must be justifiable with reference to principles and ideas intended to hold for "everybody" in the new sense. Husserl is likely thinking of cases like "liberty" and "right" in politics or "faith" and "salvation" in religion. These are not philosophical-scientific ideas, but they are analogously infinite in that their significance motivates movements of interest with universal scope (286/333). As such, they become the common property of European humanity: "Hence there are, for us Europeans, many infinite ideas ... which lie outside the philosophical-scientific sphere (infinite tasks, goals, confirmations, truths, 'true values,' 'genuine goods,' 'absolutely' valid norms)" (279/325). The orientation toward such ideas does not build a single European culture that might rival national or folk cultures. Instead, the infinite task that animates European humanity remains "divided into various infinite spheres" (289/336). The implication is that every people enters into European history by means of its own Renaissance and the programs of critical reform that follow therefrom.

10. Europeanization

The tendency to spread is inherent to Husserl's Europe. This is because the expansion of Europe *as Europe* is the result not of the political-historical machinations of nations but of the universality of the philosophical mode of existence, which is, in itself, "for everybody." Considered both as a vocational pursuit and a broader movement of cultural transformation, philosophy is "unlike all other cultural works" in that it "is not a movement of interest which is bound to the soil of the national tradition" (1970, 286/333). Obviously, non-philosophical endeavors are appropriable in foreign contexts. Husserl must mean that philosophical ideas and projects are peculiar in that they alone are not appropriable *as foreign* in the customary sense. For example, one cannot qualify as French the philosophical idea "cogito" or the analogically infinite idea "liberty." The presumed empirical origin of these ideas in the mental activity of Frenchmen is completely incidental to non-Frenchmen (and Frenchmen) who understand them in their infinity. As ideas, they are equally foreign to Frenchmen and non-Frenchmen because they are unbound to the "soil of national tradition." At the same time, the universal foreignness of philosophical ideas is an eminent *mineness* because it elicits an orientation toward autonomy. The Greek *Daseinsform* is not a cultural peculiarity, but "the first breakthrough to what is essential to humanity as such" (15/13). The recognition of this breakthrough in European humanity by non-European humanity "becomes a motive for them to Europeanize themselves even in their unbroken will to spiritual self-preservation" (275/320).

If our interpretation of European historicity reflects Husserl's intent, then it is clear that his vision of Europeanization excludes political-historical processes that assimilate, subordinate, or destroy foreign home worlds. The Europeanization of the world is a proliferation of Renaissances through which a variety of human communities and their traditions are renewed. This movement does not spread through cultural imperialism.[15] At any given time, Europe is a "relatively closed" unity in relation to non-European humanity. As new communities Europeanize, rationally reshaping their traditions, they enrich the exchange of ideas constitutive of the European synthesis and Europe itself is changed. When Husserl compares the relatively closed Europe of the present to a future, globalized Europe, he goes so far as to claim that "the expanded Europe will not be Europe any longer" (1993, 16). The incorporation of new mentalities (*Geistigkeit*) on a global scale promises a "tremendous deepening" of the currently European cultures (ibid.). By claiming that the globalized Europe will not even be Europe, Husserl guards against the identification of Europeanization with the globalization of institutions or cultural forms already established within European nations. Only with respect to Europe's fundamental character as a rational internationalism is global Europeanization a continuation (*Fortsetzung*) of Europe (ibid.).

Complications arise because Husserl can only root the inherent expansionism of philosophical history in an interpretation of the given historical background by finding it at work in the political-historical expansion of European nations and Europe as a whole. The historical reference for this moment of the Europe concept is nothing other than "the spectacle of the Europeanization of all other civilizations" (1970, 16/14). Once again, Husserl avoids spelling out which process of Europeanization he has in mind. One can only assume he refers to the entire history of modern European expansion that begins with the Spanish and Portuguese conquests and extends into Husserl's own day. Is not this history best explained by the kind of motives Husserl characterizes as political-historical? While Husserl concedes that Europe's globalization has the look of "historical non-sense," his attitude seems to be that it has created the conditions for a genuine, global Europeanization and is therefore redeemable as a development "that bears witness to the rule of an absolute meaning" (ibid.). Husserl's conception of Europeanization would include the transformation of humanity through "movements of interest" that explicitly combat the finitization of European ideas as nationally, culturally, or racially bound.[16] However, even on this interpretation, a Husserlian position on Europeanization has to contend with the problem of European hypocrisy and the consequences it has for the viability of Europe as a subject of crisis.

11. The Problem of European Hypocrisy

Hypocrisy is a charge normally leveled at persons rather than communities, let alone a historical community on the scale of Husserl's Europe. Yet, the accusation of not practicing what one preaches can properly target any agent that makes statements about its character or principles. The conditions for the possibility of European hypocrisy are therefore that European persons make statements as representatives of European communities about the character or principles of Europe (conventionally: "The West"), and that European persons act "as Europeans" or "in the name of Europe." As a matter of fact, these conditions are fulfilled, most importantly in the action and discourse of those institutions that organize European life at the national and international levels, but also in the social life of groups and individuals. Husserl himself, in the *Vienna Lecture*, understands his philosophical engagement in terms of his aspiration to be a "good European" (1970, 299/348). Assuming that hypocrisy on a historical scale is possible, we will consider the meaning of such a charge against Husserl's Europe, and the consequences for the crisis problematic should it prove justified.

The relevant hypocrisy charge would point to a history in which Europe consistently invokes as a norm the orientation toward infinite ideas without practicing it. Let us recall what it means to practice it. According to Husserl's formula, European humanity "lives in finitude, toward poles of infinity." This means that infinite ideas (in the threefold sense outlined above) count as norms for all finite ideas and that finite ideas are habitually subjected to the infinite framework of critique. Through this orientation, the common world correlated to the life-praxis of a community loses its function as an ultimate ground for justifications. At the same time, European humanity lives in finitude. Interests relative to common worlds continue to shape activity and discourse at every level of life. At the highest levels of collective action, nations continue to operate in view of political-historical interests. What is decisive is that these interests (which play out in "commerce" and "power struggles") are continually relativized with a view toward the development of an "ideally directed society" (1970,

289/336). Where the orientation toward infinite ideals is not "fully developed," as in "personalities of higher order," its attainment counts as a practical necessity, giving ever broader scope to "the spirit of norms that are valid for all" (276/322).

The justification for the relevant hypocrisy charge is not that Europe continues to live in political historicity. It is rather that the "infinite ideas" to which Europe appeals as principles do not actually reorient its existence, functioning instead *within* the purview of political-historical interests. Following Statman's suggestion with respect to hypocrisy generally, we can conceive the charge as targeting a spectrum of hypocritical attitudes arrayed between the poles of dissimulation and self-deception.[17] In the first case, infinite ideals are cynically deployed in order to mask the pursuit of finite interests. The "for everybody" in the infinite sense is understood to mean "for everybody" in some finite sense. In the second case, infinite ideals are the object of sincere belief, coupled with bad faith strategies for evading evidence that they are consistently finitized. The "for everybody" in the infinite sense is understood in the infinite sense, but consistently fails to motivate critique of finite ideas as it should, and this failure is ignored.

As is well known, the charge of hypocrisy does not directly bear upon the principles advanced by the hypocrite. However, the *tu quoque* fallacy is largely irrelevant to the issue of hypocrisy as a component of the crisis problematic. What is at stake is not the idea of philosophical culture, but rather the authority of Europe as a bearer of that culture. A principle may be sound without its utterance being authoritative. One may indeed assent to a principle without accepting it from (or "listening to") the one invoking it. As Aikin points out, the problem with the hypocrite "is not just about her insincerity with regard to the claims, but with regard to what a model she is and whether she genuinely holds her proposals" (2008, 159). The proposition that the only appropriate response to failures of philosophical culture is the promotion of philosophical culture does not entail that the only appropriate response to the failures of European civilization is the promotion of European civilization. It is this latter claim that is made by Husserl. Its truth is strictly a matter of historical judgment (we will consider this issue shortly).

Given the natural tendency toward finitization, the practicability of infinite ideals is inherently questionable. A pattern of hypocritical invocation only further volatizes their status for a community. There are several critical attitudes toward principles in this situation. First, one may endorse the hypocrite's principles despite the fact that their invocation lacks authority, and one may do so in two different ways. On the one hand, the principles may be endorsed exclusively on one's own authority, in the knowledge that they do not motivate the hypocrite. The one charging hypocrisy and the one charged with hypocrisy do not stand in a community of purpose. On the other hand, the one charging hypocrisy may intend to endorse the principles as a member of the hypocritical community, thereby partially restoring its authority. Aikin draws attention, however, to a second kind of case in which the hypocrisy of the invoker actually does serve, indirectly, to undermine the very principles she invokes. The failure of the hypocrite to abide by her own principles here functions as "meta evidence" for their impracticability (2008, 165). Aikin also considers a third kind of case in which the hypocrisy of the invoker actually heightens the urgency of making her principles practicable insofar as her failure highlights conditions, which she also critiques, that make their implementation difficult. Here, hypocrisy only "demonstrates the poignancy of [the hypocrite's] critical project" (167).

If we apply these various attitudes to the problem of European hypocrisy, we arrive at the following schema of positions: (1) European hypocrisy motivates the project of redeeming the idea of philosophical culture by redefining the subject of crisis; (2) European hypocrisy motivates the project of redeeming Europe by pursuing the idea of philosophical culture it has purported to pursue; (3) European hypocrisy demonstrates the impracticability of the very idea of philosophical culture, which should be exposed as mere pretense or illusion; (4) European hypocrisy demonstrates the difficulty and urgency of pursuing the idea of philosophical culture, which should be critically refined and pursued with greater vigilance. These positions are related in the following ways: positions 1 and 2 need not be compatible, but can be if 1 is understood as a means to 2 or 2 a welcome by-product of 1; position 3 is incompatible with 1, 2, and 4, while 4 is compatible with both 1 and 2; decisions between positions 1 and 2 turn on an historical assessment of the viability of Europe as a subject of crisis (i.e., its degree of cynicism, self-deception, and "conscience" with respect to its principles), whereas decisions between 3 and 4 turn on a philosophical stance about the role of ideas in history.

Let us examine each position more closely with respect to the crisis problematic. In position 1, winning clarity of purpose about the ideals of philosophical culture requires suspending the historical interpretation of the community dedicated to their realization. It is now a matter of reconceiving the story in which the "we" of this community plays its part, the past struggles and accomplishments it might redeem, the historical transformations to which it owes its existence, and so on. This interpretive work effectively discovers a new subject of crisis, anthropologically indeterminate (open to "everyone"), yet defined by historical provenance, limits, and prospects. The core motivation here is the conviction that Europe's "ideally directed society" is actually bound to a specific matrix of political-historical power. The critique cannot, without irony, accuse Europe of not being European enough because its pattern of hypocritical universalism has undermined its authority. Instead, the critique pursues a dialectic through which Europe's contradictions are exposed and overcome by an emergent community that becomes who it is through this very overcoming. Position 2 is simply Husserl's own. Clarity of purpose remains possible as a participant in the European story. The principled critique of European hypocrisy is inevitably an immanent critique that holds Europe accountable for its own principles. Here, "its own" refers not just to what has been stated but to what has been willed. That it has not been willed sufficiently is due to blindness, prejudice, lack of courage, or a satisfaction with false consolations. The worst outcome is that these partial failures weaken confidence in Europe, thereby undermining its resolve to fulfill its telos: "Europe's greatest danger is weariness" (1970, 299/438). Weakness of will, not self-deception or dissimulation, is the primary threat to the spiritual health of Europe.

Position 4 intersects with 1 and 2 to generate critical hermeneutic programs. Maldonado-Torres and other theorists of "decoloniality" exemplify a hermeneutic orientation toward a post-European philosophical culture (the synthesis of 4 and 1). In an interpretation that inverts Husserl's approach to the Renaissance, it is now the project of modern European conquest that initiates a new mode of historicity. This is predicated upon the theoretical and practical attempt to divide humanity into human and subhuman classes, the latter having not even the "capacity for autonomy and self-determination" (2016, 17). An invocation of autonomy in this context of division that does not explicitly target the context itself is either an evasion or a dissimulating rationalization; it is a hypocrisy that, as Césaire observed, "is all the more odious because it is less and less likely to deceive" (2000, 31).[18] Whereas Husserl interprets the great historical fact of Renaissance as the *Urstiftung* of an orientation toward autonomy, for Maldonado-Torres it is the great historical fact of modern colonialism that institutes coloniality, a regime of norms and practices that distorts the very conditions of sociality by soliciting and reinforcing a "permanent suspicion" regarding the humanity of colonized peoples (2007, 245). From this regime arises the West's self-understanding as modern: "the modern West, its hegemonic discourses, and its hegemonic institutions are themselves a product, just like the colonies, of coloniality" (2016, 10). Imperialism is not a departure from, but is "constitutive of" Western modernity (2007, 244), including its philosophical dimension (2007, 245). From this perspective, a culture of infinite ideals begins precisely by overcoming, in theory and practice, the hypocrisy of coloniality, the fruits of which should be met with methodological skepticism: "many of the ideas and practices [of Western modernity] … are entangled with and can easily reproduce coloniality … The project of critique, construction and reconstruction is massive" (2016, 11).

A complementary hermeneutic orientation (the synthesis of 4 and 2) characterizes Patočka's approach to Europe. Like the theorists of decoloniality, Patočka diagnoses a deformation in European life that begins with the modern period. The interest in the "care of the soul," which he sees as the fundamental European inheritance from the Greeks, is now overtaken by a new interest "that might be deemed a concern or care about *dominating the world*" (2002, 89). This interest infects "one area after another, politics, economics, faith and science, transforming them in a new style" (1996, 83). The key figure in this genealogy is Bacon, who subjects knowledge itself to the new interest: "knowledge is power, only effectual knowledge is real knowledge, what used to apply only for practice and production now holds for knowledge as such" (84). European culture is henceforth an expansive culture of mastery and control based on the deployment of scientific-technological power (2002, 9). Patočka's reflections are an explicit attempt to revisit the crisis problematic as set forth by Husserl (152). He begins, however, from the position that Europe's "moral situation" has become untenable (11). Through war and the perpetual mobilization for war, Europe has "definitely wrecked itself" (9). Europe itself, he writes, "*has disappeared*, probably forever" (89). Unlike the decoloniality theorists, Patočka regards Europe as the only viable subject of crisis (9, 221). The possibility of philosophical culture depends upon the resurrection of Europe. His focus is thus to revisit suppressed elements of Europe's spiritual heritage in the attempt to find "something that could to some extent be believable even for us, that could affect us in a way so that we could again find hope in a specific perspective, in a specific future, without giving in to illusory dreams" (12). Patočka clearly endorses the conceptuality of Husserl's spiritual medicine (IIA § 5). But the Europe guided by the breakthrough of science has run its course and ended in barbarism. The new Europe, if there is one, will not be Husserl's Europe any longer.

For position 3, the program of universal critique by which Husserl defines Europe is inherently hypocritical, and to criticize it for not being universal or critical enough is to share in this hypocrisy. This position arises from a political realism for which the exercise of reason in collective life is a superstructure erected upon a fragile ordering of opposing interests that ultimately operate by force. An "apolitical" critique that would transform even political institutions in the image of philosophical ideality evades responsibility for the concrete political situation it effects, which always involves rule by a particular group. Real subjects of history, if there are any, are not defined by their relation to ideas. This position encompasses several approaches to modern ideology, but Koselleck's is especially relevant to the crisis problematic. Husserl's reconstruction of modern philosophy ignores the question, so important to that tradition, of whether it is reasonable for the critical exercise of reason to limit itself in deference to the state. Husserl ranks the problems of political philosophy below the problems of subjectivity that culminate in transcendental critique, which in turn redeems a European history oriented toward the spiritualization of politics. Koselleck would claim to see behind such apolitical designs. "Universal critique" is not a relativizing of political historicity, but a modern strategy of political dissimulation traceable to the ascendant bourgeoisie. The increasingly expansive exercise of critical judgment in bourgeois society eventually threatens the political order (1988, 11). But the rising class conceals this threat, from others and itself, by advancing under the politically neutral cover of universal normative principles (147), in light of which political initiative looks like "illegitimate, naked power" (146). Rather than reckoning with the consequences of its own power, it rules via the obfuscations of a "utopian philosophy of history" (174, 133). Its projected union of authority with public judgment and will is realized only as an ideological fiction: "the Enlightenment as such rules only by veiling its rule" (166). For Koselleck, a "crisis" discovered and resolved by the resources of critique is the concealment of real crises that demand political decision.

This brief survey of positions only serves to indicate the controversy implied in Husserl's claim to find orientation for the goals of philosophical culture in modern Europe. Is Husserl's reconstruction believable as an interpretation of what European humanity actually aims to achieve? Grand narratives of Western modernity that sum up centuries-long developments are totally alien to phenomenological-theoretical work. It seems Husserl tried to minimize this kind of storytelling by touching on philosophical history only at the two vanishing points of "Greece" and "Renaissance."[19] However, because the crisis problematic relies on historical narrative as a necessary means for purposive clarity about philosophical practice, it cannot help advancing a nascent theory of Western modernity that competes with alternatives. In this context, the fact that Husserl's reconstruction provides no detailed account of Europe's social, economic, political, or religious institutions makes it seem the sort of story one can follow so long as one forgets that it is supposed to be true.

Husserl's reconstruction is unsatisfying as a critique of modern European civilization. Its aim, though, is to clarify and affirm "our" responsibility for the kind of infinite ideals to which any principled critique of Europe appeals. Further, although Husserl sees Europe as a viable subject of crisis, the very meaning of "crisis" assumes a reckoning with its unviability. One possible end to the European crisis is "the downfall of Europe in its estrangement from its own rational sense of life, its fall into hostility toward the spirit and into barbarity" (1970, 299/347). The history of European hypocrisy raises the question of whether this downfall is occurring, and thereby the question of whether a clear consciousness of crisis can be won by reflecting on what it means to be a good European. The crisis problematic as such does not require a division between European and non-European humanity, but between "humanity which has already collapsed and humanity which still has roots but is struggling to keep them or find new ones" (15/13). It accommodates a situation in which the struggle to keep or cultivate European roots undermines the purposive clarity at which the teleological reconstruction aims. The Socratic critique of the Herodic medicine that "plays nursemaid to the disease" (*Republic* 406a), that transforms life into a lengthy process of dying, surely applies at the spiritual level as well. Perhaps the "good European" proves himself a fool in assuming that Europe is an appropriate object of medical attention.[20] Broadly construed, the crisis reflection takes cognizance of this entire field of possibilities.[21] By doing so, it protects the teleological reconstruction from blind reliance on established narratives (and counternarratives) and heightens the trial to which it subjects sincere belief (IIA § 7). The reflection is resolutely opposed only to acquiescing to spiritual collapse, to abandoning the search for a true story in which humanity becomes maximally responsible for itself.[22]

12. The Problem of European Exceptionalism

Husserl is committed to defending the viability of Europe because he believes it is the only extant historical community explicitly oriented toward the ideals of philosophical culture (1970, 273/318). This position is developed in two arguments in the *Vienna Lecture*, both of which employ general historical judgments: (1) The spirit of infinity at the heart of philosophical culture depends upon the idea of the true world first discoverable in the theoretical attitude. Greek philosophy was the first theoretical tradition, and all subsequent theoretical traditions depend upon its influence. Other wisdom traditions, including those of Babylonia, Egypt, India, and China, have discovered and preserved substantial knowledge of the world, but they themselves interpret "knowledge" and "world" in a mythico-practical way that presupposes as ultimate a local context of human and divine action. All philosophical culture is therefore Greek in origin. (2) There are no known societies currently pursuing infinite ideas other than those spurred to this pursuit by contact with the nations of the original European Renaissance. One sure sign of this is that all non-European societies have a rational motive to Europeanize, whereas the Indianization of Austria or Germany, for example, is obviously pure nonsense. Therefore, no other society contemporary with modern Europe has appropriated the Greek *Daseinsform* that developed in the wake of Greek philosophy.

These arguments really amount to an *insistence* that the "remarkable teleology" of philosophical culture is inborn "only in our Europe" (1970, 273/318). Mall has suggested that Husserl's views about European and non-European culture simply result from "prejudices of diverse provenances" that are "too public to require a learned, academic refutation" (2000, 114). It is certainly difficult to refute arguments the key premises of which articulate the "feelings" and "presentiments" that first disclose how we find ourselves responsible (1970, 275/320–1).[23] It is striking, though, that Husserl presents his European exceptionalism not as common knowledge but as a contrarian view. He references the "plethora" of contemporary works that treat Indian, Chinese, and Greek philosophy as "different historical forms under one and the same idea of culture" (279/325). When asserting the rationality of universal Europeanization, he remarks that Europeans would never Indianize "if we understand ourselves properly" (275/320), implying that this proper understanding is often lacking. Husserl's position seems informed by the conviction that the crisis problematic is incommensurable with a distinctly modern penchant for pluralism. This, at least, requires learned consideration.

If there is a crisis in Husserl's sense, then some human community under definite historical conditions has recognized autonomy, the ability to examine and rationally appropriate one's own life, as an absolute value. The attempt to understand the crisis will involve foregrounding specific events through which this transformation in human history was achieved and specific concepts through which these events are intelligible. Only in this way is clarity of purpose possible for beings who "have become what we are thoroughly and exclusively in a historical-spiritual manner" (1970, 71/72). However, this story cannot account for who one is in terms of a specific anthropological designation. Reason is not a capacity relative to the makeup and circumstances of a particular animal species, let alone some subgroup of that species. The story rather accounts for "the first breakthrough to what is essential to humanity as such," namely, seeking its "genuine human nature" precisely through the endless movement "from latent to manifest reason" (15/13). This need of the crisis problematic for a particular origin and source of responsibility for what is essential to humanity causes pluralism to appear as a threat.

A pluralism of "philosophies" and "philosophical cultures" threatens to derail the crisis problematic in two ways. The first is the tendency toward relativism. If there are foreign and familiar philosophies, this is because they belong to different cultural worlds. There are obvious ways in which such belonging is evident. Local languages, styles, manners, and contexts of relevance permeate all philosophical work. However, the theoretical content of philosophy does not belong to any local world. When one decides to neglect the cultural charms of philosophical writing, considering it as a system of propositions available identically to "everyone," one often loses a great deal, but fulfills an intention implied in the pursuit of philosophy itself. The same holds for those infinite ideals that characterize philosophical culture on Husserl's account. An observer may trace transformations in the idea of liberty, for example, as it animates various cultures. But if the idea is infinite, it is intended as a valid norm "for everyone," which means that it is not appropriable *as foreign* in the new context. If pluralism entails the reduction of philosophy and philosophical culture to the categories of home and alien, then it is at odds with the crisis problematic. Husserl thus requires a decision against the view that the philosophical culture of the Greeks "is merely a factual, historical delusion, the accidental acquisition of merely *one among many other* civilizations and histories" (1970, 15/13; my emphasis).

The other hazard lurking in pluralism is a kind of second-order ethnocentrism that can emerge when ethnocentrism in the usual sense becomes a worry. Let us describe the problem insofar as it exceeds that of simple relativism. Ethnocentrism is the disposition to take one's own culture as the normative measure of others. If one is not a relativist and wishes to avoid ethnocentrism in the crisis problematic, one is driven to the following attitude. I participate in a tradition of theoretical philosophy and a broader culture of infinite ideas. However, I recognize this as a cultural peculiarity. Other communities have different notions of philosophy and philosophical culture, and I will not set up my own notion as a measure of theirs. It is easy to see that this apparent modesty actually claims reason itself as a cultural possession. The mistake lies in thinking that "my own notion" or "our own notion" implies the cultural delimitation of theoretical philosophy and its characteristic effects. Husserl claims that the philosophical transformation of culture takes place "first within the spiritual space of a single nation, the Greek nation" (1970, 277/322). This is not a Greek transformation, but a transformation of Greece.[24] The same holds for every community within the spreading synthesis of European nations. When Husserl seeks to appropriate philosophical culture as a task "personally our own" because it arises from "*our* history" (70–1/72), he wants to track the breakthrough and clarification of a telos that belongs to everybody. If pluralism subordinates the understanding of philosophical culture to the ethics of worldliness, it is at odds with the crisis problematic.

However, these forms of pluralism would not follow from the fact that Europe is one among many historical instantiations of the teleology of reason. A plurality of acquisitions of the teleology does not render accidental or delusional what is acquired. This possibility of plurality indicates the need for a general concept for the historical formations that result from appropriative reflections linking the ideal of philosophical culture to a concrete human (or extraterrestrial) development. Europe is not a "culture" in the ordinary sense, but an open system of cultures described by those concepts that function first conventionally and then, transformed, in the reconstruction. This description lends Europe its particularity as one such historical formation. The crisis problematic dictates that there can be others, born from the cultivation of other roots. Husserl's European exceptionalism rests solely on a series of historical judgments, well-founded or not. Such judgments are necessary for any position in the crisis problematic. They determine which promises, struggles, and disappointments can enter into a coherent self-conception that supports the will to resist anthropological nihilism. The philosopher need not understand herself as European, but she cannot countenance the view that humanity is a succession of cultural types, each with its peculiar ideals and norms, that "form and dissolve themselves like fleeting waves" (1970, 7/4).

That there can be multiple philosophical histories is not of interest to the crisis reflection itself. Of interest is reclaiming that philosophical history in which we have become who we are. It is true that some such history is needed for a systematic presentation of phenomenological philosophy. What the phenomenologist needs is *our* history. While this history is universal in the sense of anthropologically indeterminate, it is unique, irreversible, and territorially bound. As Husserl emphasizes, the crisis reflection is perspectival and undertaken for existential reasons (1970, 59/60). It concerns those very possibilities in light of which I can understand what I am doing.

13. Philosophical Seriousness

The ultimate presuppositions amount to the view that what the phenomenologist is doing is participating in "philosophy." This seems a fact that is obvious enough. Philosophy is a thing to do for which accommodations have already been made: here are the means, the time, the space. The philosopher herself is a familiar cultural object. She is readily understandable as a type of person motivated to certain actions by certain interests. Like other academics, she spends her time reading and writing, teaching, attending conferences, and so on. This differentiates her, for instance, from the repairmen who spend their time attending to useful things that have become faulty, purchasing materials, pricing jobs. As a particular sort of academic, she is concerned with problems unlike those of the chemist or the sociologist. Within philosophy, there are also various specializations, and so on. The philosopher is understandable in this way not only to others but also to herself. This self-understanding makes it clear what one is doing as a philosopher. But it conceals the need for self-understanding as a subject of crisis. It conceals the disunity phenomenological awakening introduces into philosophical history, and thereby the necessity of the teleological reconstruction that would unify it.

In the introduction to his *Cartesian Meditations*, Husserl remarks that while philosophers meet at professional conferences, their philosophies, unfortunately, do not (1950, 47). This is actually an important point about the superficial unity of philosophy. Husserl takes it up again in concluding *Crisis I*. Addressing himself directly to "*we ourselves*, we philosophers of the present," he asks whether his outline of Europe's philosophical history is a mere "academic oration" after which each might happily return to his own professional preoccupations. Husserl responds that "serious" philosophers cannot "seriously" do this (1970, 17). These serious philosophers can only be what they are, namely philosophers, by understanding their participation in a community united by a "single goal," namely "philosophy as such" (ibid.). These are the audience to whom Husserl addresses the remainder of his final treatise. They alone experience the "painful existential contradiction" of needing but being unable to believe in philosophy as a working goal. For them, this ability to believe is achieved only in the course of the teleological reconstruction itself. This seriousness prevents institutional arrangements and cultural distinctions from determining what it is to be a philosopher. It is the attunement receptive to the "existential reasons" one has for engaging philosophical history in the first place.

We may understand this seriousness as a resistance to the pragmatic and epistemic illusions that occlude what has to be done to appropriate wakefully what one was doing naively. The experience of jeopardy discloses the naïve pursuit of a goal as a failure to have pursued it wakefully. I, the wakeful ego, hold myself, and those with whom I stand in a community of purpose, responsible for this failure. Success now means to accomplish wakefully the very project previously pursued in naïveté. The pragmatic illusion arises because it seems that I can accomplish "philosophy" without reinterpreting what I am doing and who I am to do it. After all, the "phenomenological approach" makes progress on established problems in light of familiar standards of academic discipline. The epistemic illusion arises because it seems that phenomenological insight renders unnecessary any attention to philosophical history. After all, such insight is authoritative regardless of what this history shows. Philosophical seriousness refuses to let the coherence of philosophical practice or the fullness of phenomenological insight stand in for clarity of purpose about philosophy as a task.[25] The phenomenological standpoint introduces a new form of responsibility in light of which the transcendentally naïve tradition could not (in fact) have understood itself. The question of what one is truly seeking as a philosopher has to be posed anew.

The serious philosopher participates in philosophy only as a task she assigns herself through the teleological reconstruction. This means she can only begin to find practical orientation by feeling responsible to the history that has made her who she is. At the origin of the entire crisis problematic, we find this attempt to feel how and as whom one is called to the philosophical task. In the *Vienna Lecture*, Husserl states that his teleological interpretation of European history is guided by a "vital presentiment." Despite its "obscurity," this feeling is the first connection to a history that will prove appropriable in a way that clarifies the practical necessity of a phenomenological conversion of philosophy: "this presentiment gives us an intentional guide for seeing in European history highly significant interconnections in the pursuit of which the presentiment becomes a confirmed certainty for us. Presentiment is the felt signpost for all discoveries" (1970, 275–6/320–1). Crisis consciousness takes shape by cultivating those ways of feeling responsible that allow one to continue to be a philosopher. Being European is Husserl's way of taking philosophy seriously.

Conclusion: Owning Philosophy

Reliance on historical feeling and judgment strands the appropriation of the ultimate presuppositions in a sphere of controversy. It seems there are no solvable philosophical problems here. Indeed, there are not. The crisis reflection does not point to the solution of philosophical problems but to an unresolved history in which the philosophical vocation itself stands. It reveals that the meaningfulness of philosophy as a human endeavor presupposes an historical interpretation imbued with a sense of who "we" are and what "we" have to accomplish. The appropriation of this interpretation lays bare and clarifies the will and self-conception of the interpreter, which previously remained anonymous. In doing so, it confronts the threat of rootlessness that accompanies every seeking of roots. Only in falling prey to illusion could philosophy abstain from this disquieting reflection. The proper object of phenomenological philosophy, transcendental life, is an apodictic presupposition for reality. But philosophy is itself a reality that depends upon a general orientation toward wakefulness as an absolute value, and this orientation is a human acquisition so fragile that the fact of its having been acquired is essentially questionable. To utilize historical reflections precisely in order to make this fragility explicit is the defining characteristic of the crisis problematic as a systematic starting point for transcendental philosophy.

Husserl sometimes understates the novelty of this starting point. He emphasizes that his historical self-reflections differ from those of his predecessors because they proceed from the *Endstiftung* of philosophy, which has finally discovered its proper method and subject matter. Husserl's claim to understand his predecessors better than they could have understood themselves rests on this conviction that phenomenology is a definitive beginning for philosophical work. But the thought that one has arrived at such an *Endstiftung* is hardly unique to Husserl. His retrospective history would only be distinguished by his being right. What distinguishes the crisis problematic as a starting point is not that Husserl actually stands at the *Endstiftung*. It is that the conviction that one stands at the *Endstiftung* is here coupled with unease about what one is doing by standing there. The conviction and the unease occur together because the phenomenologist is at once awakened and jeopardized. Phenomenological wakefulness is final because of the nature of its purview. It is nonetheless the result of an awakening that uproots ramified projects in which the awakened subject understood herself to participate. It has become impossible to continue these projects without reassessing what they aim to accomplish, and who one becomes in pursuing them. Reflection on the transcendental life of consciousness does not provide this reassessment, which is personal, practical, and existential. And yet, the reassessment belongs to the systematic development of phenomenological philosophy, which cannot properly begin without it. The crisis problematic charges the transcendental philosopher with writing us into a true story about what we are doing as agents of those projects (summed up in Enlightenment) compromised by a history of transcendental naïveté.

To philosophize then means to be responsive to ideals of wakefulness that are irreducible to one another. Human life is naïve in many ways. It is a local life insensitive to its location within the wider world. It is an irreversible, inalienable life lost in the society of lives into which it fits. It is a transcendental life captivated by and subordinated to what appears through the event of appearing. The crisis problematic places philosophical activity at the junction of these ways of naïveté and awakening. To appropriate philosophy as a human activity is to appreciate the strangeness that it is something typical to do. Everyone knows that philosophy as we know it was not always practiced. But only when we place ourselves in relation to pre-philosophical culture does this well-known fact confront us with the historical contingency of those responsibilities we shoulder as a result of the breakthrough of philosophy. Philosophical culture becomes provincial when it forgets that it too has an origin and an outside. To appropriate philosophical activity is also to comprehend it as a moment of my singular life in the world. Being a philosopher is a practical identity one can take up and honor. In doing so, certain things matter to one as a philosopher. But it is not ultimately as a philosopher that being a philosopher matters to me. Philosophical seriousness is attained only by facing down the "existential 'if'" that disempowers the guiding function of self-conceptions by referring them to the non-context of my life as a whole. Historical contingency and existential necessity are themselves open to transcendental clarification as to their very possibility. But this would not provide the clarity the philosopher seeks as a subject of crisis. When it ceases to presuppose itself, "philosophy" names the obscure fact of an unconditional human interest in wakefulness. Philosophical clarity here means taking ownership of this interest by putting oneself at stake in a history in which it is invested.

Let us return to Husserl's remark that phenomenology moves entirely in acts of reflection. This remark provides an idiom in which to state the relationship we have discerned between reflections on consciousness and reflections on crisis within a systematic phenomenological philosophy. In this idiom, to move means to make evident what lies in one's purview. Moving in reflections, phenomenology has consciousness available as an infinite, self-contained field of research. We may supplement Husserl's remark: phenomenologists also orient ourselves in reflections. We may extend the idiom: to orient oneself is to situate one's movements so as to act with clarity of purpose. Phenomenological thinkers require orientation because our tradition of thought implies transformations in the projects to which it contributes. But the transformations can only become intelligible by recovering the aims of naïve life from a wakeful perspective. For an agent who knows what she is doing, movement is simply her action in its unfolding. Orienting reflections make phenomenology willable as an action that shapes the human world. The crisis reflections, writes Husserl, arrive at a decision to resume the philosophical work that is ours.

We should understand decision here in a generally Aristotelian sense. To decide does not mean to do this action rather than that, but to do the action one does having taken stock of the circumstances that determine how it achieves the good. In the critical-historical attitude, the phenomenologist regards her work as a kind of transcendental action. It is this regard that is essentially concerned with particulars, and responsive to events that shape the present. The good at which phenomenological work aims is perhaps the highest good for human beings: a communal existence that incorporates all other attainable goods into a life of self-responsibility in the spirit of infinity. The crisis reflections begin by asking whether we philosophers are still able, in the here and now of our historical development, to believe in this good as an orienting end of our action. The clarity of purpose to which these reflections aspire does not require rescuing scientific culture from objectivism and its manifold discontents. It requires precisely that there be a crisis, a situation in which the ideals of the Enlightenment project are in danger because of the naïveté with which they have been pursued. The crisis reflections reclaim that project from the perspective of transcendental wakefulness so that the endangerment of its ideals, even their disappearance in favor of surrogates, becomes manifest.

Transcendental philosophy thereby acquires a historical significance. By disclosing the lifeworld and the scientific world from the standpoint of their apodictic presupposition, phenomenology holds a way open for an Enlightenment project that can only achieve its goals by losing the world as ground. The community of philosophers is called to preserve and protect the prospect of a "great and distant future for man," an epoch of "life-inwardness and spiritualization" (1970, 299/348). This is a future in which the capacity of our scientific culture to master the world is matched by its capacity to understand the subjectivity through which the world is what it is. In summoning us to work for this uncertain future, Husserl often sounds as if he is merely seeking to inspire with rhetoric. Indeed, the crisis reflection is not concerned with philosophical problems. It is, however, concerned with what might justifiably be called *the* philosophical problem. Husserl's appeals are not rhetorical. They draw attention to the locus for the discovery and solution of that problem: "*we ourselves*, we philosophers of the present" (16/15). The whole effort of critical-historical appropriation aims to articulate what we are truly seeking in philosophy and who we must be to be able to seek it "*if* we are philosophers in all seriousness" (1970, 17/15).

Notes

Introduction

1 I refer to sections of this study by indicating the part with a roman numeral (I or II), the division with a capital letter (A or B), and the section with "§" followed by an Arabic numeral.

Division A

1 For a succinct logical treatment of presuppositions, see Rescher (1961). Rescher equates presupposition with "necessary condition for truth, meaning or possibility." What has been presupposed fits this description. As the correlate of realization, presupposition is not a logical category. It essentially concerns the life of a jeopardized subject.
2 If our notion of what has been realized resembles a Husserlian category, it is "the overlooked" (*Das Übersehene*), which Husserl describes as something directly perceivable (*dem Wahrnehmen unmittelbar bereitliegen*) that goes unperceived. What is happening behind my back, he points out, is not overlooked in this sense because it is not directly perceivable. The overlooked "must, in a certain way, *be seen, and yet overlooked*" (2004, 89).
3 Defining reflection and realization this way does not deny the ontological specificity of what they notice. This is especially important in the case of experience, which has a different kind of being than realities that might be realized or reflected upon. On this issue, see *Ideas I* § 45; also Zahavi (2005, 63–5, 90–1).
4 In *Charmides*, Plato has Critias interpret the Delphic inscription along these lines. The god does not advise us to do something. He greets us by marking the limit that separates us from divine knowledge (164d–165a). Husserl's own allusion to the inscription at the end of his *Cartesian Meditations*, by contrast, emphasizes how the discovery of transcendental subjectivity overcomes the limit ordinarily thought to distinguish knowledge of self from knowledge of world (1950, 182–3).
5 Neither the fact that there are grades of sleep nor that we ourselves cannot mark when we have fallen asleep justifies dissolving the qualitative difference between sleeping and waking life into a difference of degree. When I wake from sleep, I realize that I was withdrawn from the world as a whole. This is not like

daydreaming or losing focus because I have become tired. The appearance that it is a mere difference of degree probably arises from the practice of trying to fall asleep, which involves withdrawing oneself from worldly concerns as much as one can while remaining awake. When Husserl takes up this issue (2014a, 12–14), he makes the methodological point that we can only assess what sleep itself is like as a limit of its precursors in the process of falling asleep.

6 The Husserlian and Heideggerian positions both regard the ego of acts as generally unavailable; they disagree as to why. For Heidegger, the ego of acts emerges for a reflection on knowing, which is itself a derivative mode of Dasein (1977, §§ 13, 43–4). For Husserl, the ego of acts is the most familiar subject of all manifestation. It resists thematization precisely because it is universally functioning in the disclosure of the things that interest world-directed life: "In truth, of course, I am a transcendental ego, but I am not conscious of this; being in a particular attitude, the natural attitude, I am completely given over to the object-poles, completely bound by interests and tasks which are exclusively directed toward them" (1970, 205/209). See also Taguchi (2006): "For Husserl, the pure ego is not the result of a deduction that builds up logically. The difficulty of thematizing the pure ego is rather an indication that we here have to do with something profoundly 'obvious' [*eine tiefe 'Selbstverständlichkeit'*]" (69).

7 The sleeping I is drawn into wakefulness, but it does not project a way into wakefulness. On the problem of how to characterize this transition, see Husserl (2014a, 34–6).

8 In *Ideas I* § 35, Husserl refers to the general "readiness" of the non-actional background to function in an actional cogito. The actualization of this background, which is already ready as mine, is what we refer to as egological inhabitation.

9 See also Hart's reflections on the amnesiac's ability to refer to herself with "I" (2009a, 65–118).

10 On this issue, see, Husserl (1985, 24): "Even where recollection is not unfolded with regard to its protentions, it nevertheless implies in itself that it carries in itself intentionally (even if undeveloped) the temporal sequence leading to the present to which it itself belongs as lived-experience."

11 In distinguishing the pure ego from the real person, Husserl, in *Ideas II*, emphasizes that the former has no capabilities (*Fähigkeiten*) (1952, 104). However, he himself adopts a version of the Kantian view that the ego "can accompany" (*begleiten können*) whatever lies in the background of consciousness (108).

12 In *Basic Problems* § 10, Husserl seems to endorse this thought, though he later crosses out the relevant passage.

13 A common opposition to Hegelianism moves hermeneutic and analytic philosophies of history in this direction. Ricoeur, for instance, writes: "The step we can no longer take is the one that equates with the eternal present the capacity of

the actual present to retain the known past and anticipate the future indicated in the tendencies of this past … We no longer seek the basis upon which the history of the world may be thought of as a completed whole" (1988, 204). Danto claims that historical awareness of the present "is to perceive both it and one's consciousness of it as something the meaning of which will only be given in the future, and in historical retrospection" (1985, 342). Because we are "temporally provincial with regard to the future" we "cannot achieve a speculative philosophy of history" (142).

14 The concept "retrodiction" is from von Wright (1971, 58–9). The awakened ego could retrodict its having presupposed without looking into the naïve life-phase at all. Suppose the realization of presuppositional content z. If experience regularly shows that a condition for the performance of an action of type x in a situation of type y is that the agent was convinced of z, and if I performed action x in situation y, then I can "retrodict" that I must have been convinced of z.

Division B

1 Hobson (2005) is downright giddy about rooting dreams in the brain of the sleeper: "Waking and dreaming are two states of consciousness, with differences that depend upon chemistry. Can you digest that proposition? Or does it stick in your craw? Do you … defend yourself against the humiliation of having your dreaming reduced to a brain state?" (58–9). This brand of naturalism builds upon the mundane judgment that dreams occur for a real organism that is really sleeping.
2 No especially phenomenological reflections are needed to see that the objective world described by science is discovered from and in the world of prescientific life. Non-phenomenological approaches tend to think this insight entails skeptical-relativist consequences. In any case, Husserl's novel accomplishment with respect to the lifeworld is not to show that it underlies mundane science but to frame it as the object of a non-mundane, scientific interest.
3 The phrase is Bernet's (2005, 23).
4 Crowell (2013) borrows the term from Korsgaard in his explication of Heidegger (241). He effectively de-intellectualizes it so that it refers to ways to be in light of which "the world matters to me in some way" (180).
5 Of course, Heidegger explicitly distinguishes between wonderment and curiosity. What we will question, with Husserl, is whether it is correct to claim that freed circumspection "has nothing to do with [*hat nichts zu tun mit*] the contemplation that wonders at being" (1996, 161; 1977, 172).
6 J. Gordon (1985) advances a plausible candidate for this essential difference. The dream agent lacks the pre-conceptual bodily grip on the world that enables the initiation and execution of effortful actions, a grip that I, the one reflecting,

evidently enjoy. The dreamer "is deprived of any sense of immediate contact with the powers of his body" (187). Descartes himself wonders whether he could feel himself extending his hand in a dream, but tellingly concludes that in dreams he has been deceived by "similar *thoughts*" (1993, 14; my emphasis).

7 de Beauvoir (1976) describes how these and other evasive attitudes emerge in the course of a typical human life. On her formulation, they fail to achieve a "synthesis of freedom and its content" (55).

8 See Husserl (2002, 15–16, 82–3).

9 See P. F. Strawson (1963): "Material bodies, therefore, are basic to particular-identification" (45).

10 See *Ideas II* § 18b-c for Husserl's analysis of the distinction between changes in semblance and merely semblant changes.

11 P. F. Strawson's arguments for the priority of "person" over "consciousness" follow from the mundane apperception of consciousness: "states of consciousness could not be ascribed at all, *unless* they are ascribed to persons" (1963, 98). Or, again: "there is no sense in speaking of the individual consciousness just as such, of the individual subject of experience" (111).

12 Berger (1972) strives to do justice to the insight that the "lived realization" of transcendental subjectivity is "a gratuitous event" (43). While the natural attitude can only be "explained" phenomenologically, each new stage of phenomenological reflection "will always conserve an air of gratuitousness in connection with the present reflection" (46).

13 Landgrebe (1981) notes that the phenomenological field is not opened "merely by inhibiting, one by one, the doxic theses of separate acts, separate believings"; instead, "their *basis* must also be affected by the *epoché*; indeed the *epoché* must relate primarily to their basis" (125). The phenomenological attitude first emerges by awakening to the naïveté of world-belief as such.

14 Kirk, Raven, and Schofield (2002, 247). Thanassas (2007, 61–89) interprets Parmenides as a critic of the "metaphysics of light."

15 See, e.g., *Ideas I* § 50, *Basic Problems* § 10, *Crisis* § 38.

16 In other texts on epoché and reduction, Husserl emphasizes their creativity rather than their finding what already lay in the natural attitude. For example, the epoché is the primal institution of transcendental subjectivity as an object of experience (2002, 76n); the transcendental reduction creates a new sphere of objects "that was never objectively constituted" (55n).

17 See Mohanty's response to Ingarden's critique of *Ideas I*: "It is only through reduction that the belief in the world first comes to be recognized as a belief. Before reduction, the world is simply there … Reduction shows that there is a belief, a taken-for-grated character, a naïveté about it" (1997, 44).

18 See Broekman (1963, 58).

19 Crowell, in his critique of Fink, dubs this the "already there" problem (2001, 264).
20 The wakefulness no longer opposed to sleep also makes possible a phenomenological reflection on the sleep to which natural wakefulness opposes itself. The mundane understanding of sleep as the condition of a real organism is here replaced with a transcendental understanding of sleep as a modification in egoic attentiveness. For Husserl's reflections on sleep, see especially *Husserliana* volumes 38 and 42. For a more recent exploration along Husserlian lines, see Jacobs (2010).
21 Husserl sometimes takes measures to avoid this connotation, employing the term more broadly to refer to everything theoretically attainable in the phenomenological reduction (2002, 90).
22 If the past world-order remains intact, annihilation will retain the sense of a mundane event and the experiment will fail. In a 1931 remark on *Weltvernichtung*, Husserl writes: "If the world was, then it still is, and if it is, then it was" (2014a, 20).
23 Husserl's *Weltvernichtung* experiment shows that he never performs the second movement of the "correlationist two-step" that Meillassoux targets in his critique of post-critical subjectivism (2015, 5). The first step, which Husserl makes, is that there can be no world apart from its givenness to consciousness. The second step, which he rejects, is that there can be no consciousness apart from its giving the world. That consciousness does reveal the world is due only to the fact that the world continues to display itself. Because the world does not conform to specifications contained in consciousness, because the world is not trapped in the shape transcendental subjectivity happens to have, the world's being for consciousness does not diminish its exteriority. Even the subjective-relative lifeworld is "outside" the acts of perception and judgment that reveal it. The overall bearing of the *Crisis* makes plain that late manuscripts focused on the founding role of the lifeworld with respect to mundane science have nothing to do with a "Ptolemaic counter-revolution" (119) that restricts "the bounds of knowledge ever more stringently within the limits of humanity's present situation" (121). Meillassoux himself seems hesitant about how to fit Husserl into the genealogy of the "Kantian catastrophe" (124). On the one hand, Husserl would seem to belong to the line of correlationists who evade the subjectivist implications of their position (18–27). On the other hand, he appears as a late proponent of the metaphysics of necessary entities rightly abandoned by correlationism (122, 137n). In truth, Husserl's conception of absolute consciousness frees the external world from its subjectivist interpretation at the hands of transcendental psychologism. In this respect, the Husserlian critique of Kantianism overlaps with Meillassoux's.
24 In his nuanced discussion of fundamentality in Husserl and Heidegger, Luft (2011) argues that "fundamentality and absoluteness are not automatically coextensive" (149). Existential analysis cannot construe transcendental constitution as a possibility of the factical self if "factical existence is the concrete 'actualization' of the transcendental as the totality of Egoic potentialities" (152).
25 All direct references to Platonic dialogues are Plato, 1997.

26 In an essay typical of the Hegelian–Marxist reaction to phenomenology, Marcuse recognizes that "in this [transcendental] dimension, speaking of essence no longer means setting reality against its potentiality" (1968, 60). From here, he seeks to subject the epoché to an ideological critique. Such a posture, he writes, betrays "a quietistic indifference … with regard to the established order" (60–1).

27 For a concise discussion of co-presentation and emptiness in perception, see McKenna (1989). The "emptiness" of concealed aspects and objects describes how they are *present* to me. Nothing is beyond the act of perception as if it lay outside the range of a light beam.

28 In *Crisis* § 18, Husserl faults Descartes for mistaking egological for psychological immanence. One symptom of Descartes' confusion is that he overlooks the problems of constitution implied in the fact of intersubjectivity. Rather than asking through what cogitations the interpersonal realities "you," "we," and "I" (this human being) are achieved, Descartes presumes the *cogito* to be the spiritual aspect of a man. Husserl's critics often mistake the egological appropriation of interpersonal experience for a derivation of your person from mine. Because it follows from a psychologistic understanding of immanence, the mistake suffers from the "Cartesianism" it mistakenly attributes to Husserl. To assert that intersubjectivity is a "fact" says nothing against Husserl's approach, which investigates this fact from the most radical perspective possible. On Husserl's adherence to the "fact" of others, see Taguchi (2006, 20). For an assessment of criticisms of Husserl on intersubjectivity, see Zahavi (2001).

29 See Williams (2002). Although there is "no such thing as 'the truth' about the historical past," making narrative sense of this past is subject to the virtue of truthfulness (234–69).

30 When Husserl writes, in the *Vienna Lecture*, that "the way of philosophy passes through naïveté," this "passage" refers to "the whole modern period since the Renaissance" (1970, 292/339). For Husserl, the conviction that the objectives of the Enlightenment project require the overcoming of transcendental naïveté is at one with the conviction that this project, from its inception, has been perverted by "the naturalization of the spirit" (ibid.).

31 This is apparently what Merleau-Ponty (1962) would have it require. In the preface to *Phenomenology of Perception* he claims that only an absolute mind could effect a "complete reduction" (xiv).

Division A

1 Just how far the crisis texts were from becoming a finished treatise is documented by Carr in his *Translator's Introduction* to the *Crisis* (1970, xviii–xix). Orth (1999) describes the situation by saying that the *Crisis* is less an actual than an "imaginary

book" (9). We embrace the implication that interpretations of the *Crisis*, including our own, are not explications of a book so much as of an idea of phenomenological philosophy.
2 I explore this criticism at greater length in Knies (2016a).
3 See Husserl's preface to the published sections of *Crisis*. The text, he writes, attempts "auf dem Wege einer teleologisch-historischen Besinnung auf die Ursprünge unsere kritischen wissenschaftlichen und philosophischen Situation die unausweichliche Notwendigkeit einer transzendentalphänomenologischen Umwendung der Philosophie zu begründen. Sonach wird sie zu einer eigenständigen Einleitung in die Transzendentale Phänomenologie" (1954, xxiv).
4 In *Teleologie in der Philosophiegeschichte*, Husserl classifies philosophy as a "knowledge vocation" that shares basic structural features with "ordinary vocations" like carpentry (1993, 363, 378, 387). Elsewhere, he compares the vocation of philosophy with tasks that produce other *Geisteswerke* (282).
5 In his 1906–7 lectures on logic and the theory of knowledge, Husserl similarly proceeds from "the fact of science" (2008b, 4/3). Here, he acknowledges that his "inductive approach" confronts the problem that "what is characteristic of science" is a matter of controversy (8/6). He anticipates settling the issue by demonstrating that there *is* a rational essence to scientific thinking. However, the issue is settled only if this essence determines the conception of genuineness that actually guides scientific practice.
6 I first worked out the following contrast with Carr in Knies (2011).
7 Husserl emphasizes that the global prejudices of the natural attitude are more intractable than those particular to an intellectual milieu. In *Crisis* § 32, Husserl acknowledges the hidden power of these latter prejudices, which are "drilled even into the souls of children" (1970, 120/123). He even claims that "the abstract general will to be without prejudice does nothing about them" (ibid.). However, he goes on, they pose "the slightest difficulties" compared to the prejudices inherent to the natural attitude (ibid.). Carr would equate the "abstract general will to be without prejudice" with the stance of epoché. The concrete will to overcome prejudice would emerge only through historical reduction.
8 This is also evident from Husserl's attitude toward *Ideas*. Even in 1937, Husserl still claims that *Ideas* presents a valid philosophical method "accessible without further ado to each of us as modern philosophers" (1993, 399). The primary problem with *Ideas* as an introduction to phenomenology is that it partakes of those presuppositions that belong to every philosophical method whatsoever. It does not, in other words, question precisely how it is "accessible," "without further ado," to "each of us" as "modern philosophers." The terms of this accessibility presuppose the taking over of a philosophical project for which the historical-teleological intervention will attempt to take responsibility. This is not to say that Husserl thought the method of Ideas was beyond criticism. See, for instance, Crisis § 43.

9   Compare *Crisis* § 15: "All judgments which count as philosophical are related back to this task, this idea [of philosophy]" (1970, 72/73).
10 See Romano: "But the idea of pure description is absurd, if by that we mean a description perfectly adequate to its object, that would ultimately limit itself to putting the object on stage, and erase itself as description" (2015, 235).
11 See Knies (2015) for an account of the dispute about why Husserl "takes history seriously" in the *Crisis*.
12 Derrida equates crisis with meaning-emptying, understood as the self-forgetting of subjectivity in its products. Given this equation, the "crisis" of science stems from an insoluble dilemma at the heart of language and time-consciousness. Husserl's hope for crisis resolution is accordingly futile (2003, 172; 1989, 92n). Orth also interprets crisis as a conflict between life and its objective creations. As such, it is a "preprogramed" feature of culture in general (1999, 60–1) and arises within transcendental subjectivism as a conflict between life and conceptual structure (145–55). While recognizing Husserl's intention to the contrary, he concludes that "to abolish the crisis would mean to deny the *conditio humana* and thereby humanity itself" (166). Dodd, too, roots crisis in a dialectic of intelligibility and unintelligibility essential to intellectual history. Rather than an exceptional state, "crisis" is thus "the norm" for any scientific pursuit (2004, 49). Most scholarship saves Husserl's hope for crisis resolution by equating the crisis with objectivism.
13 Trizio (2016) defends the heterodox view that Husserl does not think the crisis of science is the loss of its *Lebensbedeutsamkeit*. Exegetically, Trizio's reading depends upon treating as authoritative Husserl's initial definition of scientific crisis in *Crisis* § 1: the failure of a science to determine adequately its subject matter and method. According to Trizio, Husserl, after acknowledging that the sciences possess a prima facie scientificity as theoretical techniques, exposes their actual crisis as the result of a crisis of philosophy. Throughout, the definition of "crisis of science" is preserved. Philosophy fails to develop a method for metaphysics, the universal science of all being (2016, 201). As a result, the special sciences become detached from philosophy. In this condition, they cannot understand their own reason, their own determination of some domain of what truly is (203). Lacking this understanding, "the ultimate rationality of their task and method (higher-level, 'authentic' scientificity), is completely lost" (205). Trizio thereby isolates a *purely theoretical* scientific crisis remediable through the phenomenological clarification of ontological regions (203, 206).

In his response to Trizio, Heffernan (2017) argues that this purely theoretical crisis is an abstraction. Exegetically, Heffernan's reading, like ours, depends upon treating as provisional Husserl's definition of scientific crisis in §1. This first definition invokes a positivistic sense of scientificity that divorces scientific method and subject matter from the question of *Lebensbedeutsamkeit*. Beginning in §2, Husserl deploys a "philosophical" definition of the scientificity of sciences "that includes their meaningfulness for life in their scientificity" (241). A science is only genuine, argues Heffernan, if it can "collaborate with philosophy to achieve a full understanding of the human being in the life-world" (247). Detached from universal science, the special sciences fail to bring humanity into self-conscious relation with what truly is. Heffernan thereby develops a concrete conception of crisis that is "both scientific and existential" (248). What we will emphasize is that this synthesis depends upon participation in a historical community that demands of science something its positivistic form cannot deliver. Husserl first introduces the philosophical sense of scientificity by appealing to the special role "our culture" ascribes to the sciences (1970, 5/3). Here, the *Lebensbedeutsamkeit* in question is precisely that *führende Bedeutung* European humanity has invested in science. We can now say with Heffernan that, for Husserl, "the *Krisis* of the European sciences consists in a loss of their scientificity understood as a loss of their meaningfulness for life" (2017, 253).

14 In the opening section of the *Vienna Lecture*, Husserl writes: "The European nations are sick; Europe itself, it is said, is in crisis [*in einer Krisis*]" (1970, 270/315). In the *Crisis*, Husserl consistently uses "*Krisis*" rather than "*Krise*," which lacks the medical connotations of the former. See Heffernan (2013, 223; 2017, 230n6). Also note Husserl's remark in a 1923 text on ethics: "Sickness is a general title for bodily [*Leibliche*] or also spiritual transformations that bring unhappiness or interrupt a happy life" (1997, 209).

15 The most medical translation here is "tranquilizations." Husserl uses constructions built on the verb *beruhigen* (1954, 4, 9). Perhaps the knack for supplying such tranquilization is the flattery that mimics medical care for the spirit. See *Gorgias*.

16 In a 1924 reflection on the conflict between heart and mind, Husserl recognizes that this is indeed a danger (2014a, 192–3).

17 See Hart's description of Husserlian optimism as "self-displacement into a horizon of promise" (1992, 313). Husserl's stance is close to Rescher's notion of "attitudinal optimism," a "praxis-geared posture of hopeful belief" (1992, 98). Because Rescher thinks "ought" binds action even failing an accompanying "can," he requires no underlying real possibility to warrant the attitude. Rescher's arguments are primarily consequentialist, though he also implies that hope is an intrinsic good (100, 112). Despite the realism of the imperative considered here, Husserl also gestures in this direction. Dedication without utility is heroic and "valuable in the highest sense" (1997, 211). See also Szabados (1973), who defends wishful thinking provided that the agent can acknowledge the unlikelihood of the wished for outcome.

18 In the midst of the historical reconstruction, reflections on tradition as such sometimes take center stage. This occurs prominently in *The Origin of Geometry*. Even here, though, Husserl is clear about the role of history in the *Crisis* as a whole.

We are, he writes, "seeking to carry out, in the form of historical meditations, self-reflections about our own present philosophical situation in the hope that in this way we can finally take possession of the meaning, method and beginning of philosophy, the *one* philosophy to which our life seeks to be and ought to be devoted" (1970, 353–4/365).

19 The original passage: "Sie kann prinzipiell nur Ziel sein in einer Berufung, aus einem kategorischen Imperativ, die weder er noch irgend jemand ihm von außen her auferlegt haben konnte, und sein apodiktisches 'Muß' ist als sein eigenstes Telos, als sein ihm 'Lebensziel,' schon bevor er dazu kommen möchte, wenn überhaupt, es als Lebensziel zu formulieren."

20 For the position that Kant holds this view, see, e.g., Beck (1960, 242–5).

21 See Knies (2016b) for an argument that the Kantian framework of postulation, though alien to Husserl's self-conception, is the best way to understand his crisis concepts.

22 Buckley, for instance, notes that Husserl recounts the history of science's fall into objectivism from the perspective of its phenomenological redemption, and remarks that "it is a curious type of crisis, indeed, when from the beginning one knows that meaning is always there to be recovered" (1992, 28).

23 This is not to say that theological considerations are incompatible with the crisis problematic. On the contrary, some of Husserl's later ethical reflections suggest they are required. See, for instance, Husserl (2014a, 203). Notably, Husserl tries to clarify why *belief* in God is ultimately demanded in any dedication to what absolutely ought to be. Reason requires belief, but cannot identify this belief with knowledge.

24 See, e.g., Husserl's reflections on *Vernunft* and *Vernunftwillen* in a 1930 text on teleology (2014a, 443).

25 Dilman gets at the same issues by examining the phrase with which Socrates introduces the concluding myth in *Gorgias*: "What I am going to tell you, I tell you as the truth" (1979, 170–86).

26 See, for instance, Hanna's worries about the connotations of both "functionary" and "vocation" in Husserl's crisis discourse (2014, 766). Moran (2012) rightly emphasizes that "Husserl sees functionaries not merely as passive bearers or conveyers of tradition, but as actively *constituting* (filtering, validating, suppressing, affirming, maintaining, renewing) our sense of belonging to institutions" (152).

27 This distinction between philosopher as benefactor and functionary tracks Husserl's historical distinction in the *Vienna Lecture* between non-philosophical and philosophical culture (1970, 274–7/320–3). Maintaining this distinction is crucial in avoiding provincialism in the crisis problematic, despite the difficulties involved in finding the borders of philosophical culture. In any case, the distinction occurs *within* a sphere of ethical concern that Husserl regards as inherently inclusive of all humanity.

28 Ströker (1993) develops an interpretation along these lines. She sees the sections on Galileo and the manuscript on geometry as exemplary for the general function of historical reflection in the *Crisis*. It is a stepwise "constitutive-analytic procedure" applied to scientific sense formations:

> First the analysis works back to their "operative" constitution on the basis of prescientific givenness, out of which their original sense was once produced in living activity, but then remained sedimented in later sense formations. Then the analysis reaches further back, to the original syntheses of passive preconstitution in which what is pregiven to science through prescientific experience is ultimately grounded. (184)

29 Merleau-Ponty thought Husserl was expressing his own view when he referred to the notion, in a late manuscript (1954, 508), that the dream of rigorously scientific philosophy was over (*ausgeträumt*). This is in accordance with Merleau-Ponty's overall interpretation of the *Crisis*, which roughly adheres to the alterations outlined below. He presents Husserl's mature conception of philosophy as a form of cultural hermeneutics that requires attunement to foreign traditions in order to enrich its structural accounts of experience (1964, 89). For a textually detailed rebuttal to the claim that Husserl regarded *strenge Wissenschaft* as an illusory goal, see Orth (1999, 29–34). For a critique of Merleau-Ponty's hermeneutic understanding of free variation, see Derrida (1989). For an attempt to reconcile hermeneutic sensitivity with transcendental eidetics, see Aldea (2016).

Division B

1 Zhok (2011) defines this situation as a "contradiction between normative claims with intersubjective roots" (52). In such cases, "we may not be free to solve contrasts by establishing an order of priority, because the efficaciousness of the claims does not depend on us" (51).
2 Post-Husserlian thinkers of crisis tend to treat mastery itself as the central problem. See, for instance, the discussion of Heidegger and Arendt in Učník (2016).
3 For a development of Husserl's concept of territory, see Steinbock (1995, 102–4, 167–72).
4 Describing Husserl's position, Moran (2012) writes that Europe "is not a geographically or politically defined place but rather a certain constellation of intellectual and spiritual achievements, outlooks and values" (61). The idealization is full-blown in Buckley (1992), who claims that, for Husserl, "Europe" is "really just a name for the universal idea of science" (31).

5 See Mandelbaum's distinction between the "special history" of cultural forms and the "general history" of societies, where the latter consist of "individuals living in an organized community that controls a particular territory" (1977, 11). The subject matter of general history is "an infinitely dense" series of events (15). Although Husserl identifies only a few decisive events in European history, it is ultimately the continuous life of European humanity for which these events are decisive.
6 I outline these three features briefly in Knies (2016b).
7 Schuhmann (1988) points out that Husserl frequently identifies *Volk* and *Nation*, emphasizing the etymological sense of the latter (70). However, Husserl also invokes a narrower use: "Nation is better understood as a more precise concept as compared to a 'people' [*Volk*], which does not live in a politically concentrated internationalism" (1993, 10n).
8 Sophistry is a feature of the crisis problematic. Its importance for philosophical history lies in its novel attitude toward the home world. Sophistry is free from the authority of tradition, but can oppose to it nothing but the abyss. Guthrie (1971, 88–97) highlights an ambiguity in the concepts typically employed in sophistic ctirique. Mere *nomoi* are opposed to *physis*, but, because the latter is unknowable, the contrast only enables statements to the effect that *nomoi* are "just" *nomoi*. This stance reflects a distance from communal life felt now as disillusion, now as contempt. The discovery of human provinciality collapses the orienting world into an arbitrary projection of power and persuasion. Education is at once alienation and mastery. The abiding importance of Socratic elenchus is to provide an antidote to this dangerous brew.
9 Pietersma's account (1977) of "epistemic situations" provides a helpful framework for reconciling Husserl's general theory of evidence with historical shifts in the very idea of truth.
10 See Held (2002) for an approach to European identity informed by Husserl, but based upon the two pillars of science and democracy.
11 Schuhmann (1988) shows that Husserl's occasional use of "world state" to describe a universal ethical community is misleading (170–1). For Husserl, the proper function of the state, in the usual sense of the term, is to preserve an orientation toward an ethical community of mutual love (*Liebesgemeinschaft*) that eventually requires the state's transcendence (111).
12 Jaeger (1965) is close to Husserl's Renaissance historicity in his explanation of the claim that European history begins with the Greeks:

> By "begins" I mean not only the temporal commencement, but also the ἀρχή, the spiritual source to which, as we reach every new stage of development, we must constantly revert in order to reorient ourselves … Yet our return to Greece, our spontaneous renewal of this influence, does not mean that by acknowledging the timeless and ever-present intellectual greatness of

the Greeks, we have given them an authority over us which, because it is independent of our own destiny, is fixed and unchallengeable. (xv)

Jaeger also claims that Europe is connected to Greece by the "factor of race," "which we can feel by intuition" (55). We will see why this factor cannot figure in Husserl's approach.

13 See Brann's reading of this paradox: "it seems that only those will be content to accept this constitution who have accepted the 'dye' of its laws (430 a 3). The just city can only be realized by its own children: To begin it must already have begun" (2004, 129).
14 Our interpretation of Renaissance historicity is in tension with a perspective briefly suggested in the *Prague Lecture*, which places "Judeo-Christian monotheism" alongside ancient Greece as one of two sources of meaning (*Sinnesquellen*) for European humanity as such (1993, 109). Here, Husserl tasks modern humanity with realizing the unity of autonomy and religion first attempted in medieval life. This perspective apparently did not find its way into the published parts of the *Crisis*.
15 Steinbock claims that Husserl's promotion of Europeanization violates his own insight into the irreducibility of home–alien distinctions (1995, 237). This would indeed be the case if Europeanization involved "the universalization of a homeworld" (235). While Husserl's statements on this issue are inconclusive, his overall approach supports the reading that Europe is not a homeworld in the ordinary sense but rather a multiplicity of homeworlds that counts as "home" in relation to non-Europe only ambiguously. Welton also criticizes Husserl for trying to overcome the "plurality of cultural worlds" (2000, 327). See also Stähler: "Husserl's efforts to transcend the various homeworlds and alienworlds toward the one world run against his own philosophy" (2003, 233). Ströker's reading is in line with our own: "[The European supernationality] is certainly unable to obliterate geographical, historical and other sociocultural differences and neither can it in any way level down the essential, ideal-typical differences of all concrete communal life—such as the familiar and the foreign" (1996, 317). Criticisms that equate Europeanization with imperialism are likely responding to the actual history of European expansion. We will consider the importance of this history in the section on hypocrisy.
16 Moran (2011) documents how Husserl's European universalism was already clashing with such finitization in the form of the "race-based relativism" of National Socialism (476).
17 Statman (1997) argues that hypocrisy generally involves some degree of self-deception. For both practical and emotional reasons, hypocrites "get into the character" who takes their professed beliefs seriously (III).
18 Also cited by Maldonado-Torres (2016, 31).

19 He is thus safe from the kind of objections brought against Heidegger by Sheehan (2015). Unlike Heidegger's *Seinsgeschichte*, Husserl's crisis reflection never supplants historical explanations for mundane events (such as world wars) with putatively fundamental explanations that appeal to little more than "the texts of a few metaphysicians" (292). For a possible feint in this direction, see the opening of Husserl's 1917 lectures on *Fichte's Ideal of Humanity* (1987, 267–9).
20 See L. R. Gordon (1995), who introduces Fanon into the crisis problematic by evaluating the attempt to spiritually resuscitate Europe as follows:

> Humanity has died in Europe, the United States, and anywhere in the world in which Western Man—that is White Man/White Culture—*is* Man and, therefore, Reason. In other words, humanity has suffered a global death. But in Euro-man, ironically even in his "colored" manifestations, lives the fool precisely because he thinks he is morally and rationally alive. (8–9)

21 This field includes even the Derridean posture of ambivalence regarding Europe as a subject of crisis. See, for instance, *The Other Heading* (1992, 31).
22 This opposition is a practical refusal to indulge nihilism—an "existential 'if'" (1970, 17/15)—about whether human history is philosophical. Ricoeur suggests that Husserl failed to confront his "proposed reading" with "other possible readings of history" that view non-philosophical factors as decisive (1967, 168). Ricoeur understands Husserl's interpretation as a theory of history. We have argued that it is better understood as a use of history for practical purposes.
23 Peucker (2007) provides a succinct consideration of the role of feeling-consciousness in Husserl's ethics. The will, for Husserl, must be motivated by evaluations that ultimately rest on value-feelings (316). Peucker identifies the problems Husserl encounters in distinguishing correct from incorrect feelings (318). These problems are relevant to how the subject of crisis is disclosed. In the *Vienna Lecture*, Husserl writes: "I mean that we feel (and in spite of all obscurity this feeling is probably legitimate) that an entelechy is inborn in our European civilization" (1970, 275/320).
24 Husserl does not say that "Greek humanity" is itself the first genuine humanity (1970, 15/13). What is essential to humanity has *its* first breakthrough *in* Greek humanity (*im griechischen Menschentum erstmalig zum Durchbruch gekommen ist*).
25 See Husserl (2014a, 451–7) for an account of how the "attitude of seriousness" (*Einstellung des Ernstes*) operates in the disclosure of and the decision for what absolutely ought to be.

References

Aikin, Scott. 2008. "Tu Quoque Arguments and the Significance of Hypocrisy." *Informal Logic* 28, no. 2: 155–69.

Aldea, Andreea Smaranda. 2016. "Phenomenology as Critique: Teleological-Historical Reflection and Husserl's Transcendental Eidetics." *Husserl Studies* 32, no. 1: 21–46.

Beck, Lewis White. 1960. *A Commentary on Kant's Critique of Practical Reason.* Chicago: University of Chicago Press.

Berger, Gaston. 1972. *The Cogito in Husserl's Philosophy.* Translated by K. McLaughlin. Evanston: Northwestern University Press.

Bernet, Rudolf. 2005. "Husserl's Concept of the World." In *Edmund Husserl: Critical Assessments of Leading Philosophers*, vol. 5, edited by Rudolf Bernet, Donn Welton and Gina Zavota, 19–38. New York: Routledge.

Blumenfeld, David, and Jean Beer Blumenfeld. 1978. "Can I Know That I Am Not Dreaming?" In *Descartes: Critical and Interpretive Essays*, edited by Michael Hooker, 234–55. Baltimore: Johns Hopkins University Press.

Brann, Eva. 2004. *The Music of the Republic: Essays on Socrates' Conversations and Plato's Writings.* Philadelphia: Paul Dry Books.

Broekman, Jan. 1963. *Phänomenologie und Egologie*: Faktisches und transzendentales Ego bei Edmund Husserl, Phaenomenologica 12. The Hague: Springer.

Buckley, Philip R. 1992. *Husserl, Heidegger and the Crisis of Philosophical Responsibility.* Dordrecht: Kluwer Academic.

Carr, David. 1970. "Translator's Introduction." In Edmund Husserl, *The Crisis of European Sciences and Transcendental Phenomenology: An Introduction to Phenomenological Philosophy.* Translated by D. Carr, xv–xliii. Evanston: Northwestern University Press.

Carr, David. 1974. *Phenomenology and the Problem of History.* Evanston: Northwestern University Press.

Carr, David. 1986. *Time, Narrative, and History.* Bloomington: Indiana University Press.

Carr, David. 1987. *Interpreting Husserl: Critical and Comparative Studies.* Dordrecht: Martinus Nijhoff.

Césaire, Aimé. 2000. *Discourse on Colonialism.* Translated by J. Pinkham. New York: Monthly Review Press.

Crowell, Steven Galt. 2001. "Gnostic Phenomenology: Eugen Fink and the Critique of Transcendental Reason." *The New Yearbook for Phenomenology and Phenomenological Philosophy* 1: 257–77.

Crowell, Steven Galt. 2013. *Normativity and Phenomenology in Husserl and Heidegger.* New York: Cambridge University Press.

Danto, Arthur Coleman. 1985. *Narration and Knowledge: Including the Integral Text of "Analytical Philosophy of History."* New York: Columbia University Press.

de Beauvoir, Simone. 1976. *Ethics of Ambiguity*. Translated by B. Frechtman. New York: Citadel Press.

Derrida, Jacques. 1989. *Edmund Husserl's Origin of Geometry: An Introduction*. Translated by J. P. Leavy, Jr. Lincoln: University of Nebraska Press.

Derrida, Jacques. 1992. *The Other Heading: Reflections on Today's Europe*. Translated by P. Brault and M. B. Nass. Bloomington: Indiana University Press.

Derrida, Jacques. 2003. *The Problem of Genesis in Husserl's Philosophy*. Translated by M. Hobson. Chicago: University of Chicago Press.

Descartes, René. 1993. *Meditations on First Philosophy*, 3rd ed. Translated by D. A. Cress. Indianapolis: Hackett.

Descartes, René. 1998. *Discourse on Method and Meditations on First Philosophy*, 4th ed. Translated by D. A. Cress. Indianapolis: Hackett.

Despland, Michel. 1973. *Kant on History and Religion: With a Translation of Kant's "On the Failure of All Attempted Philosophical Theodicies."* Montreal: McGill-Queen's Press.

Dilman, Ilham. 1979. *Morality and the Inner Life: A Study in Plato's Gorgias*. London: Macmillan Press.

Dodd, James. 2004. *Crisis and Reflection: An Essay on Husserl's Crisis of the European Sciences*. Dordrecht: Kluwer Academic.

Dray, William. 1957. *Laws and Explanation in History*. Oxford: Oxford University Press.

Fink, Eugen. 1995. *Sixth Cartesian Meditation: The Idea of a Transcendental Theory of Method*. Translated by R. Bruzina. Indianapolis: Indiana University Press.

Gasché, Rudolphe. 2009. *Europe, or the Infinite Task: A Study of a Philosophical Concept*. Stanford: Stanford University Press.

Gordon, Jeffrey. 1985. "Dream-World or Life-World? A Phenomenological Solution to an Ancient Puzzle." *Husserl Studies* 2, no. 2: 169–91.

Gordon, Lewis R. 1995. *Fanon and the Crisis of European Man: An Essay on Philosophy and the Human Sciences*. New York: Routledge.

Guthrie, W. K. C. 1971. *The Sophists*. Cambridge: Cambridge University Press.

Hanna, Robert. 2014. "Husserl's Crisis and Our Crisis." *International Journal of Philosophical Studies* 22, no. 5: 752–70.

Hart, J. G. 1992. *The Person and the Common Life: Studies in a Husserlian Social Ethics*. Dordrecht: Kluwer Academic.

Hart, J. G. 2009a. *Who One Is. Book 1. Meontology of the I: A Transcendental Phenomenology*. Dordrecht: Springer.

Hart, J. G. 2009b. *Who One Is. Book 2. Existenz and Transcendental Phenomenology*. Dordrecht: Springer.

Heffernan, George. 2013. "Phenomenology is a Humanism: Husserl's Hermeneutical-Historical Struggle to Determine the Genuine Meaning of Human Existence in *The Crisis of the European Sciences and Transcendental Phenomenology*." In

Investigaciones Fenomenológicas, vol. 4/II (Monográfico): *Razón y vida—La Responsabilidad de la Filosofía*, edited by Javier San Martín Sala and Agustín Serrano de Haro, 213–41.

Heffernan, George. 2017. "The Concept of *Krisis* in Husserl's *The Crisis of the European Sciences and Transcendental Phenomenology*." *Husserl Studies* 33, no. 3: 229–57.

Hegel, G. W. F. 1956. *The Philosophy of History*. Translated by J. Sibree. New York: Dover.

Hegel, G. W. F. 1977. *The Phenomenology of Spirit*. Translated by A. V. Miller. Oxford: Oxford University Press.

Heidegger, Martin. 1977. *Sein und Zeit*. Tübingen: Max Niemeyer.

Heidegger, Martin. 1996. *Being and Time: A Translation of* Sein und Zeit. Translated by J. Stambaugh. Albany: State University of New York Press.

Held, Klaus. 2002. "The Origin of Europe with the Greek Discovery of the World." Translated by S. Kirkland. *Epoché: A Journal for the History of Philosophy* 7, no. 1: 81–105.

Hobson, J. Allan. 2005. *Dreaming: A Very Short Introduction*. Oxford: Oxford University Press.

Hume, David. 1993. *An Enquiry Concerning Human Understanding*. Edited by E. Steinberg. Indianapolis: Hackett.

Husserl, Edmund. 1950. *Cartesianische Meditationes und Pariser Vorträge*. Edited by S. Strasser, Husserliana I. The Hague: Martinus Nijhoff.

Husserl, Edmund. 1952. *Ideen zu einer reinen Phänomenologie und phänomenologischen Philosophie, Zweites Buch: Phänomenologische Untersuchungen zur Konstitution*, edited by M. Biemel, Husserliana IV. The Hague: Martinus Nijhoff.

Husserl, Edmund. 1954. *Die Krisis der Europäischen Wissenschaften und die transcendentale Phänomenologie: Eine Einleitung in die phänomenologische Philosophie 1934–1937*. Edited by W. Biemel, Husserliana VI. The Hague: Martinus Nijhoff.

Husserl, Edmund. 1970. *The Crisis of European Sciences and Transcendental Phenomenology: An Introduction to Phenomenological Philosophy*. Translated by D. Carr. Evanston: Northwestern University Press.

Husserl, Edmund. 1973a. *Zur Phänomenologie der Intersubjektivität. Texte aus dem Nachlass. Dritter Teil: 1929–1935*. Edited by I. Kern, Husserliana, vol. 15. The Hague: Martinus Nijhoff.

Husserl, Edmund. 1973b. *Cartesian Meditations: An Introduction to Phenomenology*. Translated by D. Cairns. The Hague: Martinus Nijhoff.

Husserl, Edmund. 1976. *Ideen zu einer reinen Phänomenologie und phänomenologischen Philosophie, Erstes Buch: Allgemeine Einführung in die reine Phänomenologie*, edited by K. Schuhmann, Husserliana III. The Hague: Martinus Nijhoff.

Husserl, Edmund. 1977. *Grundprobleme der Phänomenologie 1910/11*. Edited by I. Kern, Husserliana XIII. The Hague: Martinus Nijhoff.

Husserl, Edmund. 1981. *Husserl: Shorter Works*. Edited by P. McCormick and F. A. Elliston. Notre Dame: University of Notre Dame Press and The Harvester Press.

Husserl, Edmund. 1985. "The Apodicticity of Recollection." Translated by D. Chaffin, *Husserl Studies* 2, no. 1: 3–32.

Husserl, Edmund. 1987. *Aufsätze und Vorträge (1911–1921). Mit ergänzenden Texten*. Edited by T. Nenon and H. R. Sepp, Husserliana XXV. Dordrecht: Martinus Nijhoff.

Husserl, Edmund. 1989. *Aufsätze und Vorträge (1922–1937). Mit ergänzenden Texten*. Edited by T. Nenon and H. R. Sepp, Husserliana XXVII. Dordrecht: Kluwer Academic.

Husserl, Edmund. 1993. *Die Krisis der Europäischen Wissenschaften und die transcendentale Phänomenologie: Ergänzungsband. Texte aus dem Nachlaß 1934–1937*. Edited by R. N. Smid, Husserliana XXIX. Boston: Kluwer Academic.

Husserl, Edmund. 1997. "Wert des Lebens. Wert der Welt. Sittlichkeit (Tugend) und Glückseligkeit." Edited by U. Melle, *Husserl Studies* 13, no. 3: 201–35.

Husserl, Edmund. 2002. *Zur Phänomenologischen Reduktion: Texte aus dem Nachlaß (1926–1935)*. Edited by S. Luft, Husserliana XXXIV. Dordrecht: Kluwer Academic.

Husserl, Edmund. 2004. *Wahrnehmung und Aufmerksamkeit: Texte aus dem Nachlaß (1893–1912)*. Edited by T. Vongehr and R. Giuliani, Husserliana XXXVIII. Dordrecht: Springer.

Husserl, Edmund. 2005. *Phantasy, Image Consciousness, and Memory, 1898–1925*. Translated by J. B. Brough. Dordrecht: Springer.

Husserl, Edmund. 2006. *The Basic Problems of Phenomenology: From the Lectures, Winter Semester, 1910–1911*. Translated by I. Farin and J. G. Hart. Dordrecht: Springer.

Husserl, Edmund. 2008a. *Die Lebenswelt: Auslegungen der vorgegebenen Welt und ihrer Konstitution. Texte aus dem Nachlass (1916–1937)*. Edited by R. Sowa, Husserliana XXXIX. New York: Springer.

Husserl, Edmund. 2008b. *Introduction to Logic and the Theory of Knowledge: Lectures 1906/07*. Translated by Claire Ortiz Hill. Edited by U. Melle, Husserliana XIII. Dordrecht: Springer.

Husserl, Edmund. 2014a. *Grenzprobleme der Phänomenologie. Analysen des Unbewusstseins und der Instinkte. Metaphysik. Späte Ethik. Texte aus dem Nachlass (1908–1937)*. Edited by R. Sowa and T. Vongehr. Husserliana XLII. Dordrecht: Springer.

Husserl, Edmund. 2014b. *Ideas for a Pure Phenomenology and Phenomenological Philosophy: First Book: General Introduction to Pure Phenomenology*. Translated by D. Dahlstrom. Indianapolis: Hackett.

Jacobs, Hanne. 2010. "I am Awake: Husserlian Reflections on Wakefulness and Attention." *Revue de Phenomenologie* 18, no. 1: 183–201.

Jaeger, Werner. 1965. *Paideia: The Ideals of Greek Culture. Vol. 1 Archaic Greece The Mind of Athens*. New York: Oxford University Press.

James, William. 1956. *The Will to Believe and Other Essays in Popular Philosophy*. New York: Dover.
Kant, Immanuel. 1978. *Anthropology from a Pragmatic Point of View*. Translated by V. L. Dowdell. Carbondale: Southern Illinois University Press.
Kant, Immanuel. 2002. *Critique of Practical Reason*. Translated by W. S. Pluhar. Indianapolis: Hackett.
Kirk, Geoffrey Stephen, John Earle Raven, and Malcolm Schofield. 2002. *The Presocratic Philosophers*. Cambridge: Cambridge University Press.
Knies, Kenneth. 2011. "The Practical Obscurity of Philosophy: Husserl's 'Arbeit der Probleme der letzten Voraussetzungen.'" *Husserl Studies* 27, no. 2: 83–104.
Knies, Kenneth. 2015. "Crisis and the Limits of Phenomenological Reason." *Dialogue and Universalism* 8, no. 3: 39–50.
Knies, Kenneth. 2016a. "A Qualified Defense of Husserl's Crisis Concepts." *Metodo. International Studies in Phenomenology and Philosophy* 4, no. 1: 27–47.
Knies, Kenneth. 2016b. "Europe: A Postulate of Phenomenological Reason." *Journal of the British Society for Phenomenology* 47, no. 3: 210–25.
Koselleck, Reinhart. 1988. *Critique and Crisis: Enlightenment and the Pathogenesis of Modern Society*. Cambridge, MA: MIT Press.
Landgrebe, Ludwig. 1981. *The Phenomenology of Edmund Husserl: Six Essays by Ludwig Landgrebe*. Edited by D. Welton. Ithaca: Cornell University Press.
Luft, Sebastian. 2011. *Subjectivity and Lifeworld in Transcendental Phenomenology*. Evanston: Northwestern University Press.
McKenna, William R. 1989. "Husserl's Theory of Perception." In *Husserl's Phenomenology: A Textbook*, edited by J. N. Mohanty and W. R. McKenna, 181–212. Washington, DC: University Press of America.
Maldonado-Torres, Nelson. 2007. "On the Coloniality of Being." *Cultural Studies* 21, nos. 2–3: 240–70.
Maldonado-Torres, Nelson. 2016. "Outline of Ten Theses on Coloniality and Decoloniality." Fondation Frantz Fanon. http://frantzfanonfoundation-fondationfrantzfanon.com/article2360.html Google Scholar.
Mall, R.A. 2000. *Intercultural Philosophy*, Lanham: Rowman & Littlefield.
Mandelbaum, Maurice. 1977. *The Anatomy of Historical Knowledge*. Baltimore: Johns Hopkins University Press.
Marcuse, Herbert. 1968. *Negations: Essays in Critical Theory*. Translated by J. Shapiro. Boston: Beacon Press.
Meillassoux, Quentin. 2015. *After Finitude: An Essay on the Necessity of Contingency*. Translated by Ray Brassier. London: Bloomsbury Academic.
Merleau-Ponty, Maurice. 1962. *Phenomenology of Perception*. Translated by C. Smith. London: Routledge.
Merleau-Ponty, Maurice. 1964. "Phenomenology and the Sciences of Man." Translated by J. Wild. In *The Primacy of Perception*, edited by J. M. Edie, Evanston: Northwestern University Press.

Merleau-Ponty, Maurice. 1969. *The Visible and the Invisible*. Translated by A. Lingis. Evanston: Northwestern University Press.

Mohanty, J. N. 1997. *Phenomenology: Between Essentialism and Transcendental Philosophy*. Evanston: Northwestern University Press.

Moran, Dermot. 2011. "'Even the Papuan is a Man and not a Beast': Husserl on Universalism and the Relativity of Cultures." *Journal of the History of Philosophy* 49, no. 4: 463–94.

Moran, Dermot. 2012. *Husserl's Crisis of the European Sciences and Transcendental Phenomenology: An Introduction*. Cambridge: Cambridge University Press.

Orth, Ernst Wolfgang. 1999. *Edmund Husserls 'Krisis der europäischen Wissenschaften und die transzendentale Phänomenologie*. Darmstadt: Wissenschaftliche Buchgesellschaft.

Patočka, Jan. 1996. *Heretical Essays in the Philosophy of History*. Translated by E. Kohak and edited by J. Dodd. Chicago: Open Court.

Patočka, Jan. 2002. *Plato and Europe*. Translated by P. Lom. Stanford: Stanford University Press.

Peucker, Henning. 2007. "Husserl's Critique of Kant's Ethics." *Journal of the History of Philosophy* 45, no. 2: 309–19.

Pietersma, Henry. 1977. "Husserl's Views on the Evident and the True." In *Husserl: Expositions and Appraisals*, edited by F. Ellison and P. McCormick, 38–53. Notre Dame: University of Notre Dame Press.

Plato. 1997. *Plato: Complete Works*. Edited by J. M. Cooper. Indianapolis: Hackett.

Reinach, Adolf. 2012. *The Apriori Foundations of the Civil Law: Along with the Lecture Concerning Phenomenology*. Edited by J. F. Crosby. Frankfurt: Ontos Verlag.

Rescher, Nicholas. 1961. "On the Logic of Presuppositions." *Philosophy and Phenomenological Research* 21, no. 4: 521–7.

Rescher, Nicholas. 1992. *Ethical Idealism: An Inquiry into the Nature and Function of Ideals*. Berkeley: University of California Press.

Ricoeur, Paul. 1967. *Husserl: An Analysis of His Phenomenology*. Translated by E. Ballard and L. Embree. Evanston: Northwestern University Press.

Ricoeur, Paul. 1988. *Time and Narrative*, vol. 3. Translated by K. Blamey and D. Pellauer. Chicago: University of Chicago Press.

Romano, Claude. 2015. *At the Heart of Reason*. Translated by M. B. Smith and C. Romano. Evanston: Northwestern University Press.

Schelling, F. W. J. 1978. *System of Transcendental Idealism (1800)*. Translated by P. Heath. Charlottesville: University of Virginia Press.

Schuhmann, Karl. 1988. *Husserls Staatsphilosophie*. München: Verlag Karl Alber.

Sheehan, Thomas. 2015. *Making Sense of Heidegger: A Paradigm Shift*. London: Rowman & Littlefield.

Sokolowski, Robert. 1974. *Husserlian Meditations: How Words Present Things*. Evanston: Northwestern University Press.

Sokolowski, Robert. 2008. *Phenomenology of the Human Person*. Cambridge: Cambridge University Press.
Stähler, Tanja. 2003. *Die Unruhe des Anfang: Husserl und Hegel über den Weg in die Phänomenologie*. Dordrecht: Kluwer Academic.
Statman, Daniel. 1997. "Hypocrisy and Self-Deception." *Philosophical Psychology* 10, no. 1: 57–75.
Steinbock, Anthony. 1995. *Home and Beyond: Generative Phenomenology after Husserl*. Evanston: Northwestern University Press.
Steinbock, Anthony. 1998. "Spirit and Generativity: The Role and Contribution of the Phenomenologist in Hegel and Husserl." In *Alterity and Facticity: New Perspectives on Husserl*, edited by N. Depraz and D. Zahavi, 163–203. Boston: Kluwer Academic.
Strawson, G. 2004. "Against Narrativity." *Ratio* 17, no. 4: 428–52.
Strawson, P. F. 1963. *Individuals: An Essay in Descriptive Metaphysics*. New York: Anchor Books.
Ströker, Elisabeth. 1993. *Husserl's Transcendental Phenomenology*. Translated by L. Hardy. Stanford: Stanford University Press.
Ströker, Elisabeth. 1996. "Krise der europäischen Kultur: Ein Problemerbe der husserlschen Philosophie." *Zeitschrift für philosophische Forschung* 1, no. 2: 309–22.
Szabados, Béla. 1973. "Wishful Thinking and Self-Deception." *Analysis* 33, no. 6: 201–5.
Taguchi, Shigeru. 2006. *Das Problem des,Ur-Ich' bei Edmund Husserl: Die Frage nach der selbstverständlichen,Nähe' des Selbst*. Dordrecht: Springer.
Thanassas, Panagiotis. 2007. *Parmenides, Cosmos, and Being*. Milwaukee: Marquette University Press.
Trizio, Emiliano. 2016. "What Is the Crisis of Western Sciences?" *Husserl Studies* 32: 191–211.
Učník, L'ubica. 2016. *The Crisis of Meaning and the Life-world: Husserl, Heidegger, Arendt, Patočka*. Athens: Ohio University Press.
Waldenfels, Bernhard. 2011. *Phenomenology of the Alien: Basic Concepts*. Translated by A. Kozin and T. Stähler. Evanston: Northwestern University Press.
Welton, Donn. 2000. *The Other Husserl: The Horizons of Transcendental Phenomenology*. Bloomington: Indiana University Press.
Williams, Bernard. 2002. *Truth and Truthfulness: An Essay in Genealogy*. Princeton: Princeton University Press.
Wright, G. H. von. 1971. *Explanation and Understanding*. Ithaca: Cornell University Press.
Zahavi, Dan. 2001. *Husserl and Transcendental Intersubjectivity: A Response to the Linguistic-Pragmatic Critique*. Translated by E. Behnke. Athens: Ohio University Press.
Zahavi, Dan. 2005. *Subjectivity and Selfhood: Investigating the First-Person Perspective*. Cambridge, MA: A Bradford Book.
Zhok, Andrea. 2011. "History as Therapy of Tradition in Husserl's Thought." *Studia Phaenomenologica: Romanian Journal of Phenomenology* 11: 29–54.

Index of Names

Aikin, Scott 205–6
Aldea, Andreea 146, 231

Beck, Lewis White 230
Berger, Gaston 224
Bernet, Rudolf 223
Blumenfeld, David and Jean Beer 74
Brann, Eva 233
Brentano, Franz 182
Broekman, Jan 224
Buckley, Philip 230, 231

Carr, David 21, 54, 142–6
Césaire, Aimé 207
Crowell, Steven 80, 223, 225

Danto, Arthur 21, 30–3, 52–4
de Beauvoir, Simone 224
Derrida, Jacques 228, 231, 234
Descartes, René 27, 32, 35, 43, 47, 73–7, 86, 94–5, 99–101, 119, 122, 140, 174–81
Despland, Michel 158
Dilman, Ilham 230
Dodd, James 169, 172, 228
Dray, William 52

Fink, Eugen 97, 119, 225

Galileo Galilei 177–9
Gasché, Rudolphe 197
Gordon, Jeffrey 223–4
Gordon, Lewis R. 234
Guthrie, W. K. C. 232

Hanna, Robert 230
Hart, J. G. 38–9, 229
Heffernan, George 228–9
Hegel, G. W. F. 159–64, 222
Heidegger, Martin 28–9, 71–2, 78–80, 107–8, 234
Held, Klaus 232

Hobson, Allen 223
Hume, David 113, 178–80
Husserl, Edmund
  Basic Problems 96, 222, 224
  Cartesian Meditations 47, 93, 132, 140–1, 214, 221
  Crisis 49, 84, 89, 96, 105, 108, 111, 121–2, 130, 143–4, 147–66, 168–72, 174–215, 227, 229
  Grenzprobleme der Phänomenologie 117, 149, 222, 225, 229, 230, 234
  Ideas I 18, 28, 42, 47, 63, 81, 90–4, 99, 101, 103, 104, 138–40, 142, 222, 227
  Ideas II 222, 224
  Introduction to Logic 227
  Kaizo 120, 149, 150–1, 152–3
  Krisis (Ergänzungsband) 105, 121, 175, 188–94, 197, 199, 203, 227, 232
  Die Lebenswelt 63, 67
  Zur Phänomenologie der Intersubjektivität 67
  Zur Phänomenologischen Reduktion 103, 106, 112, 121, 224, 225
  Phantasy, Image Consciousness, and Memory 47
  Prague Lecture 95, 186, 233
  Prague Letter 80, 188, 189
  Teleologie in der Philosophiegeschichte 138, 144, 149, 157, 169, 190–1, 194–6, 198, 227
  Vienna Lecture 150–1, 159, 186–7, 194–6, 204, 210–11, 215, 226, 229, 230, 234
  Wahrnehmung und Aufmerksamkeit 221
  Wert des Lebens 152–3, 229

Jacobs, Hanne 225
Jaeger, Werner 232–3
James, William 166

Kant, Immanuel 41, 93, 110, 117, 149–50, 154, 155–9, 162–3, 165, 178, 180–2, 222, 225

Koselleck, Reinhart 209

Landgrebe, Ludwig 224
Luft, Sebastian 93, 225

Maldonado-Torres, Nelson 207
Mall, R. A. 211
Mandelbaum, Maurice 52, 232
Marcuse, Herbert 226
McKenna, William 226
Meillassoux, Quentin 105, 225
Merleau-Ponty, Maurice 93–4, 226, 231
Mohanty, J. N. 224
Moran, Dermot 230, 231, 233

Orth, Ernst 228, 231

Parmenides of Elea 89
Patočka, Jan 208
Peucker, Henning 234
Pietersma, Henry 232
Plato, 24, 56, 164–5, 169, 200, 221

Reinach, Adolf 168–9
Rescher, Nicholas 221, 229
Ricoeur, Paul 222–3, 234
Romano, Claude 228

Schelling, F. W. J. 97
Schuhmann, Karl 232
Sheehan, Thomas 234
Socrates 164–5, 200
Sokolowski, Robert 37, 92–3, 107, 118
Stähler, Tanja 233
Statman, Daniel 205, 233
Steinbock, Anthony 66–70, 162, 194, 233
Strawson, Galen 38
Strawson, P. F. 85, 224
Ströker, Elisabeth 39, 231, 233
Szabados, Béla 229

Taguchi, Shigeru 222, 226
Thanassas, Panagiotis 224
Trizio, Emiliano 228–9

Učník, Ľubica 231

Waldenfels, Bernhard 68, 70
Welton, Donn 66, 233
Williams, Bernard 150, 226
Wright, G. H. von 223

Zahavi, Dan 36, 221, 226
Zhok, Andrea 231

Index of Subjects

ability-in-principle 38–41, 55, 81–2, 91–6, 108
alien (the alien)
  phenomenology of 67–72
  in philosophical history 187–8, 193–5, 197, 201, 212
annexation 55, 94, 102, 107, 126 (*see also* subsumption)
appearance 83–7
  merely subjective 60, 100–1, 177
appropriation 49–55
  critical–historical 124–8, 131–3, 167–72
  existential 77–80
  mundane 69–70, 72–3, 76–7
  as occupation 36–43
attention 36–7, 40–1, 50–1 (*see also* inhabitation)
authenticity 80, 131, 190 (*see also* existential responsibility)
awakening
  amendable 48–9, 62–5, 72
  centrality of 45, 70, 72, 114, 126–7, 130, 150, 168
  irrevocable 48–9, 72–3, 76–7, 105–6, 149–50
  and reflection 23, 27
  and retrospect 31–3, 144
  scope of 45, 72, 76, 88, 105, 107, 114
  Socratic 113–14, 182

cogito 32, 35, 86, 99, 101, 176–8, 181–2, 226
commitment 16, 43–5, 50, 78–9
  unconditional 118–21, 126–7, 130, 149–50, 156–7, 164, 173, 183 (*see also* vocational)
consuming interest 50–1, 53, 55
  and everydayness 67–9, 78
  of natural attitude 82–90, 98, 102
  of phenomenological–theoretical attitude 121–4

crisis
  and collapse 151–3, 158–9, 210
  and consolation 130, 152–3, 169–70, 173, 184, 207
  and decision 111, 171, 174, 182–7, 212
  definition of 15, 129–31, 147–50
  as exigency 132
  and nihilism 80, 213, 234
  and optimism 152–3 (*see also* wishful thinking)
  and purpose 155, 164, 167, 209–10
  as sickness 150–3, 210
critical–historical attitude 90, 124, 167
curiosity 71–2
  in philosophical history 194–5

dimensions (of appropriation)
  historical 167–70
  mundane 63–4, 107
  spatiotemporal 39–41, 105, 115
  transcendental 73, 87, 94–6, 124
dream skepticism 46–9, 98–102
dualism 94–5, 107–8, 177

ego 28–9
  basic integrity of 35–43
  first–personal 114–17
  and occupation 36–7
  psychological 61–2, 85, 88–9, 91, 105, 107, 113, 179–82, 226
  transcendental 97–8, 100, 117, 177–8
Endstiftung (final establishment) 144, 160, 161, 217–18
Enlightenment 118–20, 128–32, 150, 153–4, 156–8
  contestation of 141, 162, 165–6, 182–7, 206–10, 217
  presupposition of 120–4
epistemic illusion 57, 107, 137, 215
Europe 122, 137, 154–5, 157–8, 168, 173, 185–7
  definition of 187–9

exceptionalism of 210–14
globalization of (Europeanization) 189, 202–4, 211, 233
hypocrisy of 204–10
origin of 189–202
everydayness 28, 65–71, 76, 106, 111, 112, 145
  in philosophical history 190–1, 197
  in philosophical vocation 214
existential contradiction 156, 162, 164, 214
existential responsibility 78–80, 90, 107, 127, 170–1, 213 (*see also* authenticity)

Greece 189, 194, 198–202, 209, 213, 232
ground (of a presupposition) 13–16, 20, 32
  in appropriative reflection 48–50, 56–7
  and jeopardy 42–4
  nation as 192–4, 204
  reliability of 34–5, 42
  world as 72, 88, 102, 104, 106, 111–12

historical judgment 173, 205, 210, 213
history
  and appropriation 33, 52–5
  in crisis problematic 129–33, 141–6, 154–72, 188–9
  in critical–historical appropriation 118–20, 123–9
  and mundane appropriation 67
  and realization 17, 20
hypocrisy
  and Europe 204–10
  and provinciality 70

identity
  and jeopardy 43–5, 50, 64, 78
  practical 70, 79–80, 173–4, 218,
  subject of crisis 129, 154–5, 157–8, 162–7, 186–7, 200, 211, 213, 215, 232
illusion of false modesty 56, 72, 128
illusion of recollection 56, 93, 95, 119, 126
infinite task 144, 161, 169–70, 198–9
  definition of 196–7
inhabitation 36–7, 40–2 (*see also* attention)

jeopardy 43–5, 49–50, 56–7
  and crisis 147, 150, 215
  definition of 15

existential 79–80, 90
mundane 70, 76–7
and phenomenological attitude 111–18
and philosophical history 118–22, 124–6, 186

Lebensbedeutsamkeit (life-significance) 80, 90, 131
and crisis 148–9, 162, 183–5, 228
life–attitude 108–10, 113–14, 117–18, 131, 157, 169

naïveté
  devaluation of 34–43
  existential 79–80, 90
  historical 120–4
  and inability 26–7
  as negligence 26–7, 32, 42, 51, 56, 98, 111
  as provinciality 64–73, 106–7, 167, 194–6
  and sleep 25–6
  transcendental 91, 106–11, 118–21, 129–33, 138, 145, 146–7, 154, 157, 160, 215
narrative
  and appropriation 29–32, 50, 52–4
  established 125, 128, 130, 210
  plausibility of 157–8, 164–6, 209
  sentences 21, 30–2
natural attitude
  devaluation of 110–11, 119
  general thesis of 90–2
  and mundane attitude 81, 89–90
  as past 105–6
  precedence of (antecedence of) 119–20, 123, 132, 176, 190

objectivism 147–8, 162, 168, 173–80, 185–6, 195
occasion 51, 56
  of critical–historical awakening 119, 132, 175
  of existential awakening 77, 79
  of mundane awakening 69–70, 73
  of transcendental awakening 83–7, 98
orientation
  and crisis 150–61, 172–4, 215, 217–19
  critical–historical 125–7

disorientation 35, 70, 77
  mundane 24–6, 62, 64–9, 71–2, 77, 80, 91, 145
  mythical 166–7, 193–4, 211
  in philosophical history 188, 193, 196, 201, 204
  reorientation 43, 137, 146

phantom acts 21, 28, 51
phenomenological attitude
  and natural attitude 92–6, 108–11
  and phenomenological-theoretical attitude 122
phenomenological epoché 81, 83–4, 88, 90–2, 95, 98, 107, 112, 132, 224, 226, 227
phenomenological reduction 81, 95, 105, 107, 224, 225, 226
philosophical epoché 139–40, 142–3, 146
pragmatic illusion 50, 57, 127, 215
predicament 15–16, 43, 45, 57, 70, 111, 121, 174
  and crisis 130
presupposition
  apodictic 108, 176, 182, 217, 220
  independence of 13–14, 102–3
  missingness of 17, 29–31, 53, 55, 64, 69, 103
  subject of 27–33, 80
  truth of (correctness of) 13–14, 33
  ultimate 124, 132, 135, 137–8, 142, 144, 150, 154–5, 183, 214
  universal 72–3, 76–82, 86–9, 96, 106–7, 182
  unrealized 21–3
principle of all principles 140–1
principle of epistemic authority 48, 56, 92–5, 119, 127, 144, 161
principle of maturity 48–9, 56–7, 72, 106–7
pseudo-presupposition (pseudo-awakening) 16, 43–4, 48, 75–6, 78, 111
purview
  definition of 17–18
  mundane 69, 95, 119
  and presupposition 19–20, 31, 51
  transcendental 123

realization
  of presuppositions 15–16, 20–3
  and reflection 17–19, 23–4, 27, 95
  self- 98
relativism
  historical 23, 48–9, 128, 131, 171–2, 222–3
  as pluralism 211–13
  psychological 85, 113, 179–80
relevance (irrelevance)
  and awakening 44, 79, 114
  and curiosity 71
  and everydayness 66–7, 76
  of phenomenology 117–18, 122, 131, 138

seriousness 43–5, 50, 68–9, 71–2
  in history of philosophy 148, 177–9
  in philosophical history 214–15
sophistry 196, 198, 232
subsumption 32, 50, 55, 106 (*see also* annexation)

teleological reconstruction 50, 124–6, 156–7
  interventionist 139, 142, 144, 160–4
  irresponsible 126–7
transcendental apperception 81, 107
  discretional use 117–18
  non-discretional use 130–1
transcendental motif (transcendentalism) 154–5, 158, 173–83, 186

universal critique 148–9, 159, 162, 196–9, 201
  critique of 208–9

Verendlichung (finitization) 67, 159, 170, 198, 203–5, 233
vocation 127
  vocational attitude 129
  vocational commitment 130 (*see also* unconditional commitment)
  philosophy as 138, 145, 159, 168–9, 171, 195–6, 227

wakefulness 24, 32, 56
  and basic attitudes 49, 59, 73, 80–1, 89–90, 98

diurnal 25, 31, 45–8, 60
  phenomenological 88, 99–103, 105–6, 119
  value of 34–43
  will to wakefulness (maxim of wakefulness) 43, 113, 118, 137
  world-wakefulness 64, 69, 72–3, 76–7
Weltvernichtung (world annihilation) 102–6, 225

wishful thinking 127, 152–3, 229
world 62–4
  life– 155, 170, 181, 185, 195, 219–20, 223, 225
  local (home) 64–72, 161, 187, 203, 212, 232, 233
  national 189–94
  worldliness 64, 71–3, 112, 131, 145, 172, 190, 198, 213

www.ingramcontent.com/pod-product-compliance
Lightning Source LLC
Chambersburg PA
CBHW072140290426
44111CB00012B/1935